THE MEMORY WORKBOOK

BREAKTHROUGH TECHNIQUES TO EXERCISE YOUR BRAIN AND IMPROVE YOUR MEMORY

DOUGLAS J. MASON, PSY.D. & MICHAEL L. KOHN, PSY.D.

FOREWORD BY KAREN A. CLARK, PH.D., MEDICAL GERO-PSYCHOLOGIST

New Harbinger Publications, Inc.

Distributed in Canada by Raincoast Books

Copyright © 2001 by Douglas J. Mason and Michael Lee Kohn
New Harbinger Publications, Inc.
5674 Shattuck Avenue
Oakland, CA 94609

Cover design by Blue Designs
Edited by Carole Honeychurch
Text design by Tracy Marie Powell-Carlson

Library of Congress Card Catalog Number: 01-132287

ISBN-10 1-57224-258-2
ISBN-13 978-1-57224-258-6

Printed in the United States of America

New Harbinger Publications' website address: www.newharbinger.com

17   16   15

20   19   18   17   16   15   14

To my wife, Brenda, for her never-ending friendship, support, and love. To my beautiful daughter Stephanie, who every day teaches me the value of a child's innocence, wonderment, and continued curiosity. Finally, this book is dedicated to my mother, Mable Mason, who has shown me the power of faith, a positive loving outlook, and the miraculous healing properties of her spirit in her continued struggle against cancer.

—DJM

To Teresa—my thoughts, feelings, experiences, and memories are all considered as to how I'll tell you about them at the end of the day. I would have been in poverty without you. But you got the silver, you got the gold. And to baby Elijah, we love watching you grow and having you in our lives—our diamond from the mine.

—MLK

Contents

Foreword: A New Wrinkle in Old Age

There's something new about getting old in our current culture. As the elders among us live longer and healthier lives, the fear of hearing from the family physician that we have the "C" word has been overshadowed for some by the terror of hearing that we have the "A" word. Why for some of us has the fear of having Alzheimers disease outstripped the fear of having cancer? One reason is the vast media attention focused on the dismal plight of Alzheimer's patients, including some well-known Americans such as former President Ronald Reagan. It isn't any wonder that at the first sign of memory loss many aging individuals think the worst.

For the first time in history, today's aging cohort is worried—panicked might be a more apt description of the phenomenon—about memory loss. Many people equate any and all memory loss with Alzheimer's Disease, and the reality is very different. Forgetting the names of a new acquaintance at a party is light years away from the inability to remember the names of your own children, as can so sadly occur as Alzheimer's disease progresses. Or, as the joke goes, forgetting where you left you car in the parking lot at the mall is nothing compared to forgetting that you drove your car there in the first place.

However, as a clinician who has been working with the memory impaired for the past eleven years, I can assure you that telling patients their memory lapses are normal changes that many people can expect as they age is not as powerful as the patient experiencing a renewal in his or her capacity to remember. Now Dr. Doug Mason and Dr. Mike Kohn, both experts in the field of normal memory loss in aging, have written a much-needed book that can help readers actually experience memory renewal through a series of exercises, new information, and strategies. Combining hard science with a real concern for their readers' plight, the authors, both neuropsychologists with years of education and experience in memory function and the operation of the human brain, have written a user-friendly workbook.

Echoing Pogo's famous comment—"We've met the enemy and they is us"—Drs. Mason and Kohn aptly emphasize the need for us to recognize and accept that memory is imperfect at any age. They compare the aging memory to an out-of-shape muscle, debilitated by years of flabby thinking habits, that needs to be exercised and revitalized with a new regimen of skill building and positive attitude development. After all, there is truth to the aphorism "use it or lose it." The brain is like any other part of the body in its need for exercise, and we need to find new ways to flex its capacity to remember.

Their *Memory Workbook* is based on a successful memory-training program, the RARE DREAM Program, developed and piloted by Drs. Mason and Kohn at the East Central Florida Memory Disorder Clinic in Melbourne, Florida. The program guides participants through a series of exercises designed to help them learn new ways to flex the function of memory. The self-paced format of the workbook permits the authors to persistently coax on the one hand while providing gentle reassurance on the other as readers work through the exercises and drills in the text and begin to test and improve their own memory skills. *The Memory Workbook* addresses fears of memory loss in a straightforward style with common-sense strategies that can help readers understand and improve the aging brain.

There's no magic involved—Drs. Mason and Kohn ask the reader to begin a rigorous process of re-examining how they experience the world. Their goal is to teach readers new methods of improving their memory retrieval and retention based on the readers' personal style of learning. The targeted exercises teach readers how to pay attention to their experiences and begin to develop a new way of decoding what they see, feel, smell, hear, and even taste. They challenge readers to take a hard look at their belief systems and make solid changes in their attitudes, much like the process that occurs in psychotherapy. Indeed, they call their approach "therapy for the memory."

Drs. Mason and Kohn have packed the workbook with cutting-edge information that helps the reader understand what healthy aging means and how our brains change and function differently as we age. The authors approach the task of teaching their memory program with a combination of professionalism mixed with a healthy sense of humor to keep things interesting.

Finally, Drs. Mason and Kohn provide readers and their families who suspect more serious memory deficits with a comprehensive discussion of Alzheimer's disease and medications that are being developed to slow the progress of this insidious disease. Always the supportive professionals, the authors provide a thorough listing and description of potentially reversible memory problems as well. A guide to a complete neurological workup for the diagnosis of an irreversible memory disorder is also included in this section so readers will know what to expect when they see their physician about their memory concerns.

The Memory Workbook is a book that I look forward to passing on to my patients who have questions and concerns about their memory. They'll be in the best of hands with Drs. Mason and Kohn.

> —Karen A. Clark, Ph.D. Medical Geropsychologist VA Medical Center, Memphis, Tennessee Assistant Professor, University of Tennessee Health Sciences Center

Preface

What Began as a Bad Dream Left a Lot of Rare Memories

This book presents a comprehensive, interactive program designed to enhance the many facets of memory functioning. The exercises we'll be presenting are intended for people who are beginning to notice changes in their memory functioning associated with aging. Memory does change as we age, but these changes are not necessarily the first signs of senility. We will educate you about what these age-related changes in your memory are and will provide methods and approaches designed to improve your memory and compensate for these normal changes. Although we'll be primarily focusing on encoding information (putting data into your memory), we will also offer suggestions on retrieval strategies (pulling data from your memory). Memory is a complex process and like most human traits, does not function the same for everyone. This book will help you to identify and access your personal memory style and tailor strategies toward your individual strengths. You will gain insight into your talents and, through this understanding, learn to implement new strategies that compensate for the changes in your memory that are the result of normal aging.

The model we provide originates from our research on memory. The research revealed a statistically significant improvement in memory functioning in a pilot clinical trial. The original memory-training program was conducted at the East Central Florida Memory Disorder Clinic in Melbourne, Florida, a comprehensive community resource and multifaceted health-care system for older adults. Based on multiple memory-assessment measures, this memory-training program was found to be effective in improving the participant's memory functioning. At the end of the program, the participants evidenced "significant improvement" based on empirical testing. Subsequently our memory approach has been successful with multiple individuals and groups.

This empirical approach differs from other memory-training programs as it simultaneously incorporates the importance of emotional components of memory while focusing on the techniques to improve attention and encode information in a personal and meaningful way. We will provide step-by-step tools to help you improve your memory and to help you examine and adjust both emotional and rational aspects of your memory functioning. This book contains valuable information from the current literature on memory, memory disorders, medications, medical considerations, contacts for additional help, aging, what to expect during a neurological exam, along with memory-enhancement techniques. There is no need to memorize all the material in this book. Instead, read through the information at your own leisurely pace. Take from the material strategies that are most effective for you. The goal is to relax, learn about how memory works, gain a greater understanding of your personal habits for remembering, and then, through strategies presented in this book, incorporate techniques that will enhance your memory functioning. To simply state that your memory will improve does not do justice to the intentions of this book. Instead, by applying the strategies in this book, your mindset about memory and aging will evolve.

This book contains a comprehensive, individually tailored memory-enhancement program that realistically presents what can be done to improve memory. The goal of this program is to improve both memory functioning and any negative perceptions of memory and aging that you may hold. If the program is followed closely and with the appropriate mindset, it is designed to provide lasting effects.

Before we move on, a brief description of our original memory-training group will shed light on what our intentions are for this book. As clinical psychology doctoral students working at the memory clinic, we noticed a distinct type of older adult coming through the doors of the clinic for a memory evaluation. These were people who complained about significant changes in memory and could spend the day enumerating a litany of examples to prove their claims. However, when tested, their memory performance was within the normal range or just below the normal range when compared to their same-aged peers.

Although the "within normal limits" finding would often be a relief to people, we sensed that ultimately we were leaving them with an empty feeling. Their concerns and fears about their memory functioning were very real and were going to persist once they left our office. So what do you say to the woman who comes back into the office because she locked her keys in the car, after having just been told that her memory was fine? Or, how should we react to the more benign but frequent occurrence of informing an older gentleman that his memory was within normal limits, only to have him respond with embarrassment because he couldn't remember your name as he attempted to thank you? Certainly we couldn't just ignore their forgetfulness in the face of normal test results.

The memory problems that they were complaining about were a reality. Changes and declines may have been present in their memory functioning, but likely only in comparison with their functioning at a younger age. The changes in memory were real to the individual, but were clinically considered to be those of "healthy aging." Unfortunately, this did not make the issue any less disconcerting to these individuals.

Upon evaluating many of the people who complained of significant memory problems but who tested within normal limits, we noticed a strong emotional flavor intertwined within their complaints. There was a tone of fear and anxiety beneath the complaints. In fact, it was hard not to admit that the emotional reactions were a major contributor to their memory problems. A good indicator of this was the emotional reaction that we would experience when listening to someone with "normal" memory list off all the memory lapses he or she experienced. As one complaint would follow the next, a sense of hopelessness would permeate the room, a sense of being helpless to respond would overcome us. Often these experiences would distract us from our mission of giving objective feedback on their memory functioning. Our intuition told us that we were witnessing briefly what they were likely feeling on a daily basis.

As we continued to review the research related to memory problems with age, our intuition about emotional factors was further validated. We became far more aware of the vague notions we held about age-related memory changes. Quite simply, we became aware of a vicious cycle involving the aging process, emotional difficulty adjusting to the change, and continued memory complaints. We will fill you in on our findings and provide ways to make positive change throughout the book, but suffice it to say here, we discovered that the source of memory problems with older adults was multidimensional but very treatable. If we were to address these problems, our treatment would likewise have to be multidimensional. And we did want to address memory problems!

After a great deal of research, we created a memory-training group that was dual focused. One focus would be on strategies to enhance the encoding of information. The other focus would be on rectifying the emotional components that contributed to memory problems. As these two components are interwoven in memory functioning, so, too, would they be interwoven in our memory-training design. In addition, we incorporated another layer within the intervention that offered methods to help participants retrieve information from their memories and practical ways the participants could compensate for common memory problems. And thus, our memory-training group began.

Initially there was a very negative tone to the group. As the group members relentlessly listed their memory problems, there was a sense of demoralization that fell over the group. As they made their skepticism known, we began to wonder if we could instill the hope necessary for change. Having openly identified the increasing anxiety, we were honest with our feelings and observations, yet we refused to let these negative emotions paralyze potential progress. The goal of adapting to normal changes experienced during aging became as important as learning new strategies to improve memory.

And then, a rather amazing thing began to occur—the pall began to lift from the group. As the group members learned more about the functions of memory, implemented strategies to combat memory deficits, and began to see how emotional components contributed to their lapses in memory, they began to regain a sense of confidence in themselves. They began to see that their memories could improve and actually were improving. A sense of empowerment and control replaced the sense of demoralization and helplessness. The group began to have fun! And the same could be said about the two group leaders. By the end of the group there was a spontaneity and joviality that we could have never predicted at the start. The group started with people walking in and immediately sharing their failures; but by the end of the training program, the group was sharing their successes. Memory lapses continued to be mentioned in passing but without the burdensome emotional weight that they once carried. Bonds were formed within the group and these bonds were extended to us. By the end of the group several members gave us the best present imaginable; they gave us their dedication and continual confidence in allowing us to share in their growth.

In sum, our memory-training group celebrated memory. What began with a very negative tone, with deficits dominating the group conversation, ended with a sense of confidence and pride. We had fun. The people may have entered the group complaining of a *bad* memory, but they left the group with an improved memory and a lot of *good* memories. They felt better about their memories and therefore better about their lives and themselves.

The author John Steinbeck once advised that before starting any book, the author should be able to summarize the entire story in one line or phrase. Well, if we had to state in a simple phrase what we sought to accomplish in our memory-training group it would be "therapy for memory." Just like in any good use of therapy, which should include trust, respect, and a search for root causes, we respected memory, we appreciated memory, we sought to find the source of memory difficulties, and we sought to then improve memory, all utilizing the inherent strengths found in the older adults within the group. Unfortunately, many people hold a negative perception about the idea of therapy. Therapy, as in the term "therapeutic," simply means the healing power of treatment. In this book, we will offer a treatment approach to improving your memory, and we believe your memory will be treated well.

Finally, speaking of therapy, Sigmund Freud comes to mind for several reasons. For one, Freud deeply appreciated and valued the complex and dynamic workings of human beings. We hope that we did, too, in the writing of this book. For another, Freud's quest was to find the source of human problems and find ways of alleviating suffering in order to make life better for others. We hope to accomplish the same in the writing of this book. Lastly, and most relevant to the principles of this book, Freud demonstrated incredible flexibility throughout his life. He developed concepts and principles that almost single-handedly defined a field of science, and his influence permeated all of society. Yet, at the age of seventy, he made significant changes and revisions to many of his most fundamental and longstanding principles. Freud felt that his work and his life were always a work in progress, an unfinished product. We hope that you do, too. The people who participated in our memory group felt that way, although they may not have been aware of this attitude when they started. You may not be, either. Although by the very fact that you picked up this book, we have our suspicions . . .

We have attempted to capture the essence of the original program in the form of this self-paced workbook that is designed to be fun, challenging, and insightful. We had a lot of fun designing and implementing our memory-enhancement program and hope that you find it both helpful and entertaining. We will end the preface and begin the book with a vignette that we feel captures the essence of the following pages. It is a story of the joy of learning and the excitement of new challenges that lie ahead. The story is about Mrs. Franklin, one of the author's college professors, who shortly after the death of her husband took the time to convey to us some of the lessons that life had taught her.

A Valuable Lesson

As the early morning sunlight came streaming in through the classroom windows and the class was nearly over, Mrs. Franklin moved a few things aside on the edge of her desk and sat down. With a deep breath and a gentle look of reflection on her face, she paused and said, "Before class is over, I would like to share with all of you a thought that is unrelated to class, but which I feel is very important. Each of us is put here on earth to learn, share, love, appreciate, and give of ourselves. None of us knows when this fantastic experience will end. It can be taken away at any moment. Perhaps this is God's way of telling us that we must make the most out of every single day." With a hushed yet determined tone she continued, "So I would like you all to make me a promise. From now on, on your way to school or on your way home, find something beautiful to notice. It doesn't have to be something you see—it could be a scent, perhaps of jasmine blooming in the early spring, or it could be the sound of the breeze slightly rustling the leaves in the trees, or the way the morning light catches one autumn leaf as it falls gently to the ground. Please, look for these things and cherish them. For, although it may sound trite to some, these things are the 'stuff' of life—the little things we are put here on earth to enjoy, the things we often take for granted. We must make it important to notice them, for at any time, it can all be taken away."

A deafening silence fell over the classroom. Slowly, we all picked up our books and filed out of the room. That afternoon, I noticed more things on my way home from school than I had that whole semester. Every once in a while, I think of Mrs. Franklin and remember what an impression she made on me, and I try to appreciate all of those things that sometimes we all overlook. The lesson I learned from that story was to take notice of something special I may see on my lunch hour; to go barefoot or walk on the beach at sunset; to stop off on the way home tonight to get a double-dip ice cream cone. For as we get older, it's not the things we did that we often regret, but the things we didn't do.

You might say that this story captures the essence of *The Memory Workbook*: taking the time to look at things as though for the first time; recapturing the wonderment of a child, seeing things in a different light through the fascination of discovery; recapturing the zest for learning. This attitude is the foundation for effective memory functioning. It is with Mrs. Franklin's grounding advice that we introduce our memory-enhancement program entitled RARE-DREAM.

Acknowledgments

The authors would like to thank Tom Peake, Ph.D., and Frank Webbe, Ph.D., for their support and guidance in the initial process of the research. A special thanks to Karen Clark, Ph.D., for her continued support and invaluable clinical training in the provision of comprehensive care for the special needs of the geriatric population. We'd like to acknowledge Carol Waters and the East Central Florida Memory Disorder Clinic in Melbourne, Florida, for allowing us to conduct the research that helped us formulate our memory model. The East Central Florida Memory Disorder Clinic is funded through grants from the Alzheimer's Disease Initiative of the State of Florida, Department of Elder Affairs. Next, we'd like to thank our editor, Carole Honeychurch, for her hard work and guidance in preparing this book for publication. In addition, we'd like to thank Mari Szymanski, RN, C, Roberta Wallace, LCSW, Lisa Gwyther, MSW, Deborah Koltai, Ph.D., Kathleen Welsh-Bohmer, Ph.D., and Karima Rasheed, MHS, PA-C, for their assistance in reviewing the work and offering guidance in their respective areas of expertise, and Brenda Mason, Patricia Aten, Bob Walker, and Alice Ghigliotty for contributing their helpful wisdom. Finally we can't forget the influence that Troy Flippen has had on the following pages.

★ 1 ★

How to Use This Book

What Is RARE-DREAM?

Congratulations! You have taken the first step toward positive change with the purchase of this book. You've stopped dreaming about improving your memory and decided to put the gears into motion. You are one of the "rare" individuals with the determination to do what it takes to effect positive change and fulfill your "dream." You have made a decision to fulfill what may be considered a "RARE-DREAM." We use RARE-DREAM as an acronym that will help you enhance your memory and develop a greater sense of mastery and confidence.

RARE-DREAM stands for:

★ **Relax**

★ **Attend**

★ **Rehearse** and

★ **Envision**

while

★ **Developing**

★ **Rational** and

★ **Emotionally**

★ **Adaptive**

★ **Mindsets**

Sound complicated? Don't worry—as you will soon see, it's really very simple, and we will take you through the program a step at a time. By the time you're finished you will be relaxed with yourself and your environment. This relaxed state will allow you to be attentive to the important aspects of the world around you as you effectively focus your attention on things to be remembered. With efficient attention, you will effectively encode memories through rehearsal and you will envision and see things from a new perspective. While doing this, you will learn to identify and adjust any beliefs that may be hindering your memory. You will develop rational and emotionally adaptive mindsets (DREAM) or beliefs that replace negative thoughts and feelings about memory and aging.

By replacing these unhelpful beliefs, you will rid yourself of roadblocks that may be getting in the way of efficient memory functioning. Along with the RARE-DREAM program we will educate you on how memory works in general. But more importantly, we will guide you through the process of discovering how your memory functions and then help you to establish and implement an individually tailored memory repertoire based on your individual cognitive strengths that will serve you in maintaining an efficient memory.

It's that simple. Read and incorporate the RARE-DREAM techniques and your memory can begin to serve you rather than enslave you. Unfortunately, when it comes to the complexities of memory, there are no guarantees. We certainly can't promise you that your memory will perform flawlessly or even in the way that it once did. However, we do feel that your potential for improving your memory will be greatly enhanced if you follow the steps and complete the exercises in this book. We will guide you through this process of incorporating RARE-DREAM as your personal memory model and teach you each step, from R to M.

Essentially, the RARE-DREAM model consists of strategies to improve your memory while simultaneously providing a guide on how to embody and maintain a positive attitude and open belief system about your memory functioning. We will invite you to rid yourself of any fears that may bind you and to accept yourself for who you are, with all of your glorious faults. This includes the ability to occasionally laugh at yourself and even forgive yourself if you happen to forget. Memory-enhancement strategies (the RARE component) are useless if applied to unhealthy attitudes and incongruent beliefs (the DREAM component). Working at memory strategies without an open mind and flexible belief system will only lead to frustration and eventually discouragement. So, as you can see, to adequately address the complexities of the aging memory, we must conceptualize and target the challenges that lie ahead at multiple levels. And that's exactly what we're going to do!

The Power of Knowledge

This book is intended for those who have noticed changes in their memory through the years. It is not intended for those who have a debilitating neurologically based memory disorder that impairs daily functioning. If you believe that you have memory impairment that is impacting your day-to-day life, we strongly suggest that you have your memory evaluated by a professional, such as a neurologist or a neuropsychologist. Diagnosing memory impairment is complex and well beyond the scope of this book. These professionals can most likely help you to either ease your mind or get the assistance that you might need. Most people experiencing memory problems agree that it is the fear and anxiety of the unknown that bothers them most. Most people find that a certain level of comfort is usually found from consulting a memory professional, no matter what the diagnosis or prognosis. Many memory problems can be treated effectively, so don't be afraid to ask for help.

Knowledge itself is power.

—Francis Bacon

Effort Is Essential

This book provides exercises designed to enhance memory and to help you to identify and utilize your existing strengths. Each exercise builds upon the previous one and serves to enhance upcoming lessons. The benefits that you derive from this book will be directly proportional to your commitment to reading the material in order and participating in each exercise. Proceed with enthusiasm and determination, and you will reap maximal benefit. Proceed with less, and the benefits derived will most assuredly be less. Effort, an open mind, and commitment are essential to improve your memory.

Action is the proper fruit of knowledge.

—Thomas Fuller, M.D.

Memory Push-ups—Exercise Your Mind

Many memory experts view the workings of the mind to be similar to a muscle, and propose that exercise will serve to build and strengthen it. As such, your memory is adaptive, pliable and can be shaped, but this shaping takes some education, effort, and energy. This energy must be continuously and strategically applied, for the muscle to grow, thrive, and flourish. In completing the exercises, we will guide you in tailoring this program to fit your personal style. You will not only be guided in sculpting and shaping your memory and in applying these learned skills to your everyday life, but also in maintaining your healthy memory functioning as you gracefully age.

One older adult who completed our program reported that his marriage had improved dramatically. Puzzled, we asked him to what he attributed this improvement. He enthusiastically replied that, through his participation in the RARE-DREAM program, when he listens to his wife now, he focuses only on her, and tunes out distractions. He has learned how to sustain his attention and just as importantly, be a more active participant in his relationship. We certainly don't make the claim that this book will improve your marriage or get your spouse to listen to you, but with devotion you will begin to notice changes in both your memory functioning and its impacts throughout your life. Just as it takes becoming an adult to realize how naïve you actually were as a self-righteous teenager, you can only realize how lapses in your memory affected your life once your memory has improved. You may even notice an increased self-esteem and a new sense of confidence.

One Step at a Time

This book is intended to be read in the order presented. Although some of you may want to read only the portions that most apply to you, we recommend that you don't. Follow the outlined program as presented. Many of the skills are hierarchically based, going from one important gradient to the next with each new task building upon previously learned skills. There will be times when it's necessary to take a break and work in a specific area before progressing any further. This is fine, and you are encouraged to proceed at your own pace.

Pay special attention to words or concepts that are *italicized* throughout the text, as these are key concepts. When a concept is italicized, it is being introduced for the first time and a definition will follow. We recommend that you slow down your reading when you come across these introductions and be sure that you understand the concept being introduced. We would like to emphasize that there is also an index of terms in appendix

A that can help clarify any new concepts. As a caveat to our previous statement that effort is essential, good effort is respectful of limits. There is a limit to how much new information the mind can absorb in one sitting, and this limit should be respected. Therefore we recommend not reading more than two or three chapters per any one sitting; however, ultimately you're the best judge of your own capacity.

Randomly placed throughout the book, we've included "Memory Tips." These tips are designed to fulfill two purposes. First, they will break up some of the more intense reading, and secondly, they will offer specific strategies that will help enhance your memory functioning. Exercises that will offer a more direct way to learn are also scattered throughout the book. We feel that learning is better facilitated through experience, because once experienced, the information begins to take on personal meaning.

Forget the Reasons We Forget and Remember the Reasons We Remember

When it comes to memory, we often focus on the reasons we forget, be it old age, Alzheimer's disease, a "senior moment," or never-had-a-good-memory disease. This type of thinking often creates and fosters a negative concept of memory functioning. We want to do things a little bit differently with this book. In other words, we are asking you to take a leap of faith and begin to look at things a little differently. Instead of focusing on reasons why you forget, focus on the reasons why you remember. As you do this, you will also do some investigation and discover what conditions exist that increase the likelihood that you will remember information. You can begin to identify why and how you remember and then consciously transfer this mode of learning and remembering to other situations. When you are going somewhere in your car, you certainly don't focus on all the possible ways not to get lost. Instead, you focus on the best possible way to get to where you're going. So, do the same with your memory, beginning right now! Focus on where you are going, not on how lost you may become.

The first exercise that we will introduce is intended to show you how memory works and the best possible way to get where you're going—toward reliable memory functioning. It is a hands-on experiential exercise that will allow you to begin to experience the intricacies of memory. This exercise will set the tone for the remainder of the exercises within the book. So, have fun and let your memory reap the fullest rewards of its possibilities.

For the only time in this book we are going to ask you to apply only a little effort to this next exercise. The instructions are simple. Just read the following story. We want you to read the story just one time through at the casual speed that you typically read the newspaper. It's a story about Edgar, the protagonist of our book, and his day of cleaning his garage. Just read on and be grateful that you are not cleaning out your garage today.

✎ ✗ Exercise: Edgar's Garage

After years of meandering and broken promises, the day came when Edgar finally decided to clean out his garage. It had not been exhaustively cleaned for over twenty years. It was filled with toys, tools, and just plain junk, including a couple of old garbage bags that didn't make it out to the curb one Tuesday night long ago. As he weeded through the piles of memories, the first thing he decided to throw out was a box of old, broken watches that had been collecting dust for years. After that he threw out some busted lamps that were the cornerstone of his first apartment. He found an old radio that he decided to throw out, along with a stack of newspapers that had accumulated over the years. He then found a pile of books. One of the books was *Moby-Dick*, the first book he had ever fallen in love with. As a boy he fantasized about battling the huge, white whale. Edgar believed that in some way his love for *Moby-Dick* had had a large impact on his decision to join the Navy.

He then found some old hubcaps and gently placed them in the garbage pile. He found an old pile of records, including an old Bing Crosby record so warped that it looked like a miniature mountain range. "Poor Bing, all warped and scratched," he thought to himself. He then threw out a small and unusable barbecue grill that had deteriorated over the years. Some old phone books saved for no apparent reason went directly into the trash. His eyes lit up when he uncovered an old glass bottle he had found on the beach years ago. He picked up the bottle, and, running his hand across it, he noted the cold feel of the glass on his skin. He enjoyed the smoothness of the feel. He thought that he could still smell a hint of saltwater and the coarse feel of sand on the bottle. He decided to keep this bottle. He found the power drill he thought he had lost years ago underneath a dusty table. He found an old unopened can of Spam luncheon meat that had somehow found its way into the garage. He thought to himself that this would go well with a couple of fried eggs and buttered toast.

He found an old hammer that he put into his toolbox. He then came across a model of Apollo 13 that he'd given to his son on that hot summer day in 1969 when Neil Armstrong had spoken those famous words, "One small step for man, one giant leap for mankind." He also found a wooden baseball bat that felt heavy in his hands. He swung the bat into his left hand and felt the sharp sting of the heavy, smooth, and refined wood in his hand. He could still hear the crack of this bat, harkening back to his son's Little League days. He then turned to the first dress that he ever wore. It was a beautiful pink silk dress that fit him perfectly. It was backless and it really turned heads when he would go shopping in it. He smiled as he gently placed it in the garbage bag. He threw away an old television set that he never got around to fixing. He decided to keep an old checkers game with all the pieces still intact. Then it was time to quit for the day and engage his wife in a sporting game of checkers.

Next we are going to introduce our first randomly placed Memory Tip. As mentioned before, these are provided throughout the text as a source of education and to break up the reading. We will return to the garage cleaning exercise shortly.

🔑 Memory Tip: Create a Story

If you have several items to remember, make up a unique story about the items to assist you. Hill and associates (1991) found this to be an effective method with older adults. This method will help you to better focus your attention and will provide a context in which to attach the items to be remembered. For example, let's say you are driving home and need to remember to call your friend Mildred, feed the dogs, pay your bills, and put the roast in the oven. You could make up a little story about Mildred and Bill feeding roast to their dogs. This simple sentence in the form of a story will help you to better remember and recall the tasks to do when you get home.

Okay, we admit that the placement of that memory tip was not completely random. In order to test your memory we needed to provide a brief distraction. Now that there's been enough of a distraction, let's return to Edgar's garage.

✎ ✗ *Exercise: What Kind of Junk Do You Remember?*

Edgar encountered a lot of junk while cleaning his garage. How many of the items do you remember from having read the story once through? List all the items that you recall in the space provided below.

1. _____
2. _____
3. _____
4. _____
5. _____
6. _____
7. _____
8. _____
9. _____
10. _____
11. _____
12. _____
13. _____
14. _____
15. _____
16. _____
17. _____
18. _____

How did you do? We expect that you probably got about one-third of the items by casually reading the story once through. Would it have helped you if the items from Edgar's garage were numbered in the story? Why? Perhaps numbering the items would have allowed you to better memorize them in order. Perhaps, in your mind's eye, you would be able to visualize each number and associate the word that was paired with the number. Perhaps numbering the items would have provided some organization or context in which to better anchor the items in your mind. Let's take a look at what made you remember the items that you did remember.

Elaboration Leads to Improved Memory

Although at times it may certainly seem that way, memory is not a random entity. There are reasons that you remember what you do. With this exercise, we wanted to create a situation where some objects were more likely to be remembered than others. In very simple terms, the deeper new information is planted into your brain, the more likely you are to remember that information. There are many ways to promote deep encoding of new information, and we will build upon this concept throughout the book. Essentially, when information is provided with a great deal of texture and richness it is more likely to grab hold deep in your mind, take root and blossom into a flourishing memory. The process of providing rich texture to information is termed *elaboration*. When we elaborate, we add details and thus texture. With elaboration, we are encoding the information at a deeper level, often within multiple levels and thus assuring the success of later recall or retrieval. There are many ways to elaborate on new information. One way is to try to involve all five of your senses when learning new information. Another way is to involve different subsystems of your memory (for instance, visual versus verbal memory).

You might elaborate by making new information unique or even ridiculous in some way. This method typically involves using visualization skills, which is the E (envisioning) portion of RARE. We will cover envisioning in chapter 12, but here is a quick example of elaboration through visualization. While driving to the grocery store, Edgar wants to remember to purchase eggs and milk. He takes a moment to visualize a carton of milk walking down the road juggling eggs. Sounds pretty ridiculous, doesn't it? But this absurd image makes it unlikely that he'll forget to buy milk and eggs while shopping. That's because by visualizing he's elaborated on the milk and eggs by making them unique. There's something interesting for the mind to hold onto, leading to increased attention. Remember, there are reasons that we remember what we remember and forget what we forget!

Back to Edgar's Garage

In the exercises about Edgar's garage, we wanted to create a story where, through the use of elaboration or the absence of elaboration, you were more or less likely to remember items. Seven items in the story were elaborated upon and seven were not. One of the seven elaborated items so totally captures the spirit of this book we'll lay amazing odds and bet that this item was remembered. The elaborated items were: a **pile of books** *Moby-Dick*, a **pile of records (Bing Crosby record)**, a **glass bottle**, a **can of Spam**, a **model of Apollo 13**, a **baseball bat**, and a **beautiful pink silk dress**. The nonelaborated items were: a **radio**, a **stack of newspapers**, **hubcaps**, a **barbecue grill**, some **phone books**, a **power drill**, and a **hammer**.

So, what's the item that so very well captures the spirit of the book and that we bet good odds that you remembered? The pink silk dress, though the aged can of Spam comes in at a close second. Both are rather unique and surprising, making them stand out. Making items stand out this way is essential to elaboration. However, the dress probably caught you by surprise (it certainly couldn't have been expected) and therefore it particularly stands out. Also, the dress is further elaborated on with descriptions of how it looked. Can you imagine how our character Edgar might have looked in that backless, silk, pink dress? Furthermore, by abruptly sticking the dress in the story, we probably elicited some emotion within you. Perhaps you experienced unease or curiosity at the prospect of a man wearing a dress, or possibly just bemusement. This gave you something to wrap your memory around. There are multiple reasons why you remembered the items that you remembered in our first exercise, and let's briefly examine some emotional and logical reasons.

Emotional Versus Factual Memory

When you elaborate on information through an emotional connection, you further increase the likelihood of retention and recall of the memory. You are utilizing different memory systems within your brain toward the task of remembering. Emotional memory is contained and processed within your brain by different structures from those that are used to process and store factual data. By tapping into both systems, you can encode the information at a deeper level within different memory systems (for additional reading on brain structures and memory systems please refer to appendix A, "Glossary of Terms Related to Memory and Health Care," and appendix D, "Review of Major Structures of the Brain and Their Function."

The description of the pink dress contains the type of information we hope to capture in this book, details and nuances that will cement retention and streamline recall. We will teach you to encode information deeply and meaningfully, thereby significantly increasing the likelihood that you will be able to access and utilize the information when needed. Elaboration is one encoding key amongst many others that will unlock any doors in the way of future recall. As we explore why you might or might not have remembered certain items in Edgar's garage, let's compare how many elaborated versus unelaborated items that you remembered.

✎ ✗ Exercise: Sorting out Elaboration

For this next exercise, go back and use the list of items that you initially remembered from Edgar's garage (page 6). Compare these with the bold-faced listing of the items in the garage (page 7) to identify which items were elaborated items and which were not. Write down the items that you recalled in the appropriate columns below.

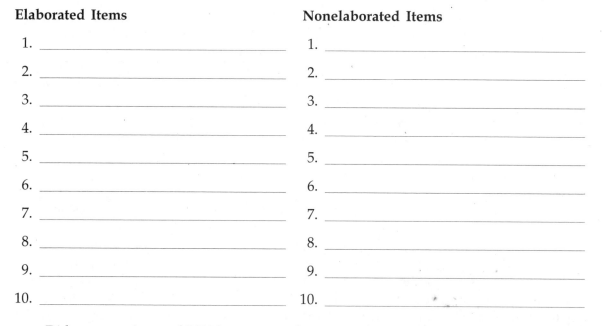

Elaborated Items	Nonelaborated Items
1. _____	1. _____
2. _____	2. _____
3. _____	3. _____
4. _____	4. _____
5. _____	5. _____
6. _____	6. _____
7. _____	7. _____
8. _____	8. _____
9. _____	9. _____
10. _____	10. _____

Did our exercise work? Did you remember more elaborated items than unelaborated items? There is a chance that some of the unelaborated items in the story hold personal significance to you and therefore contain a personal, preexisting elaboration component. For instance, although hubcaps were not elaborated on, perhaps you're a hubcap collector. In that case, hubcaps probably stood out. Perhaps your hobby is fixing radios, and therefore the broken radio stood out. Do some additional investigation to determine why you remembered what you remembered. You will usually find an explanation as to why you remember what you remember. In other words, think about your thinking as you shape your memory.

🔑 Memory Tip: Use Your Personal, Preexisting Elaboration (PPX)

Remember, *personal, preexisting elaborations* are memories that have personal significance to you. Whether you're aware of it or not, you probably use personal, preexisting elaboration (PPX) already when trying to boost recall. As an example, let's bring our friend Edgar in from the garage to show us how to use PPX elaboration when learning someone's name.

Let's say that Edgar met someone named Mary. He wants to be able to commit the name of his new acquaintance to memory quickly. To do this, he recalls a PPX that he can use. He has a cousin named Mary who has the same color eyes as the Mary he just met. By using this memory strategy to promote recall he has placed new information (the new Mary) into a previously established and elaborated memory file (his cousin Mary). His *recall*, or ability to utilize the new memory when he needs it, now becomes simple association. *Association* is tying a new memory to an old one. A memory for the name of the new Mary is now encoded at a deeper level and a safety net is created to access her name by a different means, if needed. While the memory trace for the new Mary develops and becomes more solidified within Edgar's mind, he can piggyback his ability to recall Mary's name onto a well-established memory circuit. Believe it or not, this takes less effort because a memory pattern is already laid and a new memory does not have to be created, only connected. The point is that you already use elaboration all the time to remember information. Now you can *choose* to use it when appropriate through conscious encoding and association. Because association is such a powerful memory tool, we have devoted chapter 14 to discussing it in detail.

Now let's look at a couple of other factors that might have influenced the items that you remembered in the Edgar's garage exercise.

Primacy and Recency Effects

There were four items in the story that we'd like to take a special look at. Neither the first two items listed in the story (watches, lamps) nor the last two items listed (television set, checkers game) were listed as elaborated or nonelaborated items above. However, you may have recalled these due to the phenomenon of primacy and recency effects. *Primacy effects* and *recency effects* are terms used in memory research that indicate that people maybe more likely to remember the first and/or last things encountered within a list. Go back and see if you recalled those first or last two objects. This investigation will provide you with additional information on what your personal style of memory is. If you remembered the first two, but not the last two, you may be more primacy oriented (more likely to remember the first in a given list). If you remembered the last but not the first, you are probably more recency oriented (remembering the last items in a list). You can continue to use these personal strengths as you shape and strengthen your memory. So the next time you have a list to remember, place the most important items in the front or back of the list, depending on your personal strengths.

🔑 Memory Tip: Primacy and Recency Rotation

If you have found that you have an inherent strength in utilizing either primacy or recency strategies, try taking frequent breaks when attempting to memorize a great deal of information. In doing this you can better capitalize on your inherent strengths. During the break, alter the list by moving different words into the primacy or recency positions. Allow enough time during the break for your mind to clear the link with the prior list's occupant of the primacy position. If this is a natural strength for you, it stands to reason that the more primacy or recency opportunities encountered, the better your recall of the information will be. Using this strategy of taking frequent breaks while introducing an endless supply of primacy or recency positions may actually prove to be better management of your time than more traditional strategies such as repetition. By rotating primacy and recency positions to encode information such as lists, we are creating a constant within the unfamiliar. Perhaps this familiar presence can instill just a hint of the comfort necessary to further enhance your mind's ability to process this new information.

Edgar's Garage Lays Our Foundation

The first exercise serves as the cornerstone for much of what we will discuss and teach in this book. We wanted to reveal through this exercise that memory does not work through happenstance. Memory is not arbitrary, and certain factors exist that make retention and recall more consistent and reliable. Through this exercise we introduced some of the basic concepts related to memory and specific to the RARE-DREAM model. For example, we introduced the concept of elaboration. This is a central concept interwoven throughout the RARE-DREAM memory program, one that we will explore through many different perspectives and from many different angles. We also introduced the central character in the book, Edgar. Although Edgar is modeled after an actual person, there are times when we embellish his habits a bit in order to emphasize a point. In reality, Edgar was a wonderful gentleman who participated in one of our memory groups. Edgar was the "doubting Thomas" of the group. No matter what we presented, he would voice several reasons why it wouldn't work. Edgar quickly became the barometer by which we measured the progress of the group. Upon completion of the program, he became the greatest endorser of the techniques taught in RARE-DREAM. By the way, do you remember what the overall goals of RARE and DREAM are?

Goals of RARE-DREAM

Research indicates that, as we age, we become less effective at spontaneously encoding or learning new information. The passive attention that we once relied on to absorb new information within our environment may no longer work like it once did. Changes in our attention likely account for a good part of the alterations in memory we experience with age. We hope this exercise gave you firsthand experience, showing you that elaborated information is more likely to be remembered. In this book you will learn multiple ways to elaborate on information, helping you to ensure that information is being learned effectively. That is what the RARE portion of the RARE-DREAM model will teach. Through exercises, RARE will teach you to strategically pinpoint the focus of your attention, rather than relying on the more traditional shotgun approach.

The DREAM portion of the book is equally important and well established within the literature (Yesavage et al. 1983; Best et al. 1992; Verhaeghen et al. 1992; Dellefield and McDougall 1996). The DREAM portion will assist you in developing and maintaining a realistic and adaptive attitude about memory functioning. With DREAM we will seek to adjust any perceptions or beliefs that may be working against you. A second goal of the DREAM component is to educate and assist you in adjusting to any struggles that you may be experiencing related to the progress of aging. We all live in a state of constant change. This change requires continual adjustment and adaptation, which isn't always easy. The good news is that research has shown that memory programs that incorporate multiple techniques designed to address memory at several levels, such as the RARE-DREAM Model, have been show to promote lasting changes (Neely and Baeckman 1993).

We will end this chapter with an outline of the remaining chapters and a detailed review of the RARE-DREAM approach. By providing an outline of the upcoming material, we hope to help you to begin developing some context in which to place the information as it is presented. This type of organization is essential when learning large amounts of new information.

The RARE-DREAM: Review and Overview of Chapters

In the proceeding pages you will develop methods to enhance effective learning and use strategies to improve your ability to recall the memories that you need (chapter 13). You will be able to use RARE to help you remember how to remember. You will learn to Relax and therefore maximize the receptiveness of your senses (chapter 5). You will learn specific Attention skills that will help you solidify information in the early stages of memory formulation (chapter 6). With Rehearsal, you will learn to further imprint the information you want to save into your mind so that it can be recalled later with minimal effort (chapter 10). Finally, with Envisioning you will strengthen the memory through the use of visual and sensory imagery to apply greater texture, depth, and sensory experience to the information learned (chapter 12). Together these stages compose the acronym RARE, which will guide you toward improved memory (RARE = Relax, Attend, Rehearse, and Envision). Utilizing the RARE techniques, you will continue to learn more about how memory functions and how to apply this knowledge in an effective, efficient manner that results in a more sound, reliable memory (chapters 8, 9, and 13). With RARE, your efforts will be rewarded in a way that you could only dream of before.

The second portion of our memory-enhancement program focuses on establishing realistic expectations about yourself and your memory. In this second section, we will focus on Developing Rational and Emotionally Adaptive Mindsets (DREAM). Your beliefs contain both emotional and logical components that you will examine and fine-tune to better enhance your memory functioning (chapters 3 and 11). DREAM is the foundation on which the specific RARE techniques are built. For example, in the process of improving your memory it may be necessary to accept that your memory is different than it used to be (chapter 4). In doing so, you can then replace existing ill defined or ineffective memory strategies with new strategies that incorporate your individual strengths. You will soon see there is more than one way to approach remembering.

Change and progress do not usually occur in a linear fashion, moving systematically and predictably from point A to point B. Therefore, we will weave the RARE and DREAM portions together, going back and forth from one to the other.

In the next chapter, we will establish and build a foundation for your improved memory. We will examine memory, begin to review your expectations about memory, and help you to put your memory in perspective with a trip down memory lane. The overall goal of the foundational work in the next chapter is to help you to develop or maintain accurate perceptions of your memory. With informed perceptions on memory functioning, you will be well on your way toward Developing Rational and Emotionally Adaptive Mindsets.

People are disturbed not by things but by the view which they take of them.

—Epictetus, Roman philosopher

⋆ 2 ⋆

Establishing a Foundation—Perceptions of Memory

Can memory be improved? This all depends on the perspective you hold toward memory functioning. There are two different perspectives that you may have regarding your memory: 1. the perspective that your memory functions as a distinct entity operating outside of your control; or 2. the perspective that memory is something within you that, through effort, you can make work to your advantage. Take a moment to think about this. Go back and read over the two perspectives again. Which of the two perspectives do you currently hold? Do you feel powerless toward your memory? Or do you feel like you have the ability to control your memory? Remember and continue to examine these views as you read along. And remember that we asked you to remember. We'll kick off this foundational work by providing a succinct definition of memory.

A Brief Definition of Memory

Memory consists of two phases. These phases are: 1. *encoding,* or the process of taking information from one's environment through the senses then organizing, and storing this information in the form of internal representations; and 2. *retrieval* or *recall,* which is the ability to recall these representations at a later time. In short, memory is an inner representation of our outer world and includes our ability to access and apply this information at a later time. So what is memory made up of.

Anatomy of Memory

There are multiple memory systems. These multiple systems are integrated into what we perceive as a whole, comprehensive understanding of our world. These individual memory systems work in unison to make up the central concept of "memory." You have separate memory systems for motor activities (like the ability to choose and use the correct dinner utensil to eat your soup). Other memory systems exist for sensory interactions with our environment. Multiple memory systems control and manage our complex visual memory and still others coordinate our verbal knowledge. The right side of your brain acts independently from the left. Each hemisphere works with the other by sharing its independent knowledge base and memory systems via the super information highway between the two hemispheres, the *corpus collosum*. The deep regions of your brain (subcortical) serve very different functions than the outer regions (cortical). All are interconnected through a complex network of systems and circuits. These are just a few of the individual components of the mind that make up the wonderfully complex system of memory. But as with any complex process, memory has its limitations.

Get Real!

Have you ever seen one of those characters on a television talk show or "informercial" who proclaims exceptional memory? They are usually advertising some memory-enhancement program or newly discovered substance where "you too can have a flawless memory." They perform incredible feats, such as remembering the first names of the entire 100-member studio audience. Through complex strategies, these "memory experts" put on a performance as stunning as a high-wire balancing act.

The question we pose to you is: Would you rather be trained to perform single-stunning acts worthy of a circus tent, or learn how to make your memory work for you so that you can feel good about your memory in the less dazzling but just as exciting circus of daily living? Although we will teach techniques similar to the ones used by the memory-circus performers, we are more concerned with presenting skills that will assist you in feeling confident about your memory. It's just a matter of having the correct perspective and strategically implementing techniques that will maximize your memory.

At the beginning of this chapter, we asked you which of two ways you tend to view your memory. Do you remember what the two ways were? Did you remember that we asked you to remember? Pause and take a second to see if you remember. If you can't recall, reread that section. After rereading it, close your eyes and repeat to yourself the two different perceptions. This will serve to reinforce the memory. As you will soon read, you cannot expect to remember that which you haven't examined to begin with.

The two ways to perceive memory were:

1. Memory as a distinct entity outside of your control, and

2. Memory as something within you that with effort you can control.

This "test" was our first attempt to assess how you perceive your memory and whether this perception might serve as a road block to healthy memory functioning. After all, it would be unrealistic to expect our memory to properly function and flourish while holding the belief of memory being outside of our control. Let's look closer at your expectations, as expectations are the foundation on which perceptions are built.

Expectations of Memory: Is Your Faith Misplaced?

Many of us hold unrealistic expectations about what memory is and how memory works. We seek perfection from our memory. This isn't really surprising. Like some flawless entity, we want our memory to be all-powerful, and perfect. After all, the essence of our lives is built on the foundation of memory. Memory determines who we are, what we are, and what we are capable of being and doing. From our bank account to our favorite food to the memory of our first kiss and to knowing what love feels like, all these reside under the domain of memory. Memory is the all-encompassing entity that dictates how we interact cognitively, emotionally, physically, and spiritually. Memory represents all of our interactions in our world.

One of the first steps necessary for memory improvement is to view your memory in a realistic, balanced way. Placing unrealistic expectations on your memory will only set you up for failures and endless frustration. Begin to accept that memory is imperfect and you can create your own path, finding meaning and purpose within the strengths and limitations of memory. Memory is fallible but controllable; imperfect, but beautiful. As an example of the beauty and power of memory, let's take a trip down memory lane.

The Glory of Memory

The very fact that you bought this book probably indicates that you view your memory within some negative context, at least to some degree. Chances are that any memory failure you experience is followed up by some sense of demoralization, fear, or sense of helplessness. You may battle with your memory, you might curse your memory, and you probably begrudgingly demand that it serve you better next time. You may find yourself acting as if your memory is separate from you, an entity that has failed you. Therefore, to first challenge any negativity you may hold toward memory, we want you to take a moment to embrace the glory of your memory. As you read along in this book, we will show how negative attitudes greatly contribute, biologically, emotionally, and psychologically, to daily forgetting. Let's get away from any weight of negativity and begin to feel good about your memory by placing memory in its proper perspective.

✎ ✗ Exercise: A Trip Down Memory Lane

Take a moment to allow yourself to relax. Take a deep, cleansing breath and allow all the tension within your body to float away. Allow yourself to sink deeply into your chair, letting all of the muscles in your body relax. Do this now, and then continue reading.

Think back to an earlier time, when you first fell in love. Remember the sensations within your body. You may have been aware that your heart was beating a little faster, you may remember the fluttering sensations in your stomach. Remember the sense of curiosity about that person, how you wanted to know everything all at once and to become one. Remember the sensation of a gentle touch, the smell of the loved one's hair, the brilliance of life within their bright eyes. Take a few moments to enjoy this memory. What was their name? What color were your sweetheart's eyes? Their hair? What was the color of the clothes they were wearing when you first met? Take a few moments to savor this memory, this feeling. This memory is part of you. It helps define who you are.

You may want to think back to the first time that you held your new baby. You may remember the softness of their skin, or their tiny hands and fingernails. Do you remember your overwhelming sense of pride, the baby's powdery new smell? Can you remember the spiritual realization of perfect innocence? Savor this retrospection for a while.

Now, if you've been married, remember your wedding day. What did you do when you first got up in the morning? Who was around you during the day as you prepared for the event? Remember how you felt while standing up, professing your vows. Remember the sense of nervous excitement? Picture in your mind the eye contact involved with your new spouse as you exchanged rings. Remember the first song that was played. Where did you go that night? What was the meal and drink served? Can you remember the first kiss as husband and wife? Take a few moments to really experience these feelings stored in your memory. Just close your eyes and experience.

Having the ability to reexperience these special moments may make it difficult to view your memory as weak and powerless. The feelings you created and reexperienced exemplify the power of memory. Your memory is not simply the recall of information. We tend to overlook the beautiful, multiple dimensions of memory, the memories of love and affection, and even the memories of pain and loss. All are very powerful and very much a part of who you are.

Doesn't this experience make remembering someone's name that you recently met seem trivial by comparison? Try to begin accepting your memory in all of its fallible glory. Interestingly, embracing the fallibility of your memory may actually improve your memory, just as beating yourself up for forgetting will lead to anxiety and poor memory performance. So, the next time you beat up on yourself for forgetting a name, take just a moment, smile to yourself, and remember how your memory contains all the richness of the moments that have meant so much to you. Your trip down memory lane is the starting point to establishing a positive DREAM. It is intended to highlight the power of memory—the personal power of memory that you may sometimes take for granted.

If Memory Is So Powerful, Loss of Memory Is . . .

So memory is profoundly powerful. Unfortunately, this power creates a negative side of the memory coin. The power of memory creates great fear within many of us that we will one day be without this power. Many fear that they might one day lose who they are in a fog of helplessness and dependence upon others. This fear is certainly understandable, although we hope to illustrate that unrealistic fears can really work against your health. If memory represents the power of our individuality, then deficits in memory represent the ultimate loss of our identity.

Again, we want to emphasize that having your memory evaluated might be the logical first step in your personal memory-enhancement program. If you are experiencing memory impairment to the degree that it interferes with your day-to-day functioning, then we suggest that you have your memory examined by a neurologist or other qualified person. Knowledge is power. And, if you find that there is a memory impairment, then you can turn your attention toward treatment. And if you were to find that the changes that you are experiencing are "normal aging," you will be reassured, knowing your memory changes are within normal parameters and be able to use our strategies to enhance your memory.

Changes in Memory Do Not Equal Alzheimer's Disease

Memory impairments come in many different forms and usually depend on the areas of the brain that are affected by injury or disease. There can be impairments that affect only long-term memory or impairments that affect only short-term memory. There can be memory impairment for certain types of words, for certain types of objects, and even for simple tasks.

Memory changes associated with normal aging (to be covered in more detail in chapter 6) do not equal Alzheimer's disease. Neurological disorders such as Alzheimer's disease usually progress according to a specific pattern (see chapter 16 for more information). Alzheimer's disease is the slow deterioration and continual death of cells in the brain that usually begins in the temporal lobes (memory areas). As the disease progresses forward to the frontal lobes, it usually results in compromised behavioral abnormalities. According to Ogrocki and Welsh-Bohmer (2000)*, Alzheimer's disease is characterized by a selective, severe deterioration in the consolidation and storage of new information into long-term memory. The disease is marked by rapid forgetting of newly acquired information. In contrast, memory deficits associated with normal aging are the result of poor encoding and retrieval strategies (Ogrocki and Welsh-Bohmer 2000).

Although Alzheimer's disease is the leading cause of neurological-based memory impairment in older adults, it should be noted that "by far the most common cause of memory complaints in the elderly is not brain disease, but rather the normal aging of the nervous system" (Welsh-Bohmer and Ogrocki 1998, 291).

So keep in mind: Memory lapses and memory struggles are not necessarily indicative of clinical disease. Such experiences are normal aspects of memory functioning in aging. In one study only 9 percent of patients between the ages of sixty and seventy-eight complaining of memory problems met the criteria for dementia three and a half years later (Hanninen et al. 1995, 1008).

As a final point, we would like to emphasize that even if you have memory problems that are the result of structural abnormalities within the brain, you don't have to view yourself as ineffective and powerless. Memory is fallible, just as humanity is fallible. You *choose* to feel that lapses in memory make you powerless. We are going to encourage you to "unchoose" this perception.

✎ ✗ Exercise: Are You Flexible Enough to Unchoose the Already Chosen?

Read the following story to challenge your beliefs and mindsets.

A father and his son were in a serious auto accident. Both needed surgery to live. The ambulance came and they were rushed into the emergency room. The son went into surgery room number one and the father into surgery room number two. The doctor on call for operating room number one was paged. As the doctor was informed of the child's vitals, the critical nature of the situation became clear. The doctor turned to a nearby nurse and said in a commanding voice, "Prepare the equipment for immediate surgery!" The doctor marched down the hallway and abruptly swung the doors to surgery open. Turning to the boy on the table the doctor's face quickly changed. The doctor turned to the nurse and said, "I can't work on him—that's my son!"

So how is that possible? The obvious answer is that the boy's mother is a surgeon. This might seem like an obvious explanation now, but thirty years ago, when this anecdote was circulating through American culture, all kinds of strange answers were given. The presumption was that a surgeon would certainly be a man. At that time, our culture had more rigid and fixed perceptions on the roles of males and females. In fact, the most common answer given was that the boy must have had a stepfather. At that time, it didn't readily occur to people that the mobilized surgeon could be a woman. The anecdote was used to challenge the perceptions of people, and thus challenge the biases that were keeping people from attaining their goals. Today our perspectives on gender roles have possibly changed enough to suggest the obvious answer. Perhaps you were flexible enough to come up with a quick answer and move on.

---

* Reprinted, by permission, from J. Trganowski and C. Clark, *Neurodegenerative Dementias: Clinical Features and Pathological Mechanisms*. 2000. McGraw Hill Co.

Gender roles are beginning to change, and women are beginning to feel more empowered as a result. Can the same be said for aging? Are you willing to examine and challenge any negative biases that you hold toward aging? Can you unchoose any negative biases you hold toward being an older adult? Can you unchoose your negative perceptions of the changes that accompany aging? If we described a person racing down a snowy mountain on skis, with the wind flowing through their hair, can you be just as likely to imagine a seventy-year-old on skis as a twenty-year-old? Development of a mindset that allows for a flexible, adaptive and realistic attitude about memory and aging represents the DREAM aspect of the RARE-DREAM approach. Next we will begin to induce this DREAM state.

Dreams are the touchstones of our character.

—Henry David Thoreau

★ 3 ★

Developing Rational and Emotionally Adaptive Mindsets (DREAM)

This chapter will introduce "mindset" concepts that are essential to healthy memory functioning. *Mindsets* are your beliefs, perceptions, and attitudes; in this case, beliefs and attitudes about memory and aging. Your mindset determines your emotions and any subsequent behaviors. Your current emotional state can greatly impact the quality and consistency of your memory functioning. In this chapter we will explore how misconceptions about age-related changes in memory affect your memory. As a result, you will begin to develop a more adaptive mindset, one that is based on factual or "rational" data. This adaptive mindset will in turn help to alleviate any negative emotions that result from memory lapse.

Next, we will help you to establish realistic goals for your memory functioning and ask you to begin recording your memory adventures in the form of a memory journal. Subsequently, we will further explore how to adjust your beliefs to further improve memory . We will ask you to apply the information in this chapter and readjust your goals for memory improvement in a realistic and obtainable manner. Finally, this chapter will show you how stress and negative emotions inhibit healthy memory, and we'll give you a couple of exercises to help you adjust any negative reactions during the times that your memory doesn't work as well as you think it should.

Our perceptions, our attitudes, and our internal commentary, or the things that we tell ourselves, are essential in determining how we function. Positive attitudes lead to positive outcomes. Thinking you will succeed is conducive to succeeding. Conversely, negative attitudes lead to negative outcomes. Thinking you will fail will usually lead to failure. We will talk a lot about how negative attitudes create self-fulfilling prophecies. A *self-fulfilling prophecy* means that, even if you're not conscious of it, you may do certain things that serve to fulfill your core beliefs. For example, if you fundamentally believe that you'll never learn how to operate a computer, you may do certain things beyond conscious thought to ensure that, in fact, you don't learn how to operate a computer. Self-fulfilling prophecies are often based upon fearful thoughts, which we will discuss shortly.

Your mindsets are extremely important to your health and to healthy memory functioning. In helping you to improve your memory, it is critical to assess and adjust mindsets involved with aging and memory, because a lot of unhealthy attitudes have been found to exist in older adults concerning their health in general and their memory specifically. With this said, let's take a brief look at ageism.

The future belongs to those who believe in the beauty of their dreams.

—Eleanor Roosevelt

Ageism

Although significant scientific strides have been made regarding the aging process, our society as a whole remains uneducated about this process. Due to this lack of education, a lot of myths exist regarding what happens as we age. These myths, have permeated into societal and cultural misperceptions that seem to have solidified negative attitudes in and about older adults. Misconceptions produce negative attitudes that actually work against healthy functioning. Chapter 6 will address more specifically some of the negative stereotypes attached to the aging process and will challenge you to change any ageist beliefs that you may hold.

Ageism is like any other prejudice. These perceptions pigeonhole groups of people due to the perception of shared characteristics. Prejudices ignore individual traits and focus on perceived stereotypes. They lead to negative energy, are not productive, and often act to alienate people. Ageist views are shared by young and old alike. So allow yourself to see just how powerfully influential your attitudes, your perceptions, and your thoughts are. Let's look at what some of the professionals have to say about aging and memory.

Expectations About Memory and Perceptions of Aging

One of the most common stereotypes of aging is the belief that irreversible and uncontrollable mental declines are an inevitable part of the aging process (Zarit, Gallagher, and Kramer 1981). Such stereotypes potentially create a belief among older adults that one is helpless in preventing the inevitable deterioration of their mental ability (Lachman et al. 1995).

In this book, we will refer to two types of beliefs when discussing your perceptions and attitudes regarding memory. Beliefs can either be adaptive or maladaptive. An *adaptive belief* is a belief that promotes survival and growth. An adaptive belief is flexible and strives for positive change. A *maladaptive belief* is a belief that discourages survival and growth. It is fixed, rigid, and unchangeable. Feeling that you are helpless in preventing memory decline is maladaptive. Feeling that you can take control of your memory and effect change is adaptive.

Zarit and associates (1981) provide an example of this effect when they perceptively state that "because of the prevailing expectation that memory erodes during late life, older adults may attribute each lapse of memory as further evidence of a decline in their cognitive functioning. A younger person who is free of such negative expectations can attribute the same lapse of memory to poor attention, little interest, or interference of some sort" (163). As such, the younger adult is closer to holding an adaptive belief, believing that one can take control and work toward paying greater attention, increasing interest, or blocking out distractions and interference. This belief holds the possibility of change inherent in its makeup.

The older adult's beliefs regarding memory, however, are often maladaptive, believing that one is helpless in preventing what one considers to be inevitable. Change is not possible and helplessness is the result. Indeed, the consequences of maladaptive beliefs pertaining to memory functioning may include increased dependency on others, depression, lack of motivation to tackle memory challenges, and the pursuit of unnecessary medical attention (Lachman et al. 1992). Memory is a cognitive skill that is capable of being developed and maintained with applied effort.

Right now some of you may be saying to yourselves, "Isn't it just realistic to be negative about memory declines with age?" The response to this is, "Only if your negativity is adaptive and encourages you to take control." Evidence exists to suggest that older adults may be overly critical of their memory functioning, and that this overly critical style may create unrealistic fears in them. The literature shows that subjective memory complaints in older adults more often reflect depression rather than actual cognitive decline (Lam et al 1998; Heilman and Valenstein 1985). In other words, if you have negative perceptions of your memory functioning, it's more likely caused by a depression than by deteriorating memory function. In essence, many of you hold negative evaluations of your memory ability, yet it is important to note that these negative perceptions do not necessarily reflect the actual effectiveness of your memory functioning (Scogin et al. 1985; Zarit, Cole, and Guider 1981). Essentially, you may think you are doing worse than you actually are.

Searching for Solutions

Have you ever locked your keys in your car? What a horrible experience that can be! Rectifying the situation will certainly be time consuming, possibly expensive, and perhaps embarrassing. Well, we have a proven technique to help solve this insidious problem—take an extra key with you! That's right, carry an extra key in your purse or wallet or get one of those magnetic key holders that stick beneath your car. Problem solved.

Of course, the ease with which such a problem is solved reveals a salient concern. Mainly, why don't we think of these solutions ourselves, spontaneously, in light of problems? Certainly if we had presented this problem to you and asked you to brainstorm some possible solutions, you wouldn't have just thrown your hands up after hours of deliberation and exhaustively declared, "This problem is just plain unsolvable." Indeed not—you would've come up with the same solution we came up with, or perhaps a better one. You can do the same for numerous incidents of forgetfulness. In order to improve your life for all things memory-related, the key is to put in place some external aids for memory. Examples of external aids might include leaving yourself notes or writing appointments on the calendar. Let's look at a couple of examples of minor memory lapses that you have experienced and then search for the solutions.

✎ ✗ Exercise: Silly Forgetfulness

Come up with three examples of silly forgetfulness that you may have experienced in the past and which you fear might happen again. For each example, generate one or two possible solutions. You can use a commonsense solution or you can be more creative.

Problem 1 _____

Possible Solutions: _____

_____

Problem 2 _____

Possible Solutions: _____

_____

Problem 3 _____

Possible Solutions: _____

_____

Viewing the three incidents of memory lapse above under the heading of silly forgetfulness helps to put a little different spin on the memory lapses. Writing down solutions puts you in control. If you can find humor in these memory lapses then you have changed your perspective. Human beings will go a long way to avoid emotional discomfort. Sometimes it's safer to remain unchanged just to avoid the anxiety involved in altering your perspective. When we do this we are letting our emotions rule us. Will irrational emotional fear keep you from trying new things? Do your emotions rule your memory?

Adaptive Versus Maladaptive Beliefs: How Emotions Affect Memory

How important is good memory functioning to you? Is it important enough to change some of your deepest beliefs? For example, would there be anything in the world that could convince you that something, which is known to be flat, is really round?

Most of the world in the middle fifteenth century believed that the world was flat. The general belief was that one would simply fall off the edge of the earth if they sailed too far. Spain initially refused to expand its horizons and fund Columbus because they refused to change their long-held belief system. Why finance someone who is just going to fall off the edge of the world?

Domesticated elephants are conditioned at a very young age against escape. While being trained in the circus, a baby elephant will have a single rope tied around its leg. Try as it might, the baby elephant doesn't have the strength to break away from this rope. As it grows and matures, it could easily break the bonds of this single rope, yet this rope tied to a leg is all that it takes to hold it in place. As adults, it's not the rope that holds circus elephants in place—it is the limitations of their beliefs!

If you believe that your memory is deteriorated and will continue to drastically deteriorate despite anything that you do, then all the memory training in the world will not help you. You will never truly commit yourself to improving your memory, just like Spain's reluctance to invest in Columbus or the elephant that will not walk away to freedom. Open your mind to believe that your memory is not a flat, one-dimensional entity. Your memory is a round multidimensional organism capable of adaptation and growth. Break the rope that is holding you in place so that you can stroll into the freedom of healthy memory functioning.

In helping to foster our positive DREAM, we will next help you to identify your current goals for improving your memory. Think about areas in your memory that you want to improve and list them in the space provided. Later we will examine these goals and help you to determine whether these goals are realistic or unrealistic and to establish realistic, attainable goals.

✐ ✗ *Exercise: Memory Goals*

Take a few minutes to write down, in the space provided below, ten goals that you have for improving your memory. Make these goals as specific as possible. Take some time and think carefully about what you want to write, because this is an essential component of your personal memory-enhancement program. Remember to keep your goals attainable and focused. For example, rather than saying "getting a better memory" you might say "improve my ability to recall names." Use this exercise to actually review any memory shortcomings that you have. Think about when and under what circumstances your memory fails you. Then arrive at your goals of memory improvement. Remember to be as specific as possible and take as long as you feel you need.

My Goals for Memory Improvement Are:

1. _____
2. _____
3. _____
4. _____
5. _____
6. _____
7. _____
8. _____
9. _____
10. _____

Now, next to each goal, write the word "realistic" or "unrealistic." Which of these goals can be labeled as being unrealistic? For example, the goal "never forgetting a name" is unrealistic. Expecting a perfectly functioning memory is unrealistic. Always being able to immediately recall anything and everything is unrealistic. The goal "improve my ability to remember names" is realistic. The goal "feel better about my memory" is not only realistic but is also a very soothing message to say to yourself. It is important that you not set yourself up for failure by working toward unattainable goals.

Would you like to know a good litmus test for determining whether a goal is realistic and attainable versus unrealistic and out of reach? Say each goal aloud to yourself and consider how it makes you feel when saying the goal. Does it make you feel tense or relaxed? Saying the goal, "I'd like to be able to remember the name of every member of the club," makes me feel kind of tense and nervous. Saying the goal, "remembering more names of the people at the club and feeling better about occasionally forgetting a name," makes me feel more relaxed and peaceful.

Go back now and indicate which goals sound realistic and which might border on being unrealistic.

Realistic Memory Goals

Were the goals that you listed primarily realistic or unrealistic? Fundamentally, we need to be rewarded for our efforts or we become frustrated and discouraged. When we create difficult, unattainable goals, our efforts go unrewarded, we become discouraged, and we abandon ship with a sinking sense of helplessness. On the other hand, realistic, attainable goals bring reward. With reward we become encouraged to exert more effort which results in personal growth. Now that we've put some goals on paper, let's continue to explore your perceptions of the aging process and specifically your views on aging and memory. We will do this by helping you to identify any maladaptive beliefs that may be hindering your optimal memory functioning. So, in short, our goal is to continue to help you to identify any maladaptive beliefs regarding aging and memory that may serve as obstacles toward progress and to restructure them in a way designed to promote growth. We feel that this goal is both realistic and obtainable. In order to achieve this goal, let's next examine the anatomy of a belief.

> *"One can't believe impossible things." "I daresay you haven't had much practice,"*
> *said the Queen. "When I was your age, I always did it for half-an-hour a day.*
> *Why, sometimes I've believed as many as six impossible things before breakfast."*
>
> —Lewis Carroll, 1872, Alice and the White
> Queen, in *Through the Looking Glass*, (Chap. 5).

The Belief System Model of Memory

Beliefs are the rules and values that guide us in our day-to-day activities and in interactions with others. Beliefs serve as our reference point to the outside world. They are a set of internally stored rules or opinions about how the world functions and how we function within the world. Beliefs also serve an organizational function that allows us to organize and store memories according to rules and themes. Our belief systems are based in:

1. Thoughts,

2. Feelings, and

3. Behaviors.

When we were young, our beliefs were mostly feeling based. As we grow and mature our beliefs become rooted in rational thought. Other beliefs are established or maintained through our behaviors. We can express our beliefs through behaviors or surmise the beliefs of others by observing their behavior. Our beliefs can be based in feelings, thoughts, or behaviors alone or any combination of the three, but the thought always precedes the feeling or behavior. For example, a man who has panic attacks each time he sees a strange dog may possess a belief system that all dogs are dangerous. This belief system may stem from the memory of childhood feelings or fear when his older brother would tease him and tell him that he was going to "feed him to the big dog next door." This scenario is an example of a feeling-based belief system that continues to remain unchallenged due to specific behaviors (his reaction of panic symptoms each time a dog is seen).

Belief systems related to memory can also become filled with negative feeling states such as helplessness, hopelessness, fear, and shame ("I'm losing my memory and can't do anything to stop it"). Given this example, negative perceptions can then lead toward trying to hide our failing memory from the outside world. This behavior leads to isolation which further reinforces the perception of memory being damaged beyond repair.

As you can begin to see, beliefs are intricate, dynamic, and complex entities. They're interconnected and each individual belief is composed of countless scenarios containing multiple combinations of thoughts, feelings, and behaviors. So, how do we know when we might need to adjust an unrealistic belief?

Identifying Irrational Beliefs

Albert Ellis (1976) (Gillis and Grieger 1977), the father of rational-emotive therapy, demonstrates four ways in which to identify irrational beliefs. He recommends looking for thinking patterns about a situation that involve:

1. Patterns of thoughts that reflect a situation as "**u**nbearable." For example, "My memory is failing me, and I can't stand it."

2. Thoughts that involve "**m**ustering." These include thoughts that are expressed by words such as "must," "should," or "ought." For example, "My memory *should* be working better."

3. Pattern of thoughts that represent "**a**wfulizing." In this scenario, thoughts reflect on how awful a situation seems. For example, "This is awful; I can't remember my neighbor's name."

4. Finally, Ellis identifies "**d**amning" thoughts. What about the situation is damning to you or others? For example, "My memory is getting bad and is only going to get worse."

The four patterns of irrational thoughts that Ellis identifies can be remembered by taking the first letter of each word and creating the acronym U-MAD.

- ★ <u>U</u>nbearable

- ★ <u>M</u>ustering

- ★ <u>A</u>wfulizing

- ★ <u>D</u>amning

Essentially, maladaptive beliefs involve perceptions that are distorted in some way. The way in which we identify and change these beliefs is to first examine the thought that is driving the belief. In other words, ask yourself if your thoughts reflect an unbearable situation or mustering, awfulizing, or damning thought patterns. This analysis also applies to negative feelings related to memory lapse, as negative feelings are simply the result of negative thought. In other words, you must first think a thought before an emotion can occur. For example,

Situation	Thought	Emotion	Behavior
I see a dog.	My brother used to threaten me with a dog.	Fear	Panic

By utilizing the components of the acronym U-MAD, you can begin to examine your beliefs about your memory.

Altering Your Beliefs

Maladaptive beliefs about memory that are based on negative feelings or irrational thoughts can be replaced by more adaptive thoughts. For example, let's suppose that you are unable to recall the name of an old childhood friend. Suddenly, a subtle sense of fear begins to spread throughout your body as you entertain the thought that you may be losing your memory. Identify the thought that is affecting your belief. Replace the negative thought with a more realistic and adaptive thought and the fear will be removed and the core belief altered. You might be surprised to see the irrational beliefs that you have about aging and memory. Later, we will guide you through this process by examining your entries in the form of a memory journal. Remember U-MAD, because we will ask about it later. Let's now examine your expectations about your memory.

Unmet Expectations

Our belief systems are linked to the outside world through expectations. We have expectations of ourselves and of others. We expect the sun to rise in the east every morning, our spouse to be there when we need them, and our memory to work when we need it. When our expectations go unmet it often leads to fear, frustration, anger, depression, and eventually demoralization. These feelings of anger and depression are often secondary emotions with their root in the primary feeling of fear. Three origins of fear (resulting from feeling-based beliefs) include:

1. Fear of abandonment

2. Fear of rejection

3. Fear of failure

Do your unmet expectations about your memory lead to fear, frustration, anxiety, or demoralization? Memory will not function properly if you are caught up in emotional turmoil.

Symptoms of Fear

If this primary emotion of fear is expressed outward, it can lead to crying, arguing, temper, jealousy, acting out, and the "overs" (overeating, over drinking, over exercising, etc.). If the fear is expressed inward, it can lead to withdrawal, depression, anxiety, physical ailments and, yes, even memory problems. Lapp (1984) describes the fear of failure in older adults as the main component leading to the lack of commitment necessary to improve memory functioning. The circle is now complete. Memory problems lead to fear, and fear then leads to memory problems. So, what's the solution?

Adjusting Your Beliefs and Expectations

In examining your thoughts and feelings related to your memory functioning, it is important that you be willing to challenge your belief systems and not just to blindly accept them as "truth." Adjust your beliefs by replacing maladaptive thoughts with new thoughts conducive to change and growth. Remember, your belief system is linked to the outside world through expectations. Look at your expectations and determine if the expectations were realistic, unrealistic, or unfair. Ask yourself, "Did I expect my memory to function perfectly when I got out of bed this morning?" "Did my expectation that my memory would not fail me today prove to be unrealistic?" If you find that you placed an unrealistic expectation on yourself or your memory, it is then necessary to readjust this so it doesn't result in unmet expectations and negative emotions. Revisit this chapter as you see fit to review the foundational information on which many of the upcoming DREAM exercises are built. It's not necessary to memorize all of the information presented in the belief systems model, only to gain a general working knowledge. In the upcoming pages we will guide you through the process of evaluating and adjusting any negative belief systems that may be getting in your way. Shortly, we will start examining your beliefs, feelings, and expectations in the form of a memory journal.

✎ ✗ Exercise: Realistic Memory Goals

Now let's take the above information and reevaluate your goals for memory improvement. Setting realistic goals is the way to begin to readjust your belief system. Remember, base your goals on beliefs that are rational and emotionally adaptive, and focus on realistic expectations. Your goals should be internally driven, with expectations placed on yourself and not on others. Write the goal in a way that is realistic and will lead to success. This usually involves making the goal more attainable. For example, words like "always," "never," or "should" can be replaced with words like "sometimes," "often," "can," and "could." What are your realistic goals in improving your memory? Rewrite the ten goals you have in improving your memory. Remember, be as specific as possible, be realistic, and don't set yourself up for failure.

1. _____

2. _____

3. _____

4. _____

5. _____

6. _____

7. _____

8. _____

9. _____

10. _____

We will now incorporate this information into an ongoing memory journal. The goal of the memory journal is to *think about your thinking*. Are there perceptual distortions or expectations that you may need to readjust? Remember, for the purpose of this book we are sticking to memory-related subjects. This memory journal will assist you in looking into your mind and identifying and altering the mindsets that may be hindering your memory functioning.

✎ ✗ Exercise: Memory Journal

While reading this book, keep a memory journal. In appendix B you will find an outline for the journal. If you need more space, get a pad of paper and follow the format provided. You will focus on memory lapses, memory successes, and possible explanations as to why you think they occurred. Also write down self-talk (the things you say to yourself) and feelings that occurred during the memory event and any explanations. Write down something every day for a period of at least thirty days. Review your journal every few days and patterns will emerge to help educate you on your memory functioning. Areas to target and troubleshoot will emerge.

It will take only a few minutes at the end of each day to jot down the date and to document any notations you wish to make about your memory functioning for that day. Include a note in the column for "feelings" that reflects feelings that you experienced with each notation. What were you feeling at the time? How do you feel about it now? Are you treating memory lapses as though they're utter catastrophes? This will be an important component of your enhancement training later in the book.

✎ ✗ Exercise: Identify the Words Associated with U-MAD

Do you remember what U-MAD stands for? Write the corresponding word or phrase next to each letter related to irrational beliefs. Review the section on irrational beliefs for the correct answers.

U _____

M _____

A _____

D _____

Now that we've presented our biography on beliefs, let's take a closer look at the effects of negative emotions.

Risks of Maladaptive Beliefs—Stages of Stress

As we stated before, maladaptive beliefs (mindsets) make you susceptible to thoughts and feelings of fear, frustration, anxiety, anger, depression, and demoralization. When you are faced with these feelings, your body undergoes some natural physiological changes. These changes occur in response to and as a defense against stress. These physiological changes will impact your memory function, making it much more likely that you'll have a memory lapse. Selye (1976) identified three stages of this stress response, which he dubbed the "general adaptation syndrome." These stages are outlined below and further explained in the following paragraph.

1. The *alarm reaction stage* is the point at which we are exposed to a distressing event (memory lapse). The body's adaptations to the stressors have not yet been activated.

2. The second stage is the *stage of resistance*. In this stage, resistance to the stressor is optimal.

3. The final stage is the *stage of exhaustion*. At this point, the acquired adaptation to the stressor is lost and the body begins to recover.

Reactions of Your Body to Stress

During the alarm reaction stage, messages in the form of hormones are dispatched from the brain, telling the body to prepare for "fight or flight." This means that your body must ready itself to either fight off an attack or flee to safety. The changes your body goes through bring it into the stage of resistance.

During the stage of resistance, blood flow to your muscles is increased and muscles throughout the body tense. Your heart rate and blood pressure increase and blood vessels within your skin and digestive system contract. Carbohydrates within the liver are released, breathing becomes deeper and faster as bronchial tubes widen, and sweating increases. Adrenaline is secreted and the body prepares to take action. Once the stressor is resolved, your hard-working body must reverse each of these processes, requiring a great deal of energy. This reversal takes you right into the exhaustion stage.

In order to conserve the energy necessary for the flight or fight response, the body shuts down higher cognitive processes. This includes the hippocampus, the structure of the brain that manages and stores memory. You shift from rational thinking right into a more emotional state, as the part of the brain known as the amygdala takes over the processing of emotional information (LeDoux 1994). This allows for the immediate reaction to a threat by removing the time needed for higher levels of the brain to sort out the information. When the higher levels of your brain are shut down in this way, you won't be able to store or recall factual information very well.

The biological function of fear and anxiety is adaptive in the shortterm. It serves to alert you to a threat and spur you to take action. In the longterm, however, the effects of repetitive activation and deactivation of the stress response are believed to be damaging to your body. In fact, some researchers believe that some of the hormones released during the stress response may be the agents responsible for changes in memory functioning with age (National Institute of Aging, National Institutes of Health 1999). During prolonged periods of the stress response the body saves up fat. It is speculated that this may later be converted into damaging plaques within the brain. Also, prolonged release of ACTH (one of the stress hormones) from chronic stress is believed to damage the cells in the hippocampus (the central memory system within the brain) (Carlson 1994).*

Watch for Subtle Stressors

It is important to note that not all events that activate this biological response are always obvious. Even more benign stressors that we encounter throughout the day can activate our natural response to stress. For example, if your memory is not functioning the way you want it to, and you become irritated or distressed at this, these physiological changes can be activated.

Your thoughts play a significant role in determining whether or not you experience stress as a result of some event. Negative thoughts promote a stress response by the body and, as you've learned, a stress response works against memory. Therefore, if you engage in maladaptive negative thoughts in response to a memory lapse, your body may experience a stress response that will actually make it more difficult for your memory to function properly. A vicious cycle is then initiated, wherein stress erodes effective memory functioning, impaired memory functioning leads to more negative thoughts, negative thoughts lead to a greater stress response, and on and on. Breaking this vicious cycle of stress is so important to healthy memory that we have made it the first step in our memory program. In the upcoming chapter we will teach you ways to relax in order to combat anxiety.

🔑 Memory Tip: Nutrition

Nutrition is an important component of healthy memory functioning. We can't stress enough the importance of a healthy, well-balanced diet. Your body and your brain need the appropriate nutrients to function properly. It may be necessary to limit caffeine or sweets based on your individual needs. Your individual metabolism may benefit from higher levels of protein, vegetables, or carbohydrates. There are many good nutrition books on the market, and your physician can assist you in what nutrients your body may need more of. Balance is the key. Remember that too much of anything is not good.

---

* Reprinted, by permission, N. Carlson, *Physiology of Behavior* (Needham Heights, MA: Allyn and Bacon, 1994).

✎ ✗ Exercise: How Do Your Thoughts Affect You?

The next exercise is designed to indicate to you how your thoughts affect you. In the left-hand column, we have provided a couple of memory-lapse events that one may experience. The memory-lapse events are typical examples of normal memory lapses experienced by all people at some time. The right-hand column gives an example of a maladaptive thought that one may experience as a response to the event. First, read the memory-lapse event and take a moment to really try to imagine this happening to you. Then, read the maladaptive response examples given in the right-hand column. Again, really try to imagine yourself having this type of response. Say the examples to yourself, and try to feel the thoughts within you. Pay attention to what your body's response is to the maladaptive thought. Imagine the event, and then imagine and really try to experience the resulting maladaptive response.

Event	Maladaptive Response
I forgot to get an item while at the grocery store.	Oh my god, I'm starting to lose it. Could this be the first sign of Alzheimer's?
I forgot the name of that person I just met.	What's wrong with me? This is the same thing that happened to mother before getting Alzheimer's.
	How embarrassing.
	Boy, am I stupid!

How did the thoughts make you feel? It's likely that they made you feel nervous or tense. You may have experienced your heart rate accelerate. Perhaps your breathing became more shallow and uneven. Maybe you felt a slight sweat. These are stress responses, and they may be maladaptive responses to otherwise normal events.

✎ ✗ Exercise: Experience the Adaptive Thoughts

Now repeat the exercise, but this time take a moment to experience some more adaptive thoughts. This time read the event in the left-hand column and then imagine experiencing the more adaptive responses given. Skip the maladaptive response in the middle column and focus on the adaptive thoughts in the right-hand column.

Event	Maladaptive Response	Adaptive Response
I forgot to get an item while at the grocery store.	Oh my god, I'm starting to lose it. Could this be the first sign of Alzheimer's?	Well, I remembered ten other items, and that's not bad. I guess I wasn't paying attention; I'll have to get the item on my next trip to the store.
I forgot the name of that person I just met.	What's wrong with me? This is the same thing that happened to mother before getting Alzheimer's.	Must not have been paying attention. I'll just have to ask what his name was again.

How embarrassing;
Boy, am I stupid

What's the big deal?
Everybody forgets things,
young and old.
I forgot . . . so what!

How do these responses make you feel? Was it challenging to skip over the maladaptive response and focus on the adaptive response? It's difficult to experience stress as a result of having such thoughts. Here's another little secret for you; if you think peaceful and adaptive thoughts, you cannot simultaneously experience stressful and maladaptive feelings. When you forget something, do what you did in the exercise—choose to focus on the positive response or adaptive thought and ignore the maladaptive ones! In doing this, you will find that positive feelings will follow.

Which type of thoughts do you typically experience as a result of a memory lapse? Begin to pay attention to what your natural response to a memory lapse is. Are you perpetuating a maladaptive, vicious cycle? If so, identify the thoughts that you engage in and work to change the negative thoughts into positive thoughts. Take the time to really appreciate how the different thoughts affect your biological responses. Let's look at another example.

Maladaptive Thinking Patterns

We can't emphasize enough the importance of identifying your specific maladaptive thinking patterns where your memory is concerned. How do you feel about yourself when your memory does not do exactly what you want it to do? Do you have a tendency to belittle yourself?

Continue to make entries in your journal and review the entries for maladaptive thought patterns. In fact, don't just review your memory journal; *analyze* your memory journal in order to discover even the most subtle repercussions—both positive and negative repercussions. Edgar analyzed his memory journal and discovered some interesting nuances based on his successes in changing his perspective on memory events. In chapter 11, we will ask you to do the same. We've added a couple of headings in the journal and made the memory lapses similar to help make our point that multiple reactions may occur simply from a change in perspective. Let's take a look at three of his entries.

January 1 (A Memory Success)

✸ **Memory Event:** I remembered five out of five items at the grocery store

✸ **Self-Talk:** "I'm capable"; "My memory is normal"; "It feels good to get things right."

✸ **Feelings:** Pride, contentment, confidence, and control

✸ **Immediate Physiological Reactions:** I just felt rather relaxed. I felt alert and generally attuned to my environment.

✸ **Possible Long-Term Results:** Very possibly, I may be more inclined to go out and experience new things so that I could relive some of these positive experiences.

February 1 (A Memory Disaster)

★ **Memory Event:** I forgot two out of five grocery items.

★ **Self-Talk:** I found myself engaging in negative and worrisome self-talk about the state of my memory. "I'm so forgetful," "What's the matter with me," "I'm sick and tired of disappointing myself."

★ **Feelings:** First anxiety, then fear. Finally I was left with a vague and lingering sense of depression.

★ **Immediate Physiological Reactions:** In the anxiety and fear stage, I felt my heart rate increase and my breathing became shallower. (Edgar experienced the physiological changes that occur when the general adaptation syndrome is activated.)

★ **Possible Long-Term Results:** It's possible that I might be more nervous about going to the grocery store next time for fear that I would again forget and have to go through this whole cycle again. My fears could prevent me from testing out my memory, and by not testing out my memory, I never learn just how irrational my fears are.

Edgar's March 1st event occurred after he made a commitment to change his reactions to memory lapses. This was after he examined his beliefs, expectations, and the effects of his feelings.

March 1 (A Memory Lapse and a Personal Success)

★ **Memory Event:** I forgot two out of five grocery items

★ **Self-Talk:** "Everybody forgets things. It's not necessarily abnormal, and it doesn't necessarily mean that there's something wrong with my memory." "Being able to remember all things all the time is unrealistic." "What's even more impressive than a perfect memory is the ability not to emotionally buckle under just because of minor errors. Now that's real control!"

★ **Feelings:** Pride, contentment, confidence, and control.

★ **Immediate Physiological Reactions:** I just felt rather relaxed. I felt alert and generally attuned to my environment. (No stress reaction activated.)

★ **Possible Long-Term Results:** Very possibly I may be more inclined to go out and experience new things so that I could relive some of these positive experiences. I'm not as tied down to fear of memory success or failure.

Perhaps you noticed that the March entry reflecting the feelings and possible long-term reactions to forgetting while maintaining a positive perspective were very similar to when Edgar remembered all five grocery items. Challenge and confirm Edgar's success by documenting your memory adventures and then analyzing for possible patterns. Use the "additional notes" section of your memory journal to document possible immediate physiological reactions and possible long-term results, just as Edgar did.

Remember that our feelings come from our belief system. When you're faced with a memory lapse, it is your beliefs (mindset) that guide the subsequent negative emotion. Change your beliefs and your emotions will change automatically. "I forgot—so what" will have a much less demoralizing emotion than "I forgot, my memory is going bad." Let's take a look at a related memory tip.

🔑 Memory Tip: Distract in Order to Remember

Is there an emotional component to your memory lapses? Sometimes we are unable to remember an item due to the emotionally laden material that the memory contains. Anger, anxiety, depression, and grief are common emotions that serve to distract you and lead you toward memory lapse. As an example, perhaps you can't remember the name of a previous boss with whom you could not get along. Every time you think of that person, you are immediately left with a feeling of frustration and anger. You remember the continual discord that you experienced with that person. In this instance, the stress-inducing emotional centers of your brain have eclipsed the memory centers. For memory to shine through, you will first have to part the dark emotional clouds.

As a possible strategy to combat this, put in place a strategic distraction in order to bypass the emotion and recall the nugget of information that you're searching for. If you can identify the emotion tied to that specific memory, counter it with a memory containing the opposite emotion. Instead of thinking of the tortures of working with an abrasive person, think of a specific funny memory about some work antic. Humor goes a long way in enhancing memory function. Remember, you can't feel two conflicting emotions simultaneously. Take a break from indulging yourself in the frustrating process of wading through the muck of negative memories, and think of something that makes you laugh. Without the stress response in control you can gently refocus your attention onto the word or words that you wish to recall.

If you can't identify a specific emotion tied to the forgotten word, distract yourself with a neutral memory (like the color of the first car that you owned). This allows you to gently back out of the emotionally laden path in the brain assigned to that memory, permitting you to make a later run at it. In your mind, let go of the struggle to remember and take a small break. Recite the alphabet or count to twenty. Defuse the emotion and give remembering another try. In the next chapter we will explore aging and memory.

"You know you're getting old when . . . you stoop to tie your shoelaces and ask yourself, what else can I do while I'm down here?"
—George Burns (Fischer and Noland 1991)

★ 4 ★

What Happens When We Age

Now for the million-dollar question: How much forgetting is too much? How can you tell the difference between maintaining a healthy belief system regarding memory and being in denial about a serious memory deficit? Where do the changes associated with normal aging end and memory deficits due to dementia begin? In this chapter, we will explore these questions. In the process we hope to have a little fun and help you to explore some of your views on aging and its effects on memory. Unfortunately, we can't provide a comprehensive evaluation of your memory through this book. But we can give you some glimpses into your strengths and weaknesses and help you to stand back and evaluate your personal views on aging.

Stereotypes of Cognitive Decline with Age

Many people hold the belief that cognitive decline is a normal part of aging (Zarit et al. 1981). Lachman and associates (1995) described the negative results of this view, one of which instills a belief among elders that one is helpless to alter this natural cognitive deterioration with age. Research in this area stresses the importance of education, emphasizing that memory is a body of skills capable of being developed and maintained with applied effort. Treat et al. (1978) showed that older adults interested in improving their memory are more successful if they adopt the perspective that undesirable mental functioning can be changed if one is willing to take an active role in learning new skills.

It is up to you to define a new role in your twilight years by first understanding and then embracing the aging process. Have fun and redefine this adventure of old age in this New Age. Let's start by examining some of your positive views on aging.

✎ ✗ Exercise: Positive Aspects of Aging

Sometimes we get in a rut of looking at the negatives of life. Certainly there are good phases and bad phases throughout every stage of life's journey. Often, if things seem out of whack, we must actively respond by seeking balance. Finding balance involves realistically reflecting on both negative and positive perspectives. Internal balance requires maintenance of autonomy while being able to effect change within an ambiguous environment or situation (Bandura 1977).

We won't waste time reflecting on the negatives of aging. That routine has been overplayed. We will examine the positive aspects of aging to assist you in actively embracing the aging process. Just like in the driving exercise where we asked you to see things never before noticed, we will ask you to find the often-overlooked positive aspects of aging. In this exercise, reflect on the positive side of things and list ten things you like about growing older.

1. _____

2. _____

3. _____

4. _____

5. _____

6. _____

7. _____

8. _____

9. _____

10. _____

Was it difficult for you to come up with ten things you like about growing older? Would it have been easier to list ten things you don't like about growing older? Let's continue to focus on the positives, but first we'll examine the differences between dementia and age-related memory changes.

Differences Between Dementia and Aging

What is the difference between memory changes expected with normal aging and dementia? Let's use Alzheimer's disease as an example to compare the two. According to Ogrocki and Welsh-Bohmer (2000), Alzheimer's disease is characterized by a selective severe deterioration in the consolidation and storage of new information into long-term memory. Rapidly forgetting newly acquired information marks this type of deterioration. In Alzheimer's disease, this rapid forgetting is severe, as the individual is often unaware that they forgot something. In contrast, memory deficits associated with normal aging are the result of inconsistent encoding and retrieval strategies (Ogrocki and Welsh-Bohmer 2000). There is conscious awareness that something can't be remembered, although the individual is usually able to compensate for the loss of words by circumnavigating the lost ideas with similar concepts.

Alzheimer's disease and normal aging present a much different pattern of memory difficulties. In normal aging there is a sense of frustration when we can't recall an item from a memo that we left at the office. We feel frustrated as it lies on the tip of our proverbial temporal lobe. In Alzheimer's disease, we forget the memo, the context in which the memo is to be remembered, the memory of creating the memo, and probably will deny that the memo ever existed.

With age, remembering takes more effort. Our attention begins to wander more, and we are no longer able to apply passive attention toward the item to be remembered. Other specific changes take place as we age. Our ability to judge visual-spatial relationships becomes less reliable and our ability to identify objects may begin to show lapses. This is in part due to the slowing within the connections between the inner part of the brain and its outer layers. These connections are in part responsible for the identification of visual form and for the processing of spatial relations. Motor functions and problem-solving abilities also begin to slow with age (Ogrocki and Welsh-Bohmer 2000). The general pattern seen with these changes in normal aging involves the general slowing in our ability to process visual data and slower abstract reasoning and problem solving.

What's Behind Those Senior Moments?

You obviously feel there is room for improvement where your memory is concerned, otherwise you wouldn't be holding this book right now. Maybe you don't recall things at the effortless, lightning speed that you once did. Perhaps it takes a little more effort now to recall a familiar route or the street on which to turn. Possibly once-simple tasks such as cooking or shopping have become more tedious, frustrating, and require more effort. What's the explanation for these noticeable changes? Well, quite simply, your memory changes as you age. But remember, these age-related changes do not equal deterioration. Welsh-Bohmer and Ogrocki (1998, 291)* state that "... by far the most common cause of memory complaints in the elderly is not brain disease but rather the normal aging of the nervous system ..." Different people experience these noticeable memory changes to different degrees as they age.

Unfortunately as we age, some of the effortless memory strategies that worked in the past may no longer work. With age we may find that well-established memory systems that we once relied on may no longer be as reliable, and we don't inherently know how to compensate for this. This change leads to frustration and can be the beginning of a potentially vicious cycle of perceived impaired memory. After all, which is worse? *Thinking* you have a memory impairment when you don't or having a memory impairment and adjusting to it.

Remember that memory does not necessarily worsen with age—it only changes. One of the changes identified throughout the literature is that memory becomes more accurate with age. Information may be processed at a slower speed, but there may be some silver lining found with slower processing. After all, isn't wisdom more a function of accuracy than speed? As we age we have more information to sift through before we can recall the specific kernel of knowledge that we desire. Slightly slower processing may also lead to greater awareness of nuances, shades of gray, or alternative perspectives. The wisdom we acquire through aging allows us to see things from a wider perspective. We have more internal data to bring into our working memory for comparisons before final decisions are made. Did you know that older adults have been shown to have a greater sense of understanding of these subtle qualities of life than younger adults?

Although research has shown that attention may be the most important factor in the differences noted in memory performance as we age (McCrae et al. 1987), other functions related to immediate memory usually remain relatively intact (Siegler et al. 1995). With age, memory changes often reveal themselves as difficulties in retrieval of newly learned information (Welsh-Bohmer and Ogrocki 1998).

So, in older adults, long-term memory tends to go unchanged, while short-term memory tends to slow down. This is why you can remember your wedding in rich detail but can't remember what you needed from the store. It now requires more conscious effort to move data from the working memory into long-term memory, which is what the upcoming chapters on rehearsal and envisioning will address.

---

* Reprinted, by permission, from Alexander Foster, ed., *Memory in Neurodegenerative Disease: Biological, Cognitive, and Clinical Perspectives*. 1998. Cambridge Univiersity Press.

The changes in memory may be bothersome, but they are not debilitating. We must change the false presumption that we lose the capacity to remember as we age. At the very least, this notion is overly simplistic. To compensate for the natural changes in your memory, you must take your attention off of autopilot and place it on manual. You must manually move the information from working memory into long-term memory with the new strategies outlined in this book. Items to be memorized must be meaningful and useful in order to pass your attention threshold. You must apply your concentration on things that used to come naturally to you. Therefore, learning new information takes more effort. But if the information is properly encoded, you will be less likely to notice memory difficulties in the form of retrieval frustrations. Age-related memory changes are very different from dementia.

Dementia

Dementia is a syndrome and not a specific disease. There are over seventy different diseases that may cause dementia. Like many other diseases, those leading to dementia become more common as we age. But this does not make them a normal part of aging. The *Diagnostic and Statistical Manual of Mental Disorders IV* (1994) defines dementia as a combination of multiple cognitive impairments that must include memory loss, and that results in impaired social or occupational functioning. Memory changes in aging are inconvenient and frustrating but do not limit our daily functioning like those memory changes seen in dementia.

Other cognitive problems associated with dementia include: *executive dysfunction* (impairment in planning and judgment), language problems (*dysphasia*), sensory deficits (*agnosia*), and difficulty with skilled motor movements, called *apraxias*. Dementia is different from *delirium*, an acute confusional state associated with illness or medication side effects. Deliriums are often short-term and reversible, where dementias are often not reversible. Dementia is the result of a specific disease such as head trauma, vascular disease, or Alzheimer's disease.

By the year 2050, conservative estimates indicate as many as seven to fourteen million people in the U.S. will be affected by some form of memory problem (U.S. Census Figures). Of these disorders, it is estimated that 60% will be Alzheimer's disease (Breitner and Welsh 1995). But the numbers are on your side. The number of people experiencing memory changes associated with normal aging is far greater.

"If you want to test your memory, try to recall what
you were worrying about one year ago today."

—Rotarian

Possible Explanations for Changes in Memory as We Age

For a memory to be established for later use it must be actively experienced rather than just passively noted. In normal aging, research shows that memory lapses are typically due to ineffective processes that occur when initially attempting to establish or encode what will later become a memory (Perlmutter 1978; Smith 1980; Zarit, et al. 1981; Loewen et al. 1990). Possible explanations as to why older adults may have more inconsistent memory encoding include:

★ Lifestyle changes (retirement, financial difficulties, changes in family structure)

★ Medical conditions experienced with age that effect memory

★ Emotional belief factors (fear of age-related failures, belief that memory is uncontrollable and will inevitably decline)

★ Less-receptive senses

★ Less attentive/more distractible

★ More reliance on information from within rather than from the environment

The problem resides in what you do when trying to learn new information. Given this simple premise, memory becomes something that you can gain more control over and utilize effectively as needed. You have more control over memory acquisition than retrieval. Therefore, you must actively change the way in which you go about learning information. As you've already learned, the approach we support and the techniques we teach are simply that: *techniques for remembering to remember*. Simply put, take the time and effort needed to commit something to memory. Develop effective new strategies to remember, and your memory will improve. It's time to remove the chains that bind you to the illusions of eternal youth and accept the changes that come with age and wisdom. With this said, let's examine some of the changes that take place in the brain as we age.

Structural Changes in the Brain with Age

During the teenage years through early adulthood, the brain is busy developing the covering for nerve tissue. This nerve insulator consists of a fatty substance that acts as a conductor and serves to speed up cognitive processing. There is some normal breakdown of this conductor (called *myelin*) as we reach middle and late adulthood (Hachinski et al. 1987). As a result, by middle age we begin to notice that our cognitive functioning begins to slow. We often begin to feel this slowing more as we enter our fifties and sixties. Just as hair begins to gray and skin begins to wrinkle, memory functions also make some natural changes. This is not the beginning of the end. It's not downhill from here. Through our sixties and seventies, the body's metabolism slows down as a result of normal biochemical changes taking place. As metabolism slows down, the body does not require the calories that it once did, although the same nutrients are required. Sensory and perceptual abilities begin to dull, and it takes more time to remember and to recall information. In addition, you also become more susceptible to distraction, which further derails efficient memory functioning. But remember, the trade off is that many studies have shown that the information recalled tends to be more accurate with age. Neuroscientists speculate that the complex cognitive challenges of daily life are more competently negotiated as we age. In other words, you're not losing your memory—you're just slowly getting more accurate!

There are several other normal biological changes in the brain associated with aging. Your overall brain mass decreases by as much as 10 percent by the time you reach your eighties. The greatest amount of cell decay takes place in the frontal lobes, which essentially facilitates the application of the memory process. The number of connections between nerves (synapses) in the brain decreases with age and twisting of nerve fibers (neurofibrillary tangles) and hardening of nerve fibers (plaques) may become more prevalent after the age of fifty. The brain's blood supply naturally declines and waste products accumulate in cell bodies. As you grow older, the tissues within your brain become less elastic or less sponge-like. Your brain is no longer the empty sponge capable of absorbing all the new information that surrounds you. Finally, parts of the hippocampus (the major memory structure within the brain) deteriorate and communication between the two hemispheres of the brain becomes less effective. Different people experience these changes to different degrees.

Sounds Scary, but What Does It All Mean

As a result of these changes, your memory and other brain functions also make some very natural changes when you age. It may be more difficult to recall information already stored in the brain, and also harder to learn and store new information. Verbal abilities such as vocabulary, comprehension, and speech production are fully developed in our thirties and should remain intact well into our nineties. Immediate and long-term memory also remains relatively intact with age. New learning and recent memory is also resistant to aging but not to the same degree as immediate and long-term memory (Kaye 1998, S46)*. Some older adults may experience decreased motivation and changed perceptual abilities. Elders tend to have more difficulty deliberately focusing their attention and online processing becomes more effortful. "Motor slowing and decline in visual and auditory acuity are common in the elderly" (Ogrocki and Welsh-Bohmer 2000). The trick is to not beat up on yourself in the process and to realize that these are normal memory dynamics associated with aging. These dynamics are *not* a sign that your memory will continue to get worse! Start now by getting comfortable with the discomfort of being a little different than you used to be. It's normal. Remember, patience is a virtue. It is essential that you learn how to not let your fight or flight response kick in, when you run into a memory glitch. Next, let's try an attention exercise to assist you in demonstrating the importance of not allowing yourself to become overwhelmed by negative views of the aging process.

✎ ✗ *Exercise: Selective Perspectives: How Many S's Do You See?*

Count the number of S's in the following paragraph.

Sam told his sister Sally to stop acting silly and stay in the house. Sally shrugged her shoulders and stated that she was acting silly because Sam was slurring his speech as he asked Sally to stay in the house.

Write down the answer in the following space.

Number of S's = _____28_____ .

Check appendix E for the correct answer.

Flexible Paradigms Versus Selective Perspectives

Although the above exercise is an example of selective attention (selecting to attend to letters instead of the word or narrative qualities), the crux of the exercise is to highlight the limitations of a selective perspective.

In the exercise that you just completed, we attempted to influence your perspective in order to change your view and experience of the exercise. Rather than guide you toward reading the paragraph to enjoy the sound and placement of silly words, we directed you toward a detail (the number of S's) of the paragraph. This exercise serves as a simple example of how focusing on a particular detail within a mass of information can greatly affect your personal experience of an event. Focusing on a particular detail, to the

---

* Reprinted, by permission, from J. A. Kaye, s. 1998. Lippincott, Williams, and Wilkins.

neglect of multiple alternative details, is a selective task. Sometimes our perspectives are selective to the degree that we can't see or accept alternative perspectives. We all hold certain biases, but for personal growth we need to be mindful of these biases. And, of course, our present concern is a selective perspective bias regarding aging. A selective, thus limited, perspective can blind a person from seeing other points of view and absorbing alternative experiences existing within a complex world.

If you followed our instructions and then moved on from the task, you counted the S's but selected to ignore an entertaining word play. Selecting and adhering to only one perspective may deny you the growth inherent in alternative outcomes. At times it certainly seems as if the American culture maintains a selective and limited perspective on aging. Our challenge to you is to seek out alternative perspectives related to aging and memory. (Credit goes to those readers who went through the paragraph twice—once to count and once to read and speak.) So in the service of learning, imagine that every S in the paragraph represents one more negative aspect of aging, with the silly word play being an alternative countering perspective. Transcend limited rules and views and cultivate flexible perspectives that will allow you to see qualities of wisdom, maturity, and integrity in aging.

With this said, let's now examine your current perspectives on aging.

✎ ✗ Exercise: Views on Aging

List ten words that you associate with old age. Just go with the first things that pop into your head. Don't try to overthink it.

1. _____
2. _____
3. _____
4. _____
5. _____
6. _____
7. _____
8. _____
9. _____
10. _____

List ten words that you associate with youth. Again, go with the first things that pop into your head.

1. _____
2. _____
3. _____
4. _____
5. _____
6. _____
7. _____

8. _____

9. _____

10. _____

Your Views on Aging

These words can provide a window into your views of aging. We are going to help you to review these terms and see what your own personal view of aging is. Did your list contain negative words associated with aging and positive words associated with youth? Do your words reflect alienation with youth through negative words? Do you carry any strongly held stereotypes on aging that are limiting your current memory functioning? We have met young old people and old young people. The old saying that "with age, the waist becomes broader and the mind narrower" does not have to be true for you. Let's take some of these negative stereotypes that you hold about aging and turn them around into more realistic beliefs and expectations.

✎ ✗ Exercise: Distinguishing Negative and Positive Views of Aging

Now take the twenty words from above and list them in the two categories provided, "Negative" and "Positive." It is the negative column that we must work to change, as it may be getting in the way of your memory functioning. Know thy enemy. How can you change your perspectives in the negative list? How can you open your mind just a little to see the items in the negative column differently? You can achieve balance by realistically seeing both negative and positive aspects of aging. There are some negatives associated with aging, but there are also many positives.

To win this war you must develop your DREAM. Again, DREAM is the acronym that we use to remember to **D**evelop **R**ational and **E**motionally **A**daptive **M**indsets. This is an essential step toward good memory. As a wise Zen master once said, "You must first empty your cup before it can be filled." We invite you to empty your cups of old notions of "old" and "aging" and to replace the stale, bitter liquid with sweet, refreshing new views of an identity of wisdom, activity, experience, and perceptiveness. Again, list the twenty words in the columns below.

Negative Words	**Positive Words**
1. _____	1. _____
2. _____	2. _____
3. _____	3. _____
4. _____	4. _____
5. _____	5. _____
6. _____	6. _____
7. _____	7. _____
8. _____	8. _____
9. _____	9. _____
10. _____	10. _____
11. _____	11. _____

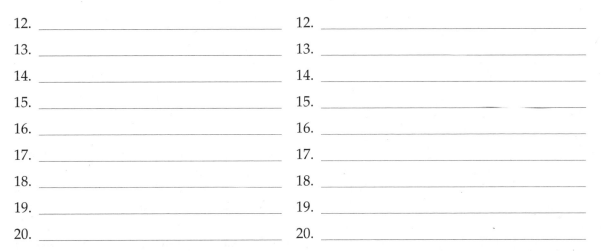

12. _____   12. _____

13. _____   13. _____

14. _____   14. _____

15. _____   15. _____

16. _____   16. _____

17. _____   17. _____

18. _____   18. _____

19. _____   19. _____

20. _____   20. _____

Which column is heavier? For those whose scale tips heavily on the negative side, remember the phenomenon of the self-fulfilling prophecy. You will work, unconsciously, to fulfill and validate your own expectations and perspectives. Let's take a look at where some of your negative perceptions of aging might come from.

With most people disbelief in a thing is founded
on a blind belief in some other thing.

—G. C. Lichtenberg

Ageism

During the 1940s through the early 1960s times were good. We had recently saved Europe and the rest of the world from certain doom and put down dictatorship in the Western world. The economy was booming. Families were expanding, with a record number of children being born. Children from this era would later be dubbed "baby boomers." As these baby boomers enter into middle age and their twilight years, we find a new strain placed on the Social Security, Medicare, and the medical systems. Due to advances in technology and health care, people are living longer than ever before. We are now living long enough to notice and even expect a difference in our cognitive functioning.

Alzheimer's disease is something that most people fear because, if we suffer from the disease, it certainly means that our bodies will outlive our minds. It is no longer uncommon to live well into your 80s, 90s, or even 100s. By the year 2030, one person out of five will be over the age of sixty-five, and there will be 8.4 million people who are eighty-five or older (Cummings et al. 1998). Essentially, the older adults of today are the neophytes of a new generational landscape. Past generations have not really had to contend with the issues that may confront a healthy ninety-year-old person today. For this reason, the term "New Ager" may be a more appropriate moniker for older adults than "the elderly," because the older adult of today is passing the threshold into a new age. The elderly (a term that, in our society, connotes frailty and dependence) of today are entering a new frontier of living life to new levels. This includes both longevity and quality of life. Older people are more active these days, with a new thirst for enjoying an adventurous life. It is a new age for the mature to take on society's archaic views and to design a new role for themselves. After all, you are the holders of wisdom and experience. It is by the sweat of your brow that the younger generations are enjoying these prosperous times. You are the foundation on which these times were built and by which future generations of New Agers will define themselves.

Aging is not something that happens to you
It's something that you choose to do well.

—Fischer and Noland

Discrimination

Regardless of the changes made by older people in this new age, discrimination based on age (*ageism*) is alive and well in modern Western society. It is up to you to distill the myths associated with age and to define a new role for yourself. Currently, the aged in America's culture have a limited role. In this technology-based, throwaway society, we usually get rid of the old to make room for the new. When the television breaks down we go out and buy a new one rather than have the old one repaired.

Unfortunately, this theme is replicated with America's seniors. By law, older adults are retired from the work force, and symbolically led to pasture and even potential poverty via social welfare policies. In this phasing out, the elderly remain invisible and unnoticed in society. Out with the old and in with the new. To blazes with learned wisdom—vitality, speed, and stamina are everything. Yes, ageism thrives in America. As a matter of fact, this bias is so ingrained within the fabric of society that New Agers often don't even realize the degree to which they buy into it and blindly accept it. "Old people's brains don't work right." "They have poor memories." "With age comes poor memory functioning and senility." "The old are the burden of the young." This view of older adults is depressing, especially if you are amongst the growing number of individuals above the age of sixty-five. Who determined that the magic age of sixty-five is "old"? It's no wonder that the New Agers are distressed, magnifying every tiny memory lapse and waiting impatiently for their certain sentence of senility. Why doesn't the mature elephant try to break the rope? Because he doesn't believe he can. Break the rope that binds *you.* You can walk away from beliefs that don't serve you and enjoy the freedom in life that you deserve.

Eastern philosophies about aging are steeped with the belief that the aged are the holders of wisdom. These elders set the norms and values in Eastern society and are held in great respect and dignity. We will tell the truth about aging. You are not ineffective because you are older. Think about your attitudes at age twenty versus now; think about how you viewed the world. How developed were your opinions? How has experience changed your view of the world?

I'm growing old by myself, my wife hasn't had a birthday in years.

—Milton Berle

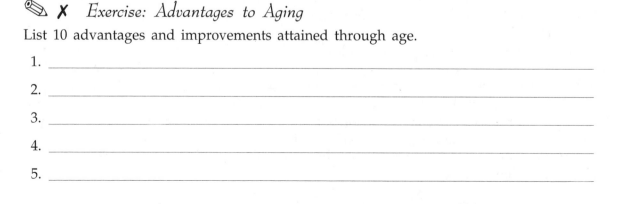

✎ ✗ Exercise: Advantages to Aging

List 10 advantages and improvements attained through age.

1. _____

2. _____

3. _____

4. _____

5. _____

6. _____

7. _____

8. _____

9. _____

10. _____

Compare this list to the list created in the beginning of the chapter in the exercise called "Positive Aspects of Aging." Do you see any differences? Have some of your perceptions of aging changed?

Expanding Your Mindset

Take a moment to remember the acronym DREAM: **D**eveloping **R**ational and **E**motional **A**daptive **M**indsets. Essentially we are asking you to open your mind to new possibilities. Use your natural strength acquired through age in viewing aging and memory from a wider perspective. We are asking for willingness and flexibility. Willingness to see things from a different point of view and the flexibility to change when old ways no longer work. We are asking you to take two steps into the dark, into the unknown in order to find balance in your view of aging. We are asking you to grow. We realize this means taking a chance. We realize this means doing something new and even frightening. We assure you that the potential rewards significantly outweigh the possible liabilities.

Preparing for RARE

Now that we've spoken frankly about ageism and established a foundation for the DREAM portion of the program, let's start to practice some of the steps for improving memory functioning within the RARE portion of the program. The next chapter will provide techniques and principles of relaxation. The chapter following relaxation will guide you to improve your powers of attention. Relaxation and attention go hand in hand and serve as the cornerstone of memory enhancement. When relaxed, you are present in your environment. Your senses are primed to absorb whatever is around you, but the absorption must be focused if it is to serve a useful purpose. This focus is where your attention becomes critical. Your attention will guide what your senses absorb. The remaining two components of RARE, rehearsal and envisioning, are the next two steps to solidifying long-term storage of information. While relaxation and attention are directed toward initially receiving information, rehearsal and envisioning are directed toward moving received information into long-term memory. Because of the distinct processes involved, techniques and principles of relaxation and attention will be presented back to back, while rehearsal and envisioning techniques will be presented later in the book (chapters 10 and 12). With this said, we will now offer you the first R in RARE.

★ 5 ★

Relaxation: An Introduction to RARE

Why Relaxation

Relaxation will be the first component taught within **R**ARE. In this chapter we will provide general methods of relaxation. With formalized methods of relaxing, we will highlight how you are functionally different when you're tense versus relaxed. Everything taught in this book is predicated upon being relaxed. When you're relaxed, you are open to the information in your environment that you choose to absorb. When you are tense, your control is usurped by distractions of both thought and feeling. For additional guidance on relaxation, we recommend a tape called "Applied Relaxation Training" by McKay, Fanning, and Sonenberg, which is available from New Harbinger Publications.

Remember that the workings of memory are multifaceted and integrative, as is our approach to memory improvement. For example, developing healthy attitudes about memory (DREAM-ing) will enhance relaxation. Employing relaxation techniques will provide the proper holding environment for maintaining healthy attitudes. A relaxed and healthy disposition will facilitate attention. Attention is the critical component to memory. When you are setting yourself up for *good* memory, you are doing many things right, not just one. If you are setting yourself up for *bad* memory, you are probably doing many things wrong, not just one.

It's less important that you memorize relaxation techniques than it is to understand the difference between being relaxed and being tense. The techniques we provide are more than just approaches that you implement to attain a relaxed state. The techniques are designed to help you learn the necessity of being in a relaxed state of mind and to differentiate relaxed from tensed. In order for a memory to be initially stored, your senses must first pick up the information. In order for your senses to effectively pick up information, your senses need to be directed to the useful information within your environment. The process of receiving the useful information in your environment is compromised if you are not relaxed.

Being in a relaxed state is not only important for effective reception of information, it is likewise important for retrieval of information. Keep in mind, a memory that has been stored in your long-term memory is only useful if it is accessible and can be appropriately retrieved. Research has shown that anxiety and stress can greatly impair attention, blocking learning and memory. When you're anxious, you're less likely to attend to information effectively, and you're also less likely to be able to access stored memories. Therefore, the first thing that we want to do is master relaxation in order to help maximize attention and retrieval capabilities. Relaxation is designed to lessen feelings of anxiety and stress and to inhibit the activation of the general adaptation syndrome (stress response). These techniques can improve memory processes and may also help to improve your general mental and physical health. Let's take a brief look at some studies that have been done on relaxation and memory.

What Does the Literature Say?

Anxiety has been implicated as having a negative effect on memory performance (Yesavage and Rose 1983; Stigsdotter-Neely and Backman 1993). As such, it has been shown that teaching relaxation techniques improves memory performance by reducing anxious thoughts and feelings (Yesavage and Jacob 1984). Sheikh et al. (1986) and Zarit et al. (1981) found pretraining in relaxation techniques to be equally effective in improving memory as pretraining specifically designed to improve imagery skills. Yesavage and Jacob (1984) demonstrated success in memory improvement in a series of studies integrating relaxation training with *mnemonic* (memory training) techniques.

The list of citations in the literature is impressively large. In general, translation of this large body of research shows that relaxation facilitates memory. By first learning relaxation skills, you will maximize your learning of what is being presented. Relaxation is the best first-wave remedy against anxiety. Anxiety will certainly impair memory abilities.

There are many relaxation techniques to choose from. We will utilize some that have proved to be successful in other programs. These include: progressive muscle group relaxation training (Yesavage and Jacob 1984) and progressive muscle group relaxation training combined with deep breathing exercises and visual imagery (Stigsdotter and Backman 1989). These studies have shown success when using a memory-training program comprised of multiple interventions, with relaxation training as the first skill taught. Before we move into the specific techniques of relaxation, let's take a look at another memory tip.

🔑 Memory Tip: Numerical Organization

Some people can better commit items to memory if they can organize them in numerical order. This organization helps to provide some context in which to anchor the individual items, and actually incorporates an additional memory system that functions to manage temporal or time and sequential organization. The next time you have something to memorize (like a grocery list), place numbers next to the items. Memorize both the items and the numbers associated with each item. If you need to pickup two loaves of bread while at the store, place the bread next to the 2 on your list as an additional reminder. If you find that this strategy enhances your ability to memorize the list, then you are probably oriented more toward sequential memorization. Trying this strategy can provide insight into your particular strengths in memory and can help you to begin to utilize and adapt memory strategies based on this identified strength.

Now let's move on to some specific techniques to aid in your relaxation. Simply follow the directions given and try the exercise.

✎ ✗ Exercise: Relaxed vs. Unrelaxed

This exercise will differentiate between what it feels like to be relaxed and unrelaxed. It is critical that you understand and are able to differentiate between being relaxed and unrelaxed because stress has become such a part of life that we are often unaware of its existence. In just a few minutes, we hope to make you aware of how unrelaxed it feels to be tense. The differences may be subtle for some of these exercises, but the effects are cumulative. Never underestimate the potential of discomfort to distract you. If you don't believe us, the next time your foot falls asleep, try to sit down with a book and fully concentrate on what you are reading! As you compare each part of your body you may want to rate the relaxed and tensed feeling on a scale from 1 to 10 (with 1 being completely relaxed and 10 being very tense). For example, rank from 1 to 10 what your hands feel like clenched and then unclenched.

For this exercise, sit in an upright chair and place your body in each of the following positions and hold the position for twenty seconds. We will start off with the unrelaxed position so that you can compare the difference in tension within your body. As we progress through each stage, relax the parts of your body that were previously unrelaxed. Take the time necessary to appreciate the difference between relaxed and unrelaxed.

1. **Shoulders**
   Unrelaxed: Shrug your shoulders and hold them as high as you can get them for twenty seconds.
   Relaxed: If your chair has armrests, place your arms there. If not, rest your hands on your upper thighs, fingers pointing in and elbows slightly bowed. Your shoulders are broad and firm. Let all the muscle groups in your shoulders and neck completely relax.

2. **Arms**
   Unrelaxed: Stretch your arms straight out in front of you, holding them parallel to the floor. Feel the tension building in your arms.
   Relaxed: Bend your arms at the elbow with your wrists resting on your thighs. Allow all the muscles in your arms to relax.

3. **Hands**
   Unrelaxed: Clinch your hands into a fist and hold.
   Relaxed: Rest your hands in your lap with the fingers slightly curled, allowing all the small tendons and muscles to completely relax.

4. **Back, chest, and stomach**
   Unrelaxed: Arch your back pushing your stomach forward. Tighten all the muscles in the front and rear of your torso.
   Relaxed: Rest your back gently against the back of your chair. Allow all the muscles in your back, chest, and stomach to completely relax.

5. **Legs**
   Unrelaxed: Cross your legs at the knee.
   Relaxed: Place your legs with your feet flat on the floor with 90-degree angle at the knees and ankles.

Did you feel any difference in your body between relaxed and unrelaxed? We spend all day applying subtle tension to our bodies. Now you can begin to become aware of the tensions your body endures.

At-Home Practice

Make an attempt once a day to:

★ Mentally review the five areas to be relaxed, and how to relax each area.

★ Take ten or fifteen minutes to practice relaxing all five areas. While relaxing, silently review each of the five areas and pay attention to your posture and the sensations of each area.

Being aware of your breathing is another essential component of relaxation. It's difficult to be anxious when your breathing is calm and controlled. Next, let's take a look at a memory tip for controlling your breathing.

🔑 Memory Tip: Conscious Breathing

Simply making a conscious effort to be aware of your breathing can serve to relax you and enhance your memory functioning. If you find that you are stressed, take a moment and focus on your breathing. Repeat to yourself "in through my nose" as you inhale and "out through my mouth" as you exhale. Allow your breathing to slow and deepen and feel yourself relax. Fill your lungs completely, starting with your abdomen and then expanding to your upper chest. Exhale completely, allowing all of your tensions to leave your body.

After you are comfortable with this first step, allow yourself to smile as you exhale. Your face contains forty-four individual muscles. Forty of these are devoted to facial expression while only four are used for chewing (National Institute of Mental Health 1995, 15-16). Different muscle groups are used with positive facial expressions than with negative facial expressions. It has been shown that in depressed patients, the activity in the large muscle in the forehead lessens as the depression decreases. Activating the positive facial muscles therefore has an effect on emotions and can serve to further relax you. So don't forget to smile!

Next we will continue enhancing your relaxation skills through further awareness of muscle groups, controlled breathing, and visualization.

Progressive Muscle Group Relaxation

Now that you are aware of the relaxed positions of your body and the importance of breathing, let's combine these to practice a relaxation exercise. This technique is called progressive muscle group relaxation. It involves focusing first on your breathing and then on different muscle groups. It may take time to get the hang of this, so try to be patient. You may want to make a relaxation tape to help you with this process. To do this, just follow the script provided and record yourself reading the steps in order. Simply read the words in the exercise verbatim, slowly and with a calm, soothing tone. If you think that the sound of your own voice might distract you, you may want to have someone else record the words. Play the tape and sit back and follow the instructions. It may take a couple of weeks before you can really get the hang of this. You should practice these relaxation techniques at least twice a day for fifteen minutes. Remember, don't get stressed over relaxation! Be patient and your senses will be ready to attend to your environment.

✎ ✗ *Exercise: Progressive Muscle Group Relaxation*

1. Sit in a comfortable chair in a safe environment with your hands lying on your lap or resting on the arms of the chair and your feet resting comfortably on the floor. Allow yourself to get comfortable and, when you are ready, slowly close your eyes. Take in a deep breath of cleansing, fresh air, filling your lungs to their full capacity. Now slowly exhale. Let go of all of the day's tensions, worries, and anxieties. Keep in mind as you become more relaxed that you have the ability to leave this relaxed state any time you wish. To do so, simply open your eyes, and all the normal sensations will return to your body.

2. Take a couple more deep breaths. Breathe in through your nose, letting the fresh air fill your abdomen, lower chest, and upper chest. Hold for a couple of seconds and slowly release the air through your mouth. Feel the tension leave your body and allow your body to relax, let go. With each breath notice how much more relaxed you become. As you become more relaxed, your breathing will return to normal. Do this a few more times. (Pause for thirty seconds.)

3. As you continue to breathe and relax more and more, allow yourself to become aware of your feet. Feel the tension of your feet against the floor. Allow the tendons in your toes to relax. Let the soothing relaxation move up your feet, across the bottoms of your feet, and across the tops of your feet. Your heels, Achilles tendons, ankles, are all very relaxed.

4. Allow this warm relaxation to now move into your lower legs. Notice how the muscles in your calves are relaxed. Let the relaxation move into your knees, into your thighs, and the backs of your upper legs. Your legs and feet are now completely relaxed and feeling heavy against the chair and floor.

5. As you continue to breathe in and out, let the warm relaxation move into your buttocks. Feel your buttocks sink into the chair. Now your waist, lower back, and all the muscles in your abdomen are becoming more and more relaxed. Going deeper and deeper into this peaceful state of relaxation, allow your upper back and chest to become more and more relaxed. Let your shoulders droop slightly, and let all the tension move out of your upper body. Now your upper arms, your biceps, and triceps are becoming more relaxed. Let all of your tensions leave your body as you exhale. Feel how heavy your forearms feel against the arms of the chair. The tendons in your hands to the tips of your fingers are now completely relaxed.

6. This calming, warm sensation of relaxation now gently moves into your neck. All the muscles in your neck are becoming more and more relaxed. Allow all of the muscles in your face to relax. Your mouth hangs slightly open, your tongue is relaxed, your cheeks feel heavy, your jaw is relaxed, your eyebrows smooth out, and your forehead is relaxed.

7. You are now completely relaxed. You may even have difficulty distinguishing where your body starts and where the chair ends. Allow your mind to drift where it wants. You amy want to picture your mind as a big, white, fluffy cloud on a warm spring afternoon . . . going whichever way the wind takes it . . . not trying to hold any specific shape . . . Blowing gently across the bright, blue sky. Notice the acuity of your senses. Notice your enhanced sense of smell and hearing. You have the ability to focus your

attention on whatever you choose. And you have the ability to remember when you choose. Take a few moments and enjoy this blissful peace. (Pause for two minutes.)

8. When you're ready, open your eyes slowly, and normal sensations will return to your body. Normal sensations will return to your feet, legs, upper body, and head. You will feel refreshed, as if you just had a good night's sleep. You will find that your memory is working better for you, and you will also find it easier to relax each time you practice.

Again it might be beneficial for you or someone else to make a cassette tape of the above transcript and listen to it to help you relax. Remember to speak slowly and allow pauses after each statement. Play the tape at least twice a day, and you will soon find that relaxation becomes a way of life for you.

Practice Mini-Relaxation

Practice relaxing parts of the body while engaged in other activities. Any or all of the areas may be relaxed in your everyday environment, depending on the activity that you're involved in. For example, your mouth and throat may be relaxed in nonsocial situations when not speaking, breathing may be relaxed in situations not requiring speech or exertion, hands can be relaxed when not in use. The opportunities to engage in relaxation are many. Try your best to think about opportunities to relax areas of your body and do it.

Cue Yourself for Relaxation

Relaxation can be achieved easily—the problem is that frequently we're too caught up in our actions to remember to relax. Therefore, use cues to remind you to engage in relaxation. Events such as hanging up after a telephone call, or completing a section of a newspaper, or when a television show you were watching ends can all be used as reminders to do your relaxation. Think of events that may cause stress for you and use these as personal reminders! Make a commitment to take a moment to relax your body and mind after being cued. Soon you will find that the cues will become automatic and that you'll be implementing relaxation principles without even being fully conscious of it. Let's take a break with a memory tip before proceeding further with relaxation.

🔑 Memory Tip: Create a Word

If there are a group of letters that you need to remember you can make up a word to represent the letters. For example, let's say you are writing your credit bureau to ask for a copy of your credit report. The credit bureau's name is TRA Enterprises. If you find that you are having difficulty remembering the name of the company, you can associate it with the word "ExTRA." TRA stands for the name of the company and the E in extra stands for enterprises.

Relax Recap

Your senses are like radar dishes that pick up the information that surrounds you. Therefore, your senses are the first step in remembering something. Remember, you can't recall that which you never picked up to begin with. Essentially, anxiety will distract your senses. Anxiety is like static that blocks your information receptors (your senses are your receptors). Relaxation techniques will serve to stop that annoying static. You know when you turn the dial of your radio just a fraction away from the station and you get that half radio-signal/half static sound? Annoying, isn't it? Well that's a lot like you trying to learn new information while experiencing anxiety. Relaxation helps tune in to that signal by keeping the static of anxiety at bay. Just as your five senses are the first step to remembering, relaxation is the first step for your senses to work at their optimum level.

We learned how to relax the parts of your body. We learned relaxing breathing techniques and progressive muscle group relaxation. *These are examples of how to relax and combat anxiety.* But remember that relaxation has to be sought. It requires effort and patience.

Slowly, slowly even an egg begins to walk.

—Ethiopian saying

✎ ✗ *Exercise: Deep Focusing*

For another relaxation technique, try deep focusing. Go outside on a nice day and find something beautiful to look at. Focus on your surroundings. Find a beautiful flower and focus all your senses on that flower. Focus your vision on the color and texture of the flower. Touch the flower and attend to how it feels on your skin. Experience how the breeze or the sun feels on your skin. Listen to all the sounds that surround you. Notice all the different sounds that you hear. Listen for sounds that you haven't noticed. Experience what the air smells like, what the flower smells like. Now eat the flower and experience what it tastes like. Just kidding about the last part. Please don't eat the flower! The next time you do a progressive muscle group relaxation, we want you to take the time to think about the flower or whatever the subject of your deep focusing exercise was. Chances are good that you will have a vivid memory of the details of the subject of your deep focus.

Deep focusing can be very relaxing, and it involves all of your senses. This exercise illustrates all the things your senses can pick up if you're relaxed, yet attentive. Many different things are relaxing to different people. The point is that you're engaging in relaxing activities to keep the static away. For some, movies are relaxing or gardening or golf. Do whatever it takes to keep your radio finely tuned.

How often are you engaging in relaxing activities? How much static are you carrying? Have you tried mini-relaxation? Remember, relaxation is the starting point upon which all of the following RARE techniques will be built. It's important that you feel comfortable with this before proceeding to the next section. If you feel that you have gained a sufficient understanding on how to relax, then you're ready to focus on attention, which is the "A" in RARE.

Relaxation techniques can further enhance your memory by allowing you to expand your attention. Through relaxation you set the stage for your senses to better pick up the information in your environment. Being in a relaxed state paves the way to being in an attentive state. The next chapter will teach you to strategically apply your attention to better encode a memory.

To be seventy years young is sometimes far more
cheerful and hopeful than to be forty years old.

—Sir Oliver Wendell Holmes

★ 6 ★

Attention

We are now entering the second component of our memory program, which is the "A" in RARE. Attention is an extremely important component of memory. Good memory functioning is the direct result of focused attention. For information to make its way into your memory stores, it must first be "attended to." Attention takes conscious effort. To absorb a piece of information into memory and to set a conscious retrieval mechanism for later recall, you must first pay attention to the information. You have to mentally take the item to be remembered and twist and turn it a couple of times in your mind before letting the information go. Your memory is only as good as the effort you put into attending. In this portion of the book, we will teach you to target your attention in an efficient, effective manner.

The true art of memory is the art of attention.
—Samuel Johnson (1759)

Passive Attention

When you were younger you probably could pay partial attention to something and later recall it. With age you can no longer rely on this passive attention to form memories. Now that you're older you probably have noticed that something as simple as paying attention takes more effort. Because of normal changes that take place in your brain and body with age, it's now necessary to give information that you want to remember your full attention.

Why Focus on Attention

Attentional deficits have been identified as a primary cause of memory difficulties encountered as we age (Smith 1980). This is especially noticeable in selective attention, our ability to focus on one thing while blocking out another (Backman and Nilsson 1985). Yesavage and Rose (1983) established the importance of concentration/attention training in memory improvement, and countless studies have replicated the importance of attention in memory training (e.g., Yesavage and Jacob 1984; Stigsdotter and Backman 1989; Stigsdotter-Neely and Backman 1993).

The first stage of memory is the sensory component, which allows information to enter the working memory through your senses for encoding. Distractions in attention will impair memory at this stage. For example, if the television distracts your attention, you're not very likely to hear what your spouse is trying to tell you. Therefore, given the changes in attention with age and the importance of attention in memory functioning, it's important to "pay attention to attention" when focusing on memory enhancement. Let's do an exercise to illustrate this point.

✎ ✗ Exercise: Method of Numerical Association

Remember the song "The Twelve Days of Christmas"? Thinking about the numbers associated with the items to be remembered will expand your attention and can be a helpful memory tool. Take five minutes and commit the items that follow to memory. In your mind, place a number beside each item. Then visualize the correct number of each of the objects. For example, if we asked you to remember a rock and a cereal box, you might first think of the number two, followed by the word "rock," and then the number three followed by the words "cereal box." Next, visualize in your mind two rocks and then three cereal boxes. The seven items to remember and visualize are: hangers, computer disks, pencils, starch, magazines, staples, and a new iron. Take the time necessary to commit these items to memory. We will test your ability to recall these items shortly.

Pay Attention!

Remember when your mother would say, "Pay attention!" Apparently we were to inherently know how to "pay attention." What does it mean to "pay attention"? Most of us would simply stop whatever it was we were doing and listen and watch. It seemed to make Mom happy. Paying attention is really more complex than you might think.

Remember, the literature shows that the difference in memory functioning between older and younger adults can be largely attributed to attention. There are several different types of attention. Stankov (1988) identified six types of attention. These include:

1. *Concentration* (sustained or focused attention): The application of mental effort in a purposeful, sustained manner (like that used in reading). Concentration is not the same as simple attention as it involves the ability to purposefully direct your attention for a sustained period of time where attention usually involves brief periods of focus (usually seconds).

2. *Vigilance:* The ability to detect rarely occurring signals over a prolonged period of time (such as watching for falling stars). Vigilance involves the ability to sustain your attention when there is nothing to pay attention to except for occasionally occurring stimuli.

3. *Divided attention:* The ability to perform two different tasks simultaneously (walking and chewing gum). This can occur with similar sensory stimulation (listening to two people talk at the same time) or with varied sensory stimulation (watching a basketball game while doing your taxes).

4. *Selective attention:* The ability to attend to one stimulus while blocking out another (like reading the paper and talking to your spouse).

5. *Search:* The ability to find a particular stimulus within the context of similar stimuli (like finding a needle in a haystack). One of the best examples of this is a traditional word search.

6. *Alternating attention* (attention switching): The ability to switch from one stimulus to another (okay, this is reading the paper and talking to your spouse).

Now that we have identified different types of attention, let's take a look at another memory tip involving attention.

🔑 Memory Tip: Decide to Divide

Obviously it's easier to divide your attention when the type of sensory information that you're taking in involves different systems within the brain. For example, it is easier to watch a sunset and listen to music than it is to read a book and listen to a lecture. Although reading and listening to verbal information involve different senses (eyes vs. ears) the information is processed in similar or competing systems within the brain. They are both different forms of verbal information. Therefore it is important to select which competing stimuli you wish to pay attention to simultaneously and not frustrate yourself on an impossible task.

✏️ ✗ *Exercise: Remembering What You Read*

Define concentration _____ .

_____

_____

For the correct answer, see page 52. Concentration and attention are often used interchangeably. Actually, concentration is a specific type of attention. More intensive than simple attention, concentration is a focused and sustained application of attention. Therefore, concentration consumes more mental energy than simple attention. However, as a result of the intensified focus, concentration will usually create a more reliable memory trace than that established by simple attention.

✏️ ✗ *Exercise: Answers to Method of Numerical Association*

Write down the items from page 52 that you associated with the seven numbers.

1. _____

2. _____

3. _____

4. _____

5. _____

6. _____

7. _____

Now check your answers in appendix E. How did you do? Is this a method that you think you might want to use in the future? In this method, your attention was expanded as the items were visualized in numbers. Sometimes you have to give it a couple of tries before you get the hang of it. If you got four or more correct, then this may be a good option for you. Next, let's examine misguided attention.

✎ ✗ *Exercise: Misguided Attention*

Put the book down for a moment and get a cotton ball. If you don't have a cotton ball, use a small wad of paper. Place it in the center of the table and concentrate on it very hard. Now, while focusing on it, make it move with your mind. Focus! You can do it! Focus! Concentrate! Move that cotton! First forward just a little, now back toward you.

Were you successful? Now blow on the cotton. Did it move? Both exercises take energy. One is positively and strategically applied; the other is not. Although it may be possible to move an object with your mind, it is much more practical to do it with the force of wind. The point is that although attention may take effort, it's important to apply that effort wisely. Don't allow yourself to become bogged down in the downward spiral shown below.

Misguided Attention → **Frustration** → **Feelings of Inadequacy** → **Poor Self-Concept** → **Poor Memory Functioning**

Let's Put All of This in Perspective

How did you feel when you were trying to move the cotton with your mind? Did you feel helpless? Did you get tired? How about when you blew on it? Did you feel more powerful? Obviously, moving objects with your mind is beyond the scope of this book. The point of this exercise is to expend the necessary energy in the correct way to move the cotton. We will not teach you to remember a hundred people's names upon meeting them, but you will be able to remember a new person's name if you choose.

✎ ✗ *Exercise: Pay Attention*

While driving a familiar route, take the time to notice something that you haven't noticed before. This is a significant exercise in revealing just how much we miss by not consciously focusing our attention. Even if the route is less than a mile, we guarantee that there will be almost an endless array of things that you haven't noticed before. On a path you've possibly traveled countless times, why haven't you noticed these things before? It's because you did not choose to focus your attention on them. You may have been thinking about what was on the radio or how much money you needed to deposit in the bank to cover this month's bills. The point is that we can only remember what we choose to place our attention and, subsequently, our memory on. Next, let's review a memory tip on limiting distractions. And, by the way, don't forget to continue to make entries in your memory journal.

🔑 Memory Tip: Find Your Way by Limiting Distractions

If you find that you often get lost while driving, it may be helpful for you to limit distractions. The more information that is contained in your environment, the more likely you are to become distracted. It may be helpful to turn off the radio. The less sensory information that you are exposed to, the more likely you will be to place your focus on the task at hand, namely navigating. Dirty windshields can also contribute to getting lost in that the sensory information coming in may be partially blocked or skewed. Carrying on a conversation, shaving, putting on makeup, talking on the phone can all serve as distractions in your ability to find your way to your destination. Internal distractions can also impede your ability to navigate. Perhaps you are thinking about an event in your day or reviewing your plans for tonight. Maybe your stomach is growling or your shoes are hurting your feet. All of these things will serve to distract you in finding your way. Make a mental note of landmarks or names of streets. Limit all distractions that are within your control and focus your attention on the task at hand. This will greatly improve your ability to navigate.

To Pay Attention: Use Effort As Your Currency

It turns out that your mother had it right all along when she told you that attention is something that must be paid. A payment requires giving something of yourself. The payment for attention is your effort. Your effort will be the currency that you use to pay attention. When asked for some additional currency to pay attention, you are asked for effort. We asked that you apply some effort in order to look for details that you have not yet seen. How many things did you see in the driving exercise that you had never before noticed? See what effort can reveal about your environment? We asked you to look at something familiar and see what you haven't before seen. Look for unseen details. With effort, you saw the world around you through new eyes.

That's the first lesson of attention—effort. Remember that applying effort to look for details focuses your attention and leads to better encoding (learning) and, therefore, better recall. Simple effort improved your memory. Actually, it's a bit of a misnomer to state that your memory actually improved. Your memory just did what it always does. Your attention is what really improved. Your memory was just the benefactor. Why? More effort, deeper encoding, better learning, better memory. See?

A method of building your attention muscle is to focus on the details around you. Make a game of it, and manually switch your attention on different settings. For example, while driving you're naturally attracted to certain elements in your environment. Without applying some effort, it's likely that you may continue to only attend to those elements that you're first attracted to. With effort, you focus your attention on details that you are typically oblivious to. Dig deep and think about where your lapses in attention lie. Mechanically switch your attention on by saying to yourself, "I'm going to pay attention to _____ . For example, if you feel that you are poor at remembering people's names, think about what you attend to when you meet new people. Is your attention primarily focused internally instead of externally on the person's name? Do you become more acutely conscious of how you're acting and what you're saying? If so, then your attention tendency is one of attending to your own performance and not to the other person's name. That person's name is much like all the things you never saw before on your drive until you focused. Right under your nose.

Now it's time to add an external aid and an organizational strategy to our tools of memory enhancement.

🔑 Memory Tip: Your Memory Spot

Establish your memory spot! Get a big beautiful bowl, basket, or cardboard box, and place it next to your phone or by your door. Put all the important things that you will need in the course of your day in this container—wallet, glasses, bills that need to be paid, and so on. Get in the habit of always checking your memory spot before leaving your house. Check it periodically, even when not leaving the house. Develop that habit; cultivate that habit. How do you develop and cultivate good habits? The same way that you get to Carnegie Hall—practice, practice, practice!

While you're practicing, work on establishing a mobile memory spot. Try always placing your car keys in your front right pocket. When you are at a restaurant, always place your purse to your right side. If you write a check, always put the checkbook to your right side. Why might these be helpful strategies? Because, if you do this enough, you will develop the habit of always looking on your right side to see if you've forgotten anything. You are becoming more conscious of your memory.

Now let's take another look at your cotton ball.

✎ ✗ Exercise: Whose Cotton Ball Is This?

Get that cotton ball from the previous exercise. Don't worry, we won't ask you to move it with your mind this time. You probably already know what a cotton ball looks like. But can you distinguish your cotton ball from another? This cotton ball is unique from all other cotton balls. Just like fingerprints and snowflakes, no two look alike. Study your cotton ball. Notice the unique patterns of its fibers. Notice the color, the shade, and the hue. It may be just a little more white or yellow than other cotton balls. Feel it. Notice its softness or its coarseness against your fingertips. Stick it to the tip of your tongue. Notice the taste and the texture against your tongue. Does it have a scent? Place it next to one of your ears and roll it between your fingers. Notice the sound that it makes. Experience the cotton ball in new ways. Remember, with conscious attention comes conscious encoding and less conscious effort during retrieval. The cotton ball is now moving from your working memory into your long-term memory within your multiple memory systems (known as temporal, procedural, perceptual, and episodic). Now, are you going to file this cotton ball to be remembered in an existing memory file (like the one for cotton), or are you going to file it by touch, sight, or time? Should you create a whole new file in which to store this cotton ball? Let's consciously place the sight, smell, taste, sound, and feel of this cotton ball in a place where it can best serve you. Utilizing the different senses creates cross-references and additional paths by which to later access the memory of the cotton ball. Memory becomes a matter of noticing the details and creating a greater number of cross-references to later access the concept. Take the time necessary to become familiar with this cotton ball, as we will ask you to recognize it later.

🔑 Memory Tip: Finding Your Car

If you often go into a building, such as a shopping mall, and find that you have difficulty remembering where you parked your car, tie a ribbon on the antenna of your car. When cars are parked side by side it is difficult to distinguish yours from others. If a large, fluorescent orange ribbon is hanging from the antenna of your car, you will be able to spot it from a distance and limit the frustration of trying to find your car.

✎ ✗ Exercise: Focus on Details

Get another cotton ball. Place it with your cotton ball and mix them up so that, from a distance, you cannot tell one from the other. Now closely examine the two cotton balls. Can you tell which is yours? We are confident that you can. If someone had asked you prior to this exercise if you could distinguish one cotton ball from another, you probably would have said no. Now you have encoded your cotton ball into your memory and have learned how to encode anything else that you choose.

Place some perfume or cologne on your cotton ball and place the cotton ball in your memory spot. The scent will serve as one more sensory modality by which to identify this spot. The perfumed scent of the cotton ball will serve as a reminder to pay attention to detail. From now on, when you smell that scent, wherever you may be, you'll remember to attend.

Persistence and determination are omnipotent. The slogan, "Press on"
has solved, and will always solve, the problems of the human race.

—Calvin Coolidge

✏ ✗ Exercise: Attend Only to Distractions

For this exercise, we want you to do something unusual. We want you to purposely pay attention to distractions. Yes, that's right—pay attention only to distractions. We want you to watch television and listen to the radio at the same time! Turn on your television and watch one of your favorite programs for ten minutes. At the same time, turn on the radio. Try to find a radio station that has some type of discussion rather than music. Focus your attention on both the radio and the television. First, try to divide your attention by attending to both simultaneously, then try alternating your attention between the radio and television, back and forth. This is more difficult than it sounds, and requires considerable effort.

Could you follow the television program? Would you be able to recite the major themes, content, and context of the show? Perhaps you can recall some, but how much effort did this take? By giving too much attention to minor memory lapses you are distracting yourself by dividing your attention between the memory lapse and the thing that you are trying to pay attention to. For example, if you become self-conscious when you meet someone new, you may not be able to later remember his or her name. Your attention would in part be diverted elsewhere. So, in essence, your memory is only as good as the quality of attention placed on information to be remembered, just as the quality of your television watching was compromised by the distraction of the radio. So don't forget to turn off the internal radio of self-doubts in order to improve the quality of the show that you want to watch. In the next memory tip, let's examine some organizational strategies.

🔑 Memory Tip: Routine Organizational Strategies

Do you ever feel you have more to remember than you can handle? As we go through our daily routine we are faced with a plethora of information that we must commit to memory for later use. Much of this information is not of the nature that we wish to commit to long-term memory. We may need it within the next hour, or tomorrow, but not beyond that. How do you handle your memory functioning for this routine information? How do you incorporate this information into your daily "routine"? How do you remind yourself of the call that you must make to the doctor at 12:15 on Wednesday to obtain lab results? How do you remember to pick up that loaf of bread at the grocery on the way home?

The trick to effective routine memory functioning is organization. Some people carry a calendar or daily planner. Others will call themselves on their home answering machines as a reminder. Computers can assist in this process, as can good old-fashioned notes. Find a method or methods that work for you and stick to them. There is no reason to cloud your long-term memory with this kind of information. Save your memory for other, more important things. The important point is to establish organized methods for supplementing your memory.

Next we will help you to experience some of those types of attention that we introduced earlier.

✎ ✗ *Exercise: Experience Tending to Your Attention*

This progressively difficult task will provide a hands-on, feet-tapping application of increasingly complex forms of attention. The task will educate you about functions of selective attention, alternating attention, and divided attention. It will also teach the use of preparatory sets—a technique that we will introduce shortly. You will use preparatory sets to facilitate your attention. For this exercise, we will first present a series of numbers. With a pencil, circle the stated number every time it appears. We will also ask you to time yourself to see how long it takes you to complete the exercise. The first exercise is an example of selective attention.

Selective Attention Task

Before starting this first exercise turn on your television with the volume turned up high. The television will serve as the competitor for your attention—a competitor you will have to block out while conducting the selective attention task. In other words, you will be selecting to place your attention on searching for a specific number while ignoring the television. Now circle the number 3 every time it appears. Time yourself and see how long it takes you to complete this exercise.

1 5 9 8 7 6 3 0 9 6 7 8 3 0 8 7 8 1 0 3 7 6 5 2 9 8 7 3 9 8 2 5 0 3 7 6 5

1 3 3 7 8 5 1 0 8 2 5 3 7 6 5 1 9 0 4 3 2 9 1 7 6 4 8 7 1 5 6 4 1 0 7 3 9

0 7 4 0 9 1 4 6 2 9 7 5 1 3 6 4 4 8 6 9 4 4 9 8 4 5 4 7 3 4 5 7 9 3 1 5 4

5 8 7 4 5 6 3 2 5 5 6 3 8 9 7 4 1 2 8 9 2 4 3 9 5 7 3 2 4 5 7 9 3 5 8 5 2

Write down the time that it took you to complete this exercise _____ .

Simple enough, right? This task also employs search and vigilance. Now lets apply the concept of alternating attention, in which you will alternate your attention between two or more things at once. Again we want you to circle every 3 that you come across. But each time a 3 is followed by a 5, we want you to switch to circling the number 6. Each time the 6 is immediately followed by a 1, we want you to switch back to circling the number 3. Aha, this is the progressively more difficult part. Again, time yourself and see how long it takes you to complete this exercise.

Alternating Attention Task

1 5 9 8 7 6 3 0 9 6 7 8 3 5 8 7 8 1 0 3 7 6 5 2 9 8 7 3 9 8 2 5 0 3 7 6 1

1 3 3 7 8 5 1 0 8 2 5 3 7 6 5 1 9 0 4 3 5 9 1 7 6 4 8 7 1 5 6 4 1 0 7 3 9

0 7 4 0 9 1 4 6 2 9 7 5 1 3 6 1 4 8 6 9 4 4 9 8 4 5 4 7 3 4 5 7 9 3 1 5 4

5 8 7 4 5 6 3 2 5 5 6 3 5 9 7 4 1 2 8 9 2 4 3 9 5 7 6 2 4 5 7 9 3 5 8 6 2

Write down the time that it took you to complete this exercise _____ .

This is obviously a little more difficult. Let's now briefly demonstrate divided attention, or the ability to perform two tasks simultaneously. Now we want you to circle every 2 and every W that you come across while simultaneously tapping your foot in measures of three. Tap one, two, three times, and then pause for one second; one, two, three, then pause for a second, all the way through, while circling 2s and Ws. Again time yourself in performing this task.

Divided Attention Task

2 9 D M 3 L 0 A V 5 M 6 0 D 2 W B 5 0 X 7 B M 3 B 5 2 C G 4 8 F Y 5

2 H V M D 2 E U 7 8 3 0 P L V W D R 3 7 4 9 F J V N W T 2 A Z 0 8 M

8 S 2 D 0 M 3 K 2 F 5 S 9 W 1 Z 8 B 0 M 3 B F 6 7 G 9 0 V 4 S H 2 M 1

3 J V W 8 C 5 A 8 X 9 2 0 4 M 3 2 6 D J W 7 G F H V C 2 4 3 I F 8 Y 3 4 F

Write down the time that it took you to complete this exercise _____ .

More Attention on Attention

You have now exercised your skills at selective, alternating, and divided attention, and you likely experienced how different types of attention require various amounts of effort. The greater the effort required, the greater the need to be properly prepared for the task at hand. In short, proper preparation is acquired in part by becoming familiar with differing demands, thereby allowing you to adequately estimate the effort needed for the mental task that lies ahead.

Using the example of alternating attention, a considerable amount of effort is required to switch your attention between different things. One of the best example of alternating attention consists of a busy day of housework involving the cooking of a big dinner. In order to get everything done, you mix preparing dinner in with the housework. You need to defrost the turkey, so you put it in the microwave. While it's defrosting, you go vacuum the rug, staying alert for the bell indicating the microwave is done. When the microwave bell goes off, you stop vacuuming and have to go back to the kitchen. Then you have to switch your attention back to remembering everything you need to do to prepare the turkey for the oven. Once it's in the oven, you decide to mop the floors and again you switch your attention to the necessary things you need to do to mop. When the timer for the turkey goes off, again you are switching your attention back to cooking. Sounds pretty complex when you think about it, and it really is. Is it any wonder, in the middle of this complicated routine, that you have difficulty remembering the name of the new couple that recently moved in next door?

Selective attention, experienced in the first attention task you just completed, often requires considerable effort, depending on the degree of competing distractions in the environment. Selective attention centers on your ability to attend when confronted with distractions. It's called selective attention because you're *selecting* where you are going to focus your attention, blocking out everything else. A situation where you might use selective attention is in a busy office or environment where there is a lot of unrelated stimulation. The worker selects to focus in on a specific job, choosing to focus out unimportant talk that is happening around him or the work that an employee next to him is doing.

Divided attention requires the most effort. It involves attempting to attend to two things at the same time. Driving your car while applying your makeup would be an example of divided attention. This is one of the most difficult and complex types of attention, and many of us find it next to impossible.

Your attention is like a magnifying glass. You have to place the lens on the object to be seen and adjust it until the image is clear. The alternative is to place your attention on autopilot and receive only what happens to stick by chance. If the task at hand demands that you select, alternate, or divide your attention, do so. But understand what you are doing and don't expect your memory to perform flawlessly when you're undertaking more complex attending tasks. Now that you've experienced the different forms of currency necessary to pay attention, let's learn how to *prepare* to pay attention.

Preparatory Set

In just a moment we're going to repeat one of the tasks that you just did, but this time we want you to do some things that will maximize your performance. Most importantly, we want you to mentally prepare yourself for what you're getting ready to do. This is called *forming a preparatory set*. It's similar to the idea of an athlete doing warm-ups before competing. To form a preparatory set, you mentally rehearse in your head all the activities, all the demands, and all the potential difficulties that may occur in a situation. It's like a mental warm-up, and it's a good way to mentally prepare yourself for the demands that lie ahead in any situation. By knowing how and where you must focus your attention, you can prepare for the task ahead of time.

Again, let's use a dinner example, preparing a three-course dinner. In order to juggle all the different things involved with making a dinner this big, you have to be properly prepared. Setting out all the necessary ingredients ahead of time is sort of like forming a preparatory set and it's a good first step. But we imagine that the best, most efficient cooks also rehearse in their heads the ingredients and utensils they will need to prepare the food they are going to make. It's a very simple process to form a preparatory set, taking only a minute or two, but it's an effective way of ensuring success in the demands that lie ahead. Too many people take attention for granted, but attention is a skill that often requires both adequate effort and appropriate preparation. The demands of a party, a business meeting, or even shopping can be overwhelming on your attention, so don't take your attention for granted. While we're practicing the preparatory set, let's also use your new relaxation skills.

Take a minute to get nice and relaxed. You may want to use an exercise that we learned earlier to ensure a state of true relaxation. Make sure you're sitting comfortably and aren't holding a lot of tension in your body.

Preparatory Set for the Divided Attention Exercise

Time to repeat the number-set exercise. Let's start by forming your preparatory set. Begin by mentally rehearsing all the demands and all the things that you need to do in this task. To practice utilizing a prepatory set we'll repeat the divided attention exercise. Circle every 2 and every W that you come across while tapping your foot to a beat of three. Before beginning, think about the 2 and the W. Prepare yourself for the task at hand and take a moment to rehearse the demands before beginning. Review the instructions on page 49. Picture in your head everything that you're going to be doing in this task. Think about how the 2 and the W will look. How are you going to be focusing your attention? Do you plan to go fast or slow? What's the first thing that you're going to be focusing on? What is the second thing you will be focusing on? Again time yourself in completing this task.

✎ ✗ *Exercise: Divided Attention*

2 9 D M 3 L 0 A V 5 M 6 0 D 2 W B 5 0 X 7 B M 3 B 5 2 C G 4 8 F Y 5

2 H V M D 2 E U 7 8 3 0 P L V W D R 3 7 4 9 F J V N W T 2 A Z 0 8 M

8 S 2 D 0 M 3 K 2 F 5 S 9 W 1 Z 8 B 0 M 3 B F 6 7 G 9 0 V 4 S H 2 M 1

3 J V W 8 C 5 A 8 X 9 2 0 4 M 3 2 6 D J W 7 G F H V C 2 4 3 I F 8 Y 3 4 F

Write down the time that it took you to complete this exercise _____ .

Compare Your Results

How was that? Did it seem easier this time? Did you improve on your time? Just to give you an idea of how well you did, we will provide you with some numbers against which you can compare your performance. These tests were administered to a group of twenty-five clinical psychology doctoral students with an average age of thirty-one. Remember, your times are expected to be a little slower than those of the students. The results were as follows:

On the **selective attention** task, the mean time for completion was twenty-eight seconds. The fastest time was twenty-two seconds and the slowest time was forty-five seconds.

On the **alternating attention** task, the mean time for completion was forty-nine seconds. The fastest time for completion was thirty seconds and the slowest time was seventy-five seconds.

Finally, on the **divided attention** task, the mean time for completion was fifty-one seconds. The fastest time was thirty-nine seconds and the slowest time was eighty-two seconds.

So, did the preparatory set help? Did you improve your score from the first time you did the exercise? Did you feel more comfortable the second time? Keep in mind, attention is the most important part of memory. If you're not paying adequate attention, *there will be limited information for you to remember*. Begin to form preparatory sets in any situation where thought is needed or memory will be called upon. Examples of when you may wish to utilize a preparatory set might include: prior to driving, before running errands, or even proceeding everyday chores. Begin each day by forming a preparatory set on what your day will consist of. Rehearse in your mind all the activities you will be involved in, all the demands you will face, and strategies to overcome obstacles. Be like an athlete, warming up as you approach the "big game" of your daily routine. Being properly prepared goes a long way in ensuring reliable memory functioning. Next we will briefly present a final preparatory strategy.

Preparatory Review

A preparatory review is similar to a preparatory set except that you do it while you're actually engaged in a task. The preparatory review serves as a mental break to ground you and allows you to review the effectiveness of past strategies and potential new strategies with which to complete the task.

During a preparatory review you will take a step back from the grind, review your progress and what you might further need to do. This review break is the time to mentally revamp any approaches that are failing. It's your halftime refresher. In the next exercise you will combine techniques that you have learned about relaxation, attention, and adaptive mindsets with preparatory strategies that were just introduced. Again you will visit Edgar's garage and commit some of his discarded junk to memory.

✎ ✗ *Exercise: Relax, Attend, and Apply an Adaptive Mindset to Edgar's Garage*

You have now learned three essential components toward fulfilling RARE-DREAM (Relax and Attend while Developing Rational and Emotionally Adaptive Mindsets). We will now apply this knowledge. Once again we will show you to Edgar's garage. The first time you were here, we asked that you just read the story once through without applying much effort. On this second reading, effort will be your tool. Before reading the story again, induce a relaxed state using all the principles we taught (breathing, progressive muscle group relaxation). After you feel relaxed and your mind is clear, consider your attention skills. Specifically, when you feel that you have obtained a relaxed state, create a preparatory set. Run through the game plan in your head. Remind yourself of the style of the narrative, the context, the task (remembering the items), and the approach you'll use for achieving the task. Then, approximately midway through the narrative, conduct a preparatory review. When you get to the middle, induce a mini-relaxation state and briefly review the task and how you're doing in achieving the goal of remembering the items (this is your preparatory review). Think back to your initial game plan and make adjustments to your approach as necessary. Don't forget to avoid self-criticisms and maladaptive thoughts about your performance. Keep a rational and emotionally adaptive mindset throughout. You will probably not get all the items, as there are many listed. But try to have fun trying out the principles discussed to this point. If you catch yourself putting undue pressure on yourself or becoming frustrated or tense, engage in another relaxation exercise. Now we will present the original story of Edgar's garage.

After years of meandering and broken promises, the day came when Edgar finally decided to clean out his garage. It had not been exhaustively cleaned for over twenty years. It was filled with toys, tools, and just plain junk, including a couple of old garbage bags that didn't make it out to the curb one Tuesday night long ago. As he weeded through the piles of memories, the first thing he decided to throw out was a box of old, broken watches that had been collecting dust for years. After that he threw out some busted lamps that were the cornerstone of his first apartment. He found an old radio that he decided to throw out, along with a stack of newspapers that had accumulated over the years. He then found a pile of books. One of the books was *Moby-Dick*, the first book he had ever fallen in love with. As a boy he fantasized about battling the huge, white whale. Edgar believed that in some way his love for *Moby-Dick* had had a large impact on his decision to join the Navy.

He then found some old hubcaps and gently placed them in the garbage pile. He found an old pile of records, including an old Bing Crosby record so warped that it looked like a miniature mountain range. "Poor Bing, all warped and scratched," he thought to himself. He then threw out a small and unusable barbecue grill that had deteriorated over the years. Some old phone books saved for no apparent reason went directly into the trash. His eyes lit up when he uncovered an old glass bottle he had found on the beach years ago. He picked up the bottle, and, running his hand across it, he noted the cold feel of the glass on his skin. He enjoyed the smoothness of the feel. He thought that he could still smell a hint of saltwater and the coarse feel of sand on the bottle. He decided to keep this bottle. He found the power drill he thought he had lost years ago underneath a dusty table. He found an old unopened can of Spam luncheon meat that had somehow found its way into the garage. He thought to himself that this would go well with a couple of fried eggs and buttered toast.

He found an old hammer that he put into his toolbox. He then came across a model of Apollo 13 that he'd given to his son on that hot summer day in 1969 when Neil Armstrong had spoken those famous words, "One small step for man, one giant leap for mankind." He also found a wooden baseball bat that felt heavy in his hands. He swung the bat into his left hand and felt the sharp sting of the heavy, smooth, and refined wood in his hand. He could still hear the crack of this bat, harkening back to his son's Little League days. He then turned to the first dress that he ever wore. It was a beautiful pink silk dress that fit him perfectly. It was backless and it really turned heads when he would go shopping in it. He smiled as he gently placed it in the garbage bag. He threw away an old television set that he never got around to fixing. He decided to keep an old checkers game with all the pieces still intact. Then it was time to quit for the day and engage his wife in a sporting game of checkers.

Edgar's spring cleaning was repeated to provide an opportunity to apply and perhaps better integrate your new skills. Shortly you will be tested, but don't be disappointed if you feel your recall did not improve or even worsened. These skills are still new to you, and therefore still a distraction. This is exactly why the exercise was repeated. It takes a lot of practice to transform yet another distraction into an integrated approach for daily living. The more you practice, the more you review, the more you absorb. In this spirit, how about a review of attention?

Concepts We Learned Related to Attention:

★ *Sustained attention:* The ability to maintain consistent, focused awareness during continuous or repetitive activities (concentration).

★ *Vigilance:* The ability to detect rarely occurring signals over a prolonged period of time.

★ *Divided attention:* The capacity for mental flexibility that allows for moving between tasks of different mental requirements.

★ *Selective attention:* The ability to maintain focused behaviors involving discrimination of stimuli. This requires activation (what you select to attend to) and inhibition (what you select to block out).

★ *Search:* The ability to find a particular stimulus within the context of similar stimuli.

★ *Alternating attention* (attention switching): The ability to switch from one stimulus to another.

Start paying attention to your attention. From now on, whenever you participate in a situation take a second to think about what kinds of attention you're using and what kinds of attention are needed for the task at hand.

Attention Strategies We've Learned

★ *Preparatory set:* A mental warm-up, preparing yourself and your mind for the specific demands required and abilities needed in an upcoming situation. Before engaging in a situation, mentally rehearse in your head all the activities, demands, and potential difficulties that may occur in a situation. With appropriate mental preparation you will facilitate optimal functioning.

★ *Preparatory review:* The act of taking a step back from a demanding task in order to review and adjust your performance. It's much the same as a preparatory set, except you're taking the time to do it after you've already started a task. It's a mental pit stop designed to prevent confusion and frustration. What should you use as a cue to stop and do a preparatory review? Fatigue, confusion, and frustration. If you feel yourself getting fatigued, confused, or frustrated, take a moment to relax and do a preparatory review.

✎ ✗ *Exercise: Second Recall of Items in Edgar's Garage*

List the items that you remember from Edgar's garage.

1. _____
2. _____
3. _____
4. _____
5. _____
6. _____
7. _____
8. _____
9. _____
10. _____
11. _____
12. _____
13. _____
14. _____
15. _____
16. _____
17. _____
18. _____

How did you do? Did a healthy mindset and relaxation and attention strategies enhance your performance? Your learning is still fresh and thus perhaps still a bit mechanical and cumbersome. With practice your skills will become more integrated into your functioning.

Applied Attention Equals Reliable Memory

Focusing on attention skills improves the encoding process. Utilizing these attention skills with a predetermined purpose and effective strategy leads to effective memory functioning. Take your attention off autopilot and place it on manual while utilizing the skills taught in this book. You will notice a difference in your memory. Remember to choose which type of attention you will use (sustained, divided, or alternating) and be willing to put in the effort. Implement preparatory sets and reviews to facilitate your memory and start absorbing the information you want to remember.

Don't choose to be random about improving your memory skills. You've already learned powerful relaxation techniques, and relaxation provides the right foundation for attention. You've already learned that stress and anxiety rob you of your attention. So don't forget that RARE is not random. Practice your relaxation techniques and attend to the world around you.

You've already got the R and the A in the RARE combination, so relax and attend and try to further cultivate healthy mindsets. A healthy mindset not only securely positions you to negotiate the demands of the world, it securely positions you to negotiate the demands of learning new skills from a new book. Before moving on to rehearsal and envisioning, which are the second R and the E in RARE, let's look at some other aspects of memory functioning. The next chapter will further explore the role of depression in memory and aging.

⋆ 7 ⋆

Depression

In this chapter we are going to examine depression and some of the causes of depression in New Agers. Depression is sometimes called "pseudo-dementia" by neurologists due to the degree to which it affects memory. Actually, there is nothing "pseudo" about it. Depression does affect memory to a degree not commonly recognized. Also in this chapter, we will take a look at what your perceptions of your memory may mean and screen for depressive symptoms you may have.

✎ ✗ Exercise: Don't Think About Your Feet

Whatever you do, do not think about your feet. Place the idea of feet out of your mind and think about anything else except your feet. Don't let those feet enter your mind.

Now put the book down and take some time to conduct this exercise. Take at least five minutes. But, if you can, see if you can take an hour. Let yourself get busy doing something else, but whatever you do, do not think about your feet. Take a break now.

Are you the type of person who tends to ruminate over things? If you have a memory lapse, such as forgetting to place the outgoing mail in the box before leaving the house, do you magnify it? Do you then use this as self-incriminating evidence to be later compared with "yet another" memory lapse, building a case for certain cognitive decline?

Rumination and Obsessive-Thinking Patterns

How did you function during your break, constantly not thinking about your feet? How many times did your feet enter your consciousness? Did they get in your way, tripping you up, so to speak? This is exactly what you are doing when you obsess about your memory. If every time you forget something you ruminate over it, then your feet are getting in your way. If your attention is consumed with one thing, then it cannot be as well applied to other things that need to be remembered. Every second consumed by your mind thinking of your feet is one second lost toward doing whatever else you wanted to do. If you become so consumed with the one item that you forgot at the grocery store, then you miss the success of remembering the other items that you did remember. You may be obsessing to the point that it is affecting your memory! Negative thought patterns will be addressed in much greater detail later, so stay tuned (but not to your feet).

Subjective Evaluations of Memory Function

Before we move on, let's discuss some issues involved in evaluating your own memory. We debated whether to include an exercise on rating your subjective memory complaints. We decided not to, primarily because there is not an opportunity to follow it up with a measurement of your actual memory performance. In essence, there was no ethical or practical way to compare your perceptions of your memory with the objective reality of how your memory actually functions. A comprehensive memory evaluation needs to be administered by a professional trained to interpret the results. Let's look at what the literature says about evaluating your own memory.

Self-assessment of memory functioning often does not reflect actual performance (McGlone et al. 1990; Dellefield and McDougall 1996). Research has shown that those older adults most likely to seek treatment for memory problems are less likely to correctly and objectively assess the functioning of their memory abilities and tend to hold negative biases regarding their memory functioning (Scogin and Prohaska 1993). Many studies have demonstrated that elder adults often have negative subjective perceptions of their memory functioning. They often perceive their memory as impaired when, in fact, it is unimpaired when tested. It has been estimated that 25 to 30 percent of healthy seniors complain of poor memory performance. Among the young elderly (under the age of eighty), there is a relatively low risk of developing dementia based simply on self-report of poor memory functioning (Kaye 1998). The consequences of maladaptive beliefs pertaining to memory functioning may include increased dependency on others, depression, lack of motivation to tackle memory challenges, and the pursuit of unnecessary medical attention (Lachman et al. 1992). So what's going on with this group of older adults who feel their memory is giving out on them when, in fact, they test normally?

What may be happening is a selective personal perspective of expected decline, leading to experiences of depression and associated memory lapses. So let's ensure that you're not missing the forest for the trees or counting S's while missing the bigger picture. According to the literature, if you feel that you have memory problems it is most likely normal changes related to aging. The second leading cause of subjective memory complaints is depression. Remember, depression can mimic a mild dementia. Finally, according to the literature, you stand the least chance of having Alzheimer's disease if you feel you have problems with your memory.

Many studies have shown that there is a high correlation between subjective memory complaints and symptoms of depression. In the pilot study we did to evaluate the RARE-DREAM approach, one-third of those referred to the study were subsequently referred for evaluation and treatment of depression and only offered memory-enhancement training after their depression was treated. Shortly, we will take a look at whether you are depressed. But before we do, let's take a look at some causes of depression, situational changes that may lead to some depressive symptoms, and pseudo-dementia.

Isolation and Longing

Modern technology has dictated that the good old days of grandparents continuing to have a central role in a large family are gone. The principle of "Go west, young man" has always permeated our nation. The ideals of expanding, chasing our dreams, and forging new opportunities have become our legacy. Unfortunately, as the opportunities and resources of our nation grew, so did the distance between generations of family members.

Generations began to grow old apart as the extended family became more and more extended. The family stories passed down from generation to generation have quickly been replaced with new forms of entertainment such as television and high-tech video equipment. Rambo has replaced Grandpa as the children's hero. Homemade cakes, cookies, and pies have been replaced with fast food in prepackaged individual containers. As we grow older, we long for the good old days of simplicity. For many, there is a feeling that the older they get, the more estranged they feel toward our ever-changing culture. Many New Agers are faced with a sense of loss and with an increased sense of isolation and alienation. Others may cling to vigorous and virtuous perceptions of youth only to have it challenged by modern views of the aged. We examine every new wrinkle and gray hair, but as hard as we try not to, we age. Depression often invariably sets in, as the quest for eternal youth is given up and the sentence of age is reluctantly accepted. In fact, the elderly are one of the largest groups that are affected by depression. Graceful aging is a rare perspective only given to a chosen few.

The older you get the stronger the wind
gets—and it's always in your face.

—Jack Nicklaus

Social and Emotional Changes Experienced with Aging

There are many changes other than the physical changes that take place as we age. From a social and emotional perspective, retirement forces us to use our brains differently. Remember, the brain, like a muscle, has to be exercised if it is to stay in shape. We may not be as active as we once were, and we may begin to experience time differently. As we age, we begin to struggle with existential issues of our own mortality while simultaneously seeking to balance the many changes encountered with growing older. We start to look for meaning in our lives, for the good we have done and the differences that we made. Perhaps a once-congested house seems big and empty as our children leave to forge lives for themselves. We may be faced with a sense of loneliness that is new and alienating. Perhaps our finances are more limited, and we find ourselves worrying about paying the bills.

Not only are there physiological changes taking place in your brain, there are social and emotional changes that may negatively impact your memory functioning. It is imperative that you continue to seek challenges and exercise your mind. There seems to be a craze presently for older adults to exercise their cardiovascular system. People line up at the malls for daily walks. Older adults are joining fitness centers in record numbers. Don't get us wrong, this is important for your health; but it is just as important to exercise your mind. Make a commitment now to exercise your mind daily. Read new books, take a college course, take on a new hobby, do puzzles, engage in challenging and interesting conversation, draw, write, work, play, and love. Each activity you engage in exercises a different part of your mind and strengthens your overall memory and cognitive functioning.

These are the soul's changes. I don't believe in aging. I believe in
forever altering one's aspect to the sun. Hence my optimism.

—Virginia Woolf

Pseudo-Dementia

Pseudo-dementia or "false dementia" is the name neurologists give to a depression that mimics the symptoms of dementia. Often it is very difficult to discriminate between the symptoms of depression and the symptoms of a dementia. However, discovering the true source of any alarming symptom is critical for effective treatment. In fact, the treatment for one may actually be a complete mistreatment for the other. For instance, if the source of memory problems stems from a depression, a possible recommended treatment may be to expand stimulating experiences by going out and doing new things. Such a recommendation may only overwhelm a person in the early stages of a dementia, who may need instead to simplify their environment.

Feelings of depression can become prevalent as we age. Our twilight years are a time when we are faced with many losses and multiple existential struggles. Issues of loss are actually a matter of bereavement and should not be attributed to "clinical depression" (major depression) unless they last longer than two months and are accompanied by functional impairment, psychotic symptoms, feelings of worthlessness, suicidal thoughts, and/or a significant, prolonged decrease in energy (Kaye 1998, S46). Whether you are suffering from depression or grief, your memory is sure to be affected. The literature shows that increased levels of depression are correlated with decreased performance on cognitive tests (Yaffe et al. 1999). It is normal to have some impairment in memory if you are depressed.

A major depression is defined by the *Diagnostic and Statistical Manual of Mental Disorders IV* (American Psychiatric Association 1994, 162) as: five or more of the following symptoms that last for two consecutive weeks with symptoms present nearly every day for most of the day. One of these symptoms must be depressed mood or a general loss of interest and pleasure.

1. Depressed mood most of the day (feels sad or empty)

2. Markedly diminished interest or pleasure in activities

3. Change in appetite or significant weight gain or loss (5% of body weight in one month)

4. Sleep disturbance (insomnia or hypersomnia)

5. Significantly increased or decreased activity level

6. Fatigue or loss of energy

7. Excessive guilt or feelings of worthlessness

8. Poor concentration or indecisiveness

9. Recurrent thoughts of death or suicide

Depression in older adults often does not involve an overt depressed mood. Instead, it may involve primary symptoms of a lack of energy, lack of enjoyment in normal activities, and the lack of a positive mood (Lawton et al. 1996). Depression is a very treatable illness. Consult your physician if you think that you might be depressed. Your memory difficulties may just be another symptom of depression. Are you depressed? Try the following exercise to see.

✎ ✗ Exercise: Depression Assessment

Answer the following questions by circling the answer you identify with (modified Geriatric Depression Scale (GDS Modified: Sheikh et al. 1991 and 1986; Yesavage et al. 1983; Brink et al. 1982).*

1. Do you feel dissatisfied with your life?   Yes / No
2. Have you dropped many of your activities and interests?   Yes / No
3. Do you feel that your life is empty?   Yes / No
4. Do you often get bored?   Yes / No
5. Do you feel your future is hopeless?   Yes / No
6. Are you bothered by thoughts that you can't get out of your head?   Yes / No
7. Are you down and in poor spirits most of the time?   Yes / No
8. Are you afraid something bad is going to happen to you?   Yes / No
9. Do you feel sad most of the time?   Yes / No
10. Do you often feel helpless?   Yes / No
11. Do you often get restless and fidgety?   Yes / No
12. Do you prefer to stay home rather than go out and do new things?   Yes / No
13. Do you frequently worry about the future?   Yes / No
14. Do you feel you have more problems with memory than most?   Yes / No
15. Do you think it is difficult and draining to be alive now?   Yes / No
16. Do you often feel downhearted and blue?   Yes / No
17. Do you feel pretty worthless the way you are now?   Yes / No
18. Do you worry a lot about the past?   Yes / No
19. Do you feel life is dull and boring?   Yes / No
20. Is it hard for you to get a start on new projects?   Yes / No
21. Are you lacking energy?   Yes / No
22. Do you feel that your situation is hopeless?   Yes / No
23. Do you feel that most people are better off than you are?   Yes / No
24. Do you frequently get upset about little things?   Yes / No
25. Do you frequently feel like crying?   Yes / No
26. Do you have trouble concentrating?   Yes / No
27. Do you have trouble getting up in the morning?   Yes / No
28. Do you prefer to avoid social gatherings?   Yes / No

* Reprinted, with permission, from Yesavage, "Imagery Pretraining and Memory Training in the Elderly." *Gerontology*. 1983. The Hawthorn Press.

29. Is it difficult for you to make decisions?   Yes / No

30. Is your mind less clear than it used to be?   Yes / No

Count the number of times that you answered yes to the above questions and put the number in the space provided.

Total Number of "Yes" Answers = _

Results of Depression Questionnaire

If you scored ten or above, then you probably have some symptoms of depression and should seek medical treatment and/or counseling. If you scored over sixteen, then the severity of your depressive symptoms are to the degree that probably require treatment. Please consult your physician.

Depression is very treatable and is probably greatly affecting your memory functioning if your score on the scale was high. While it is implicit in previous chapters that maladaptive beliefs about memory may contribute to depression, this is an entirely different issue than depression as a primary condition contributing to memory deficits. For individuals experiencing depression as a primary condition adversely affecting memory, it is possible that psychotherapy and medications may prove to be an essential component to your memory enhancement program. Treat the depression and you should see significant improvements in your memory.

🔑 Memory Tip: Check Your Exhaust

Do you notice more problems with your memory shortly after driving in your car? Do your memory problems wax and wane and include symptoms of headaches or nausea? If you are driving an older model car it may be necessary to get the exhaust of your car checked. Even small leaks can cause memory impairments and can eventually lead to permanent complications. Your neighborhood mechanic should be able to do this for you at minimal cost. Let us caution you that the chances of this causing your memory changes is remote but may be worth looking into.

Before moving on to the rehearsal aspect of RARE, let's complete the foundation of this house of memory by taking the next couple of chapters to look at memory. In chapter 8 we will examine memory and tell you everything you ever wanted to know about what it is composed of and how it works. Chapter 9 will break down memory into two broad classifications, visual and verbal memory, and help you to determine where your strengths lie.

Before we move on, here is a poem about cherished childhood memories. The poem was written by the mother of one of the authors and not only highlights the beauty of memory, but also represents the accomplishments that can continue to be achieved even late in life. The author, Mabel Mason, began to write poetry in her later years in hopes of one day getting published. At the age of sixty-six her hopes have now finally been realized.

Carefree Memories

Memories of my childhood days
Bring a smile to my aging face
No place on earth I'd rather be
Than granny's old log cabin place
Sitting by the rushing creek
That ran beside the old homestead
'Twas no need for words to speak
The entire world was fast asleep

The carefree heart of a little girl
Amazed by the beauty of a fairy-tale world
Reminiscing memories of years gone by
Her dresses long, boots ankle high

A colorful bonnet upon her head
An apron tied around her waist
A simple wrap around her shoulders
Was her humble yet graceful taste

As the creek whispered a familiar tune
Of rippling music to a steady beat
The open fireplace seemed a mile high
An old wooden chair our only seat

Gathering wild greens to prepare and to cook
In an old iron kettle on a rusty hook
Grandma so tiny with a spirit so deep
Fill my thoughts as I drift to sleep.

—Mabel Mason

∗ 8 ∗

Memory

Memory is More Complex Than You Might Think

Memory is a process that is governed by multiple systems throughout the brain. The complex intricacies of memory functioning are not completely understood, although there are many models that have been proposed. This chapter is devoted to teaching you how memory functions. By having a working knowledge of how memory works you will be in a better position to plan strategies to improve memory. For those of you wishing to gain a greater education about the workings of memory, we have included information in appendix D on specific areas of the brain and their functions. Let's start with a definition and an overview of memory.

What Is Memory?

Memory is a mental process of storage and retrieval of information and experience. Information makes its way into your memory through your senses. It is then processed by multiple systems throughout your brain and stored for later use (Parente and Stapleton 1993). Here is a visual representation of the process of memory.

Senses → Storage (Memory Consolidation) = Memory ← Retrieval

For memory to properly function, information must be correctly received through the senses. Memory is stored (encoded) *according to many different themes*. It is stored according to time (when something happened), category (animal, plant, mineral), function (a hammer is used to pound nails), and many others. These different types of memory represent individual memory systems within the brain. Once information is stored correctly within one or more of these systems it can later be retrieved. The ease and accuracy of retrieval depends upon the effectiveness of the initial encoding. Retrieval is also dependent upon what file you consciously decide to file newly learned information under. In other words, *you can choose* which file in your mind to store a particular memory in. You can even decide to place a memory in a folder that already exists. This is called *association*.

There are many ways in which to view memory. We will limit our discussion to concepts from which the RARE-DREAM model was comprised in order to set the stage for our later exercises.

Models of Memory

There are many models of memory that have been proposed through the years. We will review three that pertain directly to the RARE-DREAM model. These include the Atkinson and Shiffrin Model, Cognitive Efforts Model, and the Depth of Processing Model.

Atkinson and Shiffrin Model of Memory

Common among many models of memory is the view of memory as a system of operations that function through different phases in time (Laaksonen 1994). A generally accepted model of memory is the one proposed by Atkinson and Shiffrin (1968). In this model, the structural components of memory consist of what is called a "sensory store" (where data picked up by your senses is temporarily stored), short-term memory, and long-term memory. Information is first acquired through the senses, where it then enters the short-term memory store. Encoding may be mediated by how many senses were involved during the processing of the information while contained in short-term memory. Once the information enters the short-term memory it can either be forgotten or further processed and moved into long-term memory where a permanent record is created. The term "working memory" is often used in place of the term short-term memory because information is typically held at this level to fulfill a work function and then either forgotten or further consolidated into long-term memory. For instance, when you look up a number in the phone book, the number is held in working (short-term) memory until the number has been dialed. Once the work of dialing is accomplished, the numbers are forgotten. If it's necessary that you retain this number, you may then rehearse the number to properly encode it in your long-term memory. The next model of memory describes memory from the perspective of effort.

Cognitive Effort Model of Memory

The cognitive effort model is a dynamic model stating that the critical variable for reliable memory is related to the degree of cognitive effort used when processing the information. With increased cognitive effort, more distinct and durable memories are established. According to this model, the degree of motivation expended in establishing a memory determines the level of success of memory consolidation and later retrieval. In essence, the harder you try to encode a memory the more successful you will be. Let us caution you here that this effort must first be correctly placed in order to be effective. The final model of memory that we will introduce is the depth of processing model.

Depth of Processing

A related perspective of memory functioning is the "depth of processing" concept supported by Craik and Lockhart (1972). This concept holds that effective memory is contingent upon the kinds of operations carried out while encoding information, and that retention is determined by the characteristics that are emphasized during the initial encoding process (Reed 1992). According to this model, information that is encoded in a more personally meaningful way is more likely to be recalled. There is evidence to suggest that older adults are less likely to spontaneously apply these deeper levels of processing to their memory functioning (Zarit et al. 1981). In accordance with depth of processing concepts, recent approaches in memory training have targeted processes that occur during the encoding stage of memory (Smith 1980).

These three models of memory are the basis on which the RARE-DREAM strategy is built. In combining the three models, we can surmise that effective memory functioning is dependent upon adequate transfer of information from your senses into working memory. While the information is contained in working memory it is elaborated upon and tagged with meaningful retrieval cues before it is transferred for permanent storage into long-term memory. Now that we've examined models of memory, let's take a look at different types of memory.

Types of Memory

Ogrocki and Welsh-Bohmer identify two types of memory. The first type is *learned experiences* that are accessible through conscious awareness. The second type is *automatic changes in behavior* that are at an unconscious level (Ogrocki and Welsh-Bohmer 2000, 19). Thinking of memory in terms of unconscious or automatic processes and conscious or planned mechanisms serves as a good initial conceptualization. For our purposes, we will refer to these as "declarative" and "nondeclarative" memory, respectively.

Declarative Memory

Declarative memory is conscious memory. It is knowledge of facts and events that includes both *episodic* (time-related data of past experiences) and *semantic* (fact-related) data. Declarative memory stores information about facts (who, what, when, where) and the relationship between them.

Other terms that you may hear associated with declarative memory might include "explicit memory" or "cognitive memory." This is what most people are referring to when they state that they begin to notice lapses in their memory functioning. It is also the type of memory most affected by depression.

Nondeclarative Memory

Nondeclarative memory is memory that cannot be accessed consciously. It includes motor learning, habits, and conditioning. Nondeclarative memory includes the skills achieved through repetitious exposure, such as driving a car or riding a bike. Nondeclarative memory involves multiple senses and systems and utilizes multiple motor and cognitive pathways in its execution. Other names for nondeclarative memory include "implicit memory," "dispositional memory," or "nonconscious memory."

An example of nondeclarative memory is the slow process of learning the skilled movements to play the piano. Other examples include different types of nonconscious memory, priming, and conditioning. Nondeclarative memory is your intuition and is often represented in cartoons by the little devil sitting on one shoulder whispering in one ear and an angel sitting on the other shoulder whispering in the other ear. This is a primitive memory system and is used by both humans and animals. This system has been well proven over time, is very well established, and is an excellent vehicle on which to mount improved memory functioning.

Take a moment and describe out loud to yourself how you would tie your shoe or ride a bicycle. Name all the specific steps in singing a song or painting a picture. Explain déjà vu. If you struggled (and we expect you did), it is because essentially you were trying to utilize declarative memory functions to verbally describe nondeclarative memory experiences. In contrast, what makes the game of charades so challenging to people is that the game involves using nondeclarative processes to describe declarative concepts. This further evidences just how intricate and, frankly, awesome your memory is. The next time you feel demoralized about your memory, remember how complex the concept of memory is. Think about a nondeclarative skill that you have mastered, such as your ability to play a musical instrument, knit, or even ride a bike. After the next exercise on declarative memory, we will look at memory from an anatomical point of view.

✎ ✗ Exercise: Declarative Memory

One of the best examples of declarative memory is what is called "paired associative learning." This simple exercise involves linking groups of words together and learning them in pairs. The reason this is one of the best examples of this type of memory is that declarative memory is responsible for making sense out of internal memories and the world around us. Declarative memory provides the context in which we place the content of our memories.

Take a few minutes and memorize the following pairs of words. Link the pairs together in your mind so that if we say book, you will say staple.

* book / staple

* bag / glove

* tree / leaf

* sun / man

* plug / cord

* computer / television

* watch / shirt

* fence / grass

We will check your success later. In the meantime we will link memory functions to specific areas of the brain.

Anatomy of Memory

There are multiple systems and areas of the brain associated with memory functioning. The area of the brain called the hippocampus (located in the temporal lobe) is generally considered the central processing unit for memory. Other areas involved in memory functioning include the areas called medial temporal lobes and the diencephalon. Today it is widely recognized by neuroscientists that there is not one central area of the brain solely responsible for memory. Memory is stored and processed throughout the brain. What this means is that the idea of "your memory" going bad is not the same as your heart or kidneys going bad. This makes the function of memory more resilient than if it was contained within a single area of the brain. In other words, both the strength and proper utilization of memory lies in diversity.

Different memory functions have been localized to distinct areas of the brain. Motor memories (like limb position, knowledge of personal space) is stored near the motor processing areas of your brain. Sensory memories are stored near sensory processing areas of your brain. Different regions of the brain are wired together and work in conjunction. For example, pain sensory receptors detect that your hand is getting burned. This message is processed within the spinal cord and memory of the hand's position in space is quickly detected and adjusted to prevent further damage from heat. Given this wonderfully complex pattern of memory functioning, we do not have to concern ourselves with a single entity of memory. We can create tailored methods to encode and retrieve memories dependent upon the type of memory and where we choose to store it.

For example, let's pair a paperclip with the smell of sweat. By that single thought you have created new pathways to store new properties of a paperclip and have associated the idea of a paperclip with sweat. Now for encoding purposes picture yourself running through a hot stationery store looking for paperclips. Again, new pathways are created and the odds of recalling those items are increased. Now imagine that your goal is to remember to stop at the store on the way home and purchase some paperclips. By taking a moment and creating this unique scenario of running through a hot store, looking for paperclips and sweating, the episodic and semantic elements applied to the encoding will greatly enhance your ability to execute the errand.

Levels of Processing

You now see the importance in both *where* information is processed and how it is processed. Thereby you can begin to see how important it is for information to be processed at different stages and at progressively deeper levels to assure sound memory functioning. You will remember to pick up paperclips if you run this scenario through your memory for smell, as well as through your action or motor memory. This concept of encoding information at multiple levels is a central theme in the remaining "R and E" of the RARE techniques you will learn.

✐ ✗ *Exercise: Checking Your Declarative Memory*

Write in the appropriate word that is associated with each word below.

★ book / _____

★ bag / _____

★ tree / _____

★ sun / _____

★ plug / _____

★ computer / _____

★ watch / _____

★ fence / _____

Check your answers from the previous page. How did you do? Did you remember that "staple" goes with "book"? We elaborated on that one a bit more in introducing the preceding exercise. If you forgot a few, that's okay. Remember, it's losing both the factual and time portions of memory that you have to watch for. If you got at least five of the eight, then your declarative memory is doing pretty well. Shortly, we will take a look at your long-term declarative memory. In the meantime, let's look at the function of memory through the five systems of memory.

The Five Systems of Memory

In this next section, we will outline the five systems of memory. These include working memory, semantic memory, episodic memory, procedural memory, and perceptual memory. Remember, according to our model these different systems work together and function according to time and purpose. Don't get these confused with the two types of memory presented at the beginning of this chapter (declarative or conscious memory and nondeclarative or unconscious memory). By learning about these different memory systems, we can better utilize them for retention and recall. We will start our presentation with working memory.

Working Memory

Working memory (which could also be called "memory for now") contains all that we are conscious of and working on right now. Information is held long enough to make a decision and then either is lost or sent on to storage for later use. If it's transferred to form a memory for later use, it becomes long-term memory. Information that you are thinking about right now (reading about working memory) includes data currently entering your senses, as well as related memories associated from long-term memory stores that help you make sense of what you're reading. Working memory (also called short-term memory) is transient in nature and, unless processed and stored in long-term memory, will be lost after it is used. The phase in which working or short-term memory is transferred into long-term memory is called *memory consolidation*. This storage function allows us to bring information online for comparisons to other information contained in long-term memory, thereby enhancing problem solving and comprehension. Other terms associated with working memory include immediate memory, active memory, and primary memory.

Working memory has three major subsystems that work in unison (Gathercole and Baddeley 1993). These are the central executive, the visuo-spatial sketchpad, and the phonological loop. The *central executive* serves to regulate and manage information contained in working memory. It also serves to regulate and interact with functions of long-term memory. The *visuo-spatial sketchpad* regulates visual and spatial information and processes this information for immediate use. Finally, the *phonological loop* translates information into verbal code and is central in allowing us to read, converse, and transfer our world into verbal representations. It is our verbal information processor or our mind's "ear."

🔑 Memory Tip: Context-Dependent Memory

Context-dependent memory involves the recall of information in the same or similar place or situation as when the memory was formed. The theory of context-dependent memory assers that memories will be more easily recalled if you are within the same context as when the memory was established. Have you ever walked into a room and forgot what you went in there for? Frequently you will have to go back to where you started from to remember what you were doing. This is an example of context dependent memory, which can be used to your advantage. If you find that you can't remember something, go back to where the memory was formed. If that is not possible, try to create similar feelings or sensations to those that initially surrounded the encoding of the information. You may find that the information you are trying to remember will be much more accessible.

Now we will continue our review of memory systems with long-term memory.

Long-Term Memory

This is what most people call "memory" and it can be also considered "memory for later." It is the stored, permanent information that we have committed to memory to be retrieved for later use. This is the area where we notice a lapse when we have a name on the tip of our tongue and can't seem to get it out. Long-term memory is made up of both *semantic* and *episodic* memory (Tulving 1972). Long-term memory is not actually a system of memory per se, but rather an abstract term used to globally denote more permanently stored information.

Semantic Memory

Semantic memory includes all of the general information that we have accumulated in our long-term memories that is not linked by time or place. It involves data related to who, what, and why.

Episodic Memory

This system is in charge of the information associated with the time and place at which you learned the information and formed the memory. This is the system that is utilized in the preceding memory tip on context-dependent memory. The episodic memory acts as the memory for when and where. For example, remembering that you had a salad for dinner last night is an episodic memory (when). Remembering that lettuce is a plant that matures through the process of photosynthesis is a semantic memory (who, what, or why).

Procedural Memory

The procedural system stores information on how to do something (like how to change the spark plugs in your car, what tools to use, which way to turn the spark plugs in order to remove them, and how much pressure to apply for optimal performance). Procedural memory holds our knowledge about our skills and habits. This knowledge base represents our life's work. It is the information that was acquired slowly through continued practice. Think of someone on television who has portrayed an amnesic. If portrayed accurately, the person lost the memory of who he or she is (explicit memory), not the memory of how to do things (procedural memory). The person has no recollection of any personal history, but can still change a spark plug, if the knowledge was previously learned. The differences between these two components of long-term memory, illustrated by the amnesic who has no memory of personal events but maintains knowledge of procedural artifacts, highlights the complexity and dynamic nature of memory functioning.

Perceptual Memory

Perceptual memory serves to identify objects and the structure of language. It is also a knowledge base for evaluating overall patterns of larger groups of data. It provides the context for the content of memory and is intuitive in nature, not involving the conceptual or comparative logic utilized in other memory systems. It sees the forest and not the individual trees. The perceptual memory system is the system that allows people to be "geniuses" or gifted artists or musicians. Through this memory system, we recognize themes and are able to use intuition in order to process larger patterns of data. There are separate systems within the perceptual memory system that mediate visual and auditory information.

The perceptual memory defines a musician, a world-class chef, or even a skilled mechanic. They have built up a large knowledge base of complex patterns related to their expertise and can thus process the information using these patterns. They become intuitive in processing these patterns and can predict where the pattern is heading. Recognizing your strengths can greatly enhance your memory functioning. You will be processing the same amount of information in your working memory, but the information processed will be in chunks rather than individual bits. If you can process the information in patterns, you can process more information quicker and more efficiently. This is the optimal use of perceptual memory.

🔑 Memory Tip: Better Recall

Episodic and procedural memory can be useful in recall. If you are having difficulty getting access to something that you wish to remember, try to remember other things that were occurring during that time frame. What else happened that day? What were you wearing? Who were you with? What were you doing? Although these questions represent different memory systems, they are interconnected. Thinking about the desired memory from alternative perspectives can help to activate other related memory systems that are linked to that memory. This in turn will activate the system that holds the memory that you wish to recall.

Five Systems of Memory—A Review

The five systems of memory again are:

1. Working Memory

2. Semantic Memory

3. Episodic Memory

4. Procedural Memory

5. Perceptual Memory

(Episodic and semantic memory together make up long-term memory)

The names of these systems can be remembered by thinking of the acronym WEPPS. W = working memory, E = episodic memory, P = perceptual memory, P = procedural memory, and S = semantic memory. Remember these, because we will ask you about them later.

✎ ✗ Exercise: Declarative Memory

Remember the word pairs you first encountered on page 77? Try to remember what they were and write down the word that completes each pair.

★ book / _____

★ bag / _____

★ tree / _____

★ sun / _____

★ plug / _____

★ computer / _____

★ watch / _____

★ fence / _____

Now compare your answers to the list provided in the previous exercise. How did you do? Don't worry if you didn't do as well as you might have anticipated. We will cover declarative memory in many more forms many more times. We wanted you to get a feel for how your long-term declarative memory is working. If you got close to the same number correct that you did on the first trial, then you're doing well.

✎ ✗ *Exercise: Long-Term Memory*

Answer the following questions reflective of long-term memory.

1. What is the value of pi? _____ .

2. What was the flavor of the last piece of pie that you ate? _____ .

3. What were you wearing last Christmas? _____ .

4. What colors are in a rainbow? _____ .

5. What colors make orange? _____ .

6. How does cotton feel? _____ .

Now label 1-6 as either episodic or semantic long-term memory.

1. _____

2. _____

3. _____

4. _____

5. _____

6. _____

Check your answers in appendix E.

Since we are targeting your memory at multiple stages of functioning, we will now briefly cover the basic stages of memory functioning.

Stages of Memory Functioning

Memory works in three different stages: Encoding, storage, and retrieval.

1. **Encoding:** Once we come in contact with information to be remembered our brains develop a "code," which becomes a record of the experience. Our memory can be affected at this stage if the information is not coded in a way that makes it easy to

recall when needed. For example, we may recognize someone in the office where we work, but outside of that environment we may have difficulty in recognizing him or her. This is because the face was coded in association with work and outside of that coding strategy the memory is not recognizable. We lose the context of the memory that is guided by our semantic memory system.

2. **Storage:** This is the ability to hold and effectively store a memory. Rehearsal is one of the most important factors involved in retaining the information that we've been exposed to. Problems in this stage of memory often occur due to a lack of rehearsal.

3. **Retrieval:** This refers to the ability to recall the memory needed. Once the information is successfully stored, it must be retrievable in order to be useful. For information to be retrieved, it first must be stored effectively. Once effectively stored, cues and reminders can help us then retrieve the information. Remembering that you need to pick up milk before coming home can easily be forgotten as you go through your daily routine. As you drive home and see a convenience store your memory is jogged and you remember the errand. Often it seems as if we have forgotten something even though it was successfully stored. We simply need help in retrieving the memory; we have to remember to recall.

The importance of paying attention to detail cannot be overemphasized. If we become bogged down with too much information and preoccupied with the stress of our daily routine it becomes increasingly more difficult to remember the things we need for later. That's why relaxation is such an important component for effective memory. It is much more difficult to remember things if we add an emotional component of anxiety or depression. Also, it's important to use any tricks or tools that seem to help you. You can find some suggestions in the memory tips scattered throughout the book. But different memory tips work for some and not for others. As you go through the book, find out what works for you and incorporate it into your daily routine. And don't forget to continue to practice relaxation and to make entries in your journal.

> *Morning memory jog upon arising:*
> *It's gotten so I have to put a sign beside my bed*
> *"First the pants, then the shoes!"*
> *It helps me keep my head.*
>
> —E. Fischer and J. T. Noland

Remember Your Senses

Your senses are the first step in storing a memory. If your senses are not appropriately picking up information to begin with, there is no way that you can form a memory. Your senses are mediated by your attentional capacity (how well you can pay attention). When you're attending to information, your senses are alert and receptive to environmental information. If you're inattentive, your senses are not picking up this information. As an example, if you're not attending visually (your eyes are closed), then you're not going to pick up any visual information around you. If you are not listening, then you won't pick up any auditory information. For the visually inclined we will now present the functions of memory in another way.

Working Model Of Memory:

Sensory Registers	**Working Memory**	**Long-Term Memory**

information -----------------> encoding <----------------- retrieval
("learning")

This is equivalent to:

Sight		
Sound	**Your**	**Stored**
Touch	**Short-Term**	**Data**
Smell	**Memory**	**Files**
Taste		

Strategies to improve your memory functioning.

Relax   **Relax/Attend**   **Attend/Rehearse**   **Rehearse/Envision**

We have presented memory in different ways. This is exactly what you have to do when you encode information. By looking at the data in different ways you can form better associations and memory traces within your brain and can choose a wider context from which to draw the data.

🔑 Memory Tip: Toxins

Many toxins, even in small amounts, can lead to cognitive impairment. Are you exposed to any type of toxin on a regular basis? The most common neurotoxin is alcohol. Have you recently been exposed to some type of toxin? These include: paints, glues, fuels, oils, cleaners, etc. Remember to always use these types of solvents in a well-ventilated area. Wear masks and protective gear for your skin. Memory difficulties attributable to toxic exposure are often accompanied by other acute physical symptoms such as nausea, skin abnormalities, or headaches. The best strategy is to avoid these types of toxins, if at all possible.

✎ ✗ Exercise: Memory Systems

Write down the five memory systems.

W = _____

E = _____

P = _____

P = _____

S = _____

Check your answers in appendix E.

Memory Problems—Stages of Memory Function in New Agers

Let's apply what we have learned about memory to the aging process. Research investigating memory function in older adults has revealed little evidence that memory dysfunction occurs primarily within either the storage or retrieval stages of memory (Smith 1980). Perlmutter (1978) and Loewen and colleagues (1990) found evidence to suggest that in comparison to younger subjects, older subjects may be more limited by inconsistencies in encoding processes. It has also been shown that older adults are less likely than younger subjects to spontaneously use effective encoding strategies (Hill et al. 1990). In short, both encoding and retrieval seems to function properly in older adults, but there seems to be inconsistencies in the use of effective strategies by which to navigate the process.

What Causes Encoding and Retrieval Difficulties?

Since memory functioning relies on a complex set of variables, it is difficult to ascertain a specific cause for encoding or retrieval inconsistencies as we age. There may be a multitude of origins and several theories have been proposed. Encoding deficiencies in older adults may be a function of difficulties in producing and using visual images that may facilitate deeper levels of information processing (Sheikh et al. 1986). Other causes of deficiencies that have been proposed include: decreased organization (Yesavage 1989), decreased effort implemented in processing information (Camp et al. 1993), attentional impairments (Yesavage and Rose 1983), or more generalized distraction due to anxiety (Yesavage and Jacob 1984), depression (Zarit et al. 1981), and maladaptive beliefs regarding memory functioning (Lachman et al. 1995). These factors are far from exclusive, and it is likely to be a combination of these that contribute to changes in memory as we age.

Multiple Systems, Stages, and Types of Memory = Multiple Opportunities for Intervention

You're probably beginning to see just how complex the concept of memory is. With this wonderful complexity come endless points of intervention for improvement. With education on the function of memory comes hope for improvement in memory recall.

In short, we are accentuating the existing positives and ameliorating the negatives. Continue to implement and integrate the encoding strategies you've learned thus far, centering around relaxation and attention principles. Continue to develop your rational and emotionally adaptive mindsets and try to stick with your memory journal. Also try to use the various memory tips that work for you, including the use of external memory aids (your personal memory spot, calendars, lists). Give up the memory strategies that no longer work due to the biological, social, or emotional changes that have taken place in your life. Be willing to add some new tools to your memory toolbox. Next we will look at visual and verbal memory and find where your personal strengths lie. But first, a bit of a refresher.

RARE-DREAM Review

So what are the steps for efficient memory functioning? RARE-DREAM! What does RARE-DREAM stand for?

1. Relax

    2. Attend

        3. Rehearse

            4. Envision

              while

Developing Rational and Emotionally Adaptive Mindsets

Perched in my shorts on the edge of my bed,
With a shoe in my hand and my teeth in a cup,
I'm looking for clues, so I don't have to ask:
Am I going to bed now, or just getting up?

                    —E. Fischer and J. T. Noland

∗ 9 ∗

Visual and Verbal Memory

Your eyes and ears are integral senses in understanding your environment. They are also important sensory organs and the first step in establishing memories of their respective types. Many people have strengths in either one or both areas. Are you visually or verbally oriented? Do you do better with your visual-spatial sketchpad or with your phonological loop? Which should you rely on to remember how to get to the party on Friday or to help you remember the name of the new neighbor? In this chapter we will help you to determine your strengths and offer suggestions to enhance both visual and verbal memory functions.

This chapter contains various exercises to assist you in examining and enhancing visual and verbal memory. By knowing where your strengths lie and consciously choosing which system to utilize in memory, you will enhance attention and thus encoding. For example, if you have a list of grocery items, you can place them in visual memory by making up ways in which the items can interact (like a carton of milk throwing eggs at a tub of butter). If you are more verbally oriented, you can memorize the list through repetition or by making up an acronym using the first letter of each item ("MEB" to represent milk, eggs, and butter).

Verbal Memory Is Attention Driven

In determining whether you are verbally or visually oriented it is important to consider that verbal memory is more dependent on attention than visual memory. When we are presented with visual information we usually have more time to look at it and take in the details. Our attention can wander a bit and we can still get all of the data. With verbal memory, the information is presented in a linear fashion. If our attention wanders for only a second, we miss some of the information and thus are unable to remember it all. If you find that you're having difficulty with the verbal memory exercises, it may be due to having difficulty focusing your attention. In this case, review your performance on the attention exercises in chapter 5. If your performance time on the attention exercises is substantially inflated, attention deficits may be the cause of problems in verbal memory. Remember, some changes in attention are expected in the normal aging process. But if lapses in your attention seem severe, then we recommend that you have your memory evaluated. You may find that some of the visual memory strategies presented in this chapter may serve as an effective new strategy to enhance your memory functioning.

Are You Visually or Verbally Oriented?

It is important to recognize your strengths in the process of enhancing your memory. Some of us do better with visually oriented information and others do better with information that they hear. This can be important in improving your memory, as we often have the choice to take in information from different senses. Take the following quiz to determine if you are more visually or verbally oriented.

✎ ✗ *Exercise: Visual or Verbal Orientation*

Circle the answer that best applies to you.

1. If you are getting directions from someone do you:
   - a. Follow their verbal directions
   - b. Follow the directions using a visual representation (like landmarks)?

2. When you meet someone new do you:
   - a. Focus on what the person is saying (for instance, their name)
   - b. Focus on some physical feature?

3. In your spare time would you rather:
   - a. Listen to music
   - b. Watch television?

4. When writing down directions do you prefer to:
   - a. Write out verbal directions
   - b. Draw a map to follow?

5. If you are doodling on a piece of paper do you tend to:
   - a. Write words
   - b. Draw pictures?

6. If you had a choice would you rather:
   - a. Write a poem
   - b. Paint a picture?

7. If you were going to take a college course for fun would you rather take:
   - a. Review of English Literature
   - b. General photography?

8. When watching a movie do you:
   - a. Pay more attention to what is being said
   - b. Focus more on what is happening?

Tally up all of the times that you circled "a" and all of the times you circled "b" below.

a = _____   b = _____

If the "a" column is higher than the "b" column, then you are probably more verbally oriented. If the "b" column is greater than the "a" column, then you're probably more visually oriented. If both columns are within one point of each other, then you are equally strong verbally and visually.

🔑 Memory Tip: Which Brain Is Your Right Brain

In most cases, the left hemisphere of your brain processes verbal information and the right hemisphere of your brain processes visual information. Many people are dominant to one memory system or the other, just as we are hand dominant. Your natural strengths, whether more visually or verbally oriented, may be germane to your memory functioning and even your memory weakness. For example, if you are visually oriented and are having difficulty remembering people's names when meeting them, then it may be because you are focusing on what they are wearing or the style of their hair rather than their name. If you discover this to be true for you, you can then make a conscious effort to focus on their name. Or take it a step further, and tie the name to your natural visual strength of noticing clothes. If Edgar meets someone named Jean and notices that she is wearing jeans, then that memory is pretty well solidified and will be accessible when needed. Use the upcoming memory tips to solidify the name into your memory. If you are more verbally oriented you may find it easier to write out directions verbally rather trying to follow a map. Remember, this is just the introduction of how you can make this information work for you. Be creative and allow your memory to begin to reshape itself!

✎ ✗ *Exercise: Testing Visual Memory*

Look at the following figures for about ten seconds each. After each figure you will be asked to copy the figure from memory.

Figure 1

Review this figure for ten seconds. Now cover the figure with a piece of paper.

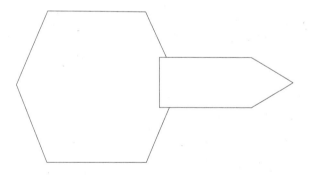

Now copy this figure in the space provided.

Figure 2

Review this figure for ten seconds. Again, cover the figure with a piece of paper.

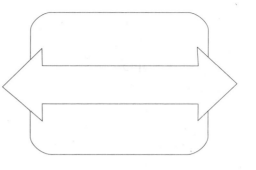

Now copy this figure in the space provided.

Score your performance on the visual memory exercise according to the following protocol. Place the correct number of points in each space provided according to the listed scoring criteria.

Figure 1

_____ Give yourself 1 point if you drew a six-sided figure.

_____ Give yourself an additional point if you correctly drew the hexagon, and it was similar in size to the original figure.

_____ Give yourself an additional point if the hexagon you drew had six equal sides.

Perfect performance = 3 points

_____ Give yourself 1 point if your drew a five-sided figure.

_____ Give yourself an additional point if you drew the pentagon correctly, and it was similar in size to the original figure.

_____ Give yourself an additional point if the parallel sides of the pentagon were about twice as long as the shorter sides that make up the point.

Perfect performance = 3 points

_____ Give yourself 1 point if you drew two figures.

_____ Give yourself an additional point if you drew two figures overlapping on their sides.

_____ Give yourself 1 point if the pentagon intersected the hexagon in the manner shown in the figure.

Perfect performance = 3points

Add the total number of points.

8–9 points = Excellent visual reproduction skills
6–7 points = Good visual reproduction skills
4–5 points = Average visual reproduction skills
2–3 points = Poor visual reproduction skills

Figure 2

_____ Give yourself 1 point if you drew a four-sided figure.

_____ Give yourself an additional point if you correctly drew the square with rounded corners, and it was similar in size to the original figure.

Perfect performance = 2 points

_____ Give yourself 1 point if your drew a double sided arrow.

_____ Give yourself an additional point if you drew the double-sided arrow that was similar in proportions to the one shown in the figure.

Perfect performance = 2 points

_____ Give yourself 1 point if you drew the arrow inside the square.

_____ Give yourself an additional point if you drew the arrow running parallel to the base of the square and cutting the square in roughly two equal rectangles.

Perfect performance = 2 points

Add the total number of points.

5–6 points = Excellent visual reproduction skills
3–4 points = Average visual reproduction skills
1–2 points = Poor visual reproduction skills

This exercise serves to give you some idea as to the strength of your visual skills. Keep in mind that if you have difficulty drawing or are not a good artist, you probably scored much lower than your actual visual skills score would be.

🔑 Memory Tip: Visual or Spatial Orientation

Are you more visually or spatially oriented? The ability to identify objects (form vision) is processed by a different system within your brain than your ability to judge angular or spatial relationships. For example, picture yourself changing the television station with your remote control. You pick up the remote, point it toward the television, and push the button to change channels. Did you identify the button to push via its pattern on the remote control or did you recall the correct button by examining the remote to find the correct button? When you look at a clock, do you decipher the time by the pattern of the hands or do you rely on the numbers? If you have a tendency to perform these types of tasks via pattern recognition verses visual recognition of the actual numbers or correct buttons, then you are probably more spatially oriented. If you tend to rely on visual iden-tification to perform these tasks, then you are probably more visually oriented. What is/was your occupation? Did it involve visual-spatial skills, good hand-eye coordination, or the ability to remember numbers or words? All of these things can give you a clue about your natural strengths and help you to develop strategies for memory-enhancement techniques.

✎ ✗ *Exercise: Verbal Translation of Visual Information*

Look at the following diagram.

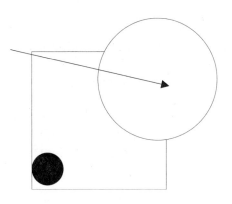

In a brief paragraph, describe the diagram so that someone who could not see the diagram would be able to reproduce it.

_____

_____

_____

_____

_____

See appendix E for a suggested description. There is no right or wrong answer. Your success depends in part on how concise the description was. If this was successful for you, then it may lend further proof that verbal skills, and thus verbal memory, is a strength for you. You should utilize this strength when trying to remember things.

Now let's try the exercise in reverse. We will give you a verbal description of a figure and we want you to draw the described figure in the space below:

✎ ✗ *Exercise: Visual Translation of Verbal Information*

Draw the following figure in the space below.

Start with a large circle in the center of your paper. Draw a large square in the center of the circle that does not touch the circle at any point. In the bottom left corner of the square draw a smaller square that is about one-fourth the size of the large square. Shade the small square in black. Draw a diagonal line that extends outside of the circle on both ends that bisects the upper left and lower right corners of the large square. See appendix E for the figure.

Were you able to do this exercise successfully? If so, you probably have strength in your visual processing of information and thus your visual memory. Compare the results to the previous exercise where you verbally described the shown figure. Does one stand out as being remarkably better than the other? If you were able to reconstruct the drawing better from a verbal description, your visual memory may be stronger than your verbal memory. If, on the other hand, you were more successful at succinctly describing the figure with words, then you may be more verbally oriented.

🔑 Memory Tip: Talk Through it

Verbal reinforcement can go a long way in helping you to remember. If there is something that you need to remember for later, say it out loud to yourself to encode the information in your memory. "I have to remember to call my sister at 4:00." This will strengthen the memory and help you to anchor it within your mind. You can also use this to help you remember that you have completed routine tasks. For example, say to yourself, "I am letting the dog out" or "I am locking the doors." Reinforce these memories with visualization or with humor. This will make these routine tasks more efficient, and you won't have to check later to ensure that you completed the task.

✎ ✗ Exercise: Memory for Verbal Information

Have someone else read the following clip from a major newspaper out loud to you. Have them read it only once. No peeking, please, or you may turn this into a visual test!

"Mr. Sam Robinson, a local merchant, announces a going-out-of-business sale. He is liquidating the entire stock of his furniture store. The store has been in the family for four generations. Upon retirement, he and his wife of forty-seven years plan to relocate to southern Florida and take up golfing."

Now write down in the space provided as much as you remember about the story.

_____

_____

_____

Now let's check your verbal memory. Place a check by each of the following words and concepts remembered. All words do not have to be recalled verbatim but should include the major details. For example, just remembering Sam would not warrant a correct response. On the other hand, you don't have to recall the complete phrase of "a going-out-of-business sale." Correct responses could include some close proximity using the words "going," "out," and "business." Words in parenthesis contain the key words that must be included for a point to be given.

_____ Sam Robinson (Sam Robinson)

_____ a local merchant (a merchant)

_____ announces (announces, states, plans)

_____ a going-out-of-business (going out of business)

_____ sale (sale)

____ He is liquidating (liquidating, getting rid of)

____ the stock (stock)

____ his furniture store (furniture store)

____ The store has (store)

____ been in the family (family)

____ for four generations (four generations)

____ Upon retirement (retirement)

____ he and his wife (wife)

____ of forty-seven years (forty-seven years)

____ plan to relocate (relocate, move, live)

____ to southern Florida (Florida)

____ and take up golfing. (begin, start playing, golf, golfing)

Count the number of checks and tally your score.

If you received a score of 15–17, you have an excellent verbal memory. If you received a score of 12–14, your verbal memory is above average. If you received a score of 9–11, your verbal memory is in the average range. If you got a score of 6–8, your verbal memory skills are slightly below average. If you got a score of 5 or below, your immediate verbal memory probably represents a weakness for you. Again, this exercise can serve as an opportunity for you to determine where your strengths lie.

✎ ✗ Exercise: Remembering Names

Review the following list of names. Focus on which first names go with which last names. Take the time necessary to encode this information, utilizing previously taught techniques. Consciously use visual or verbal strategies depending on where your strengths lie.

1. John Marshall

2. Lillie Fields

3. Marge Miller

4. Harry Filling

5. Sam Smart

6. Mike Hammer

7. Sandy Hill

8. Dedrick Waters

⚷ Memory Tip: Using Music to Make Your Memory Work for You

Are you a musician? Do you just enjoy listening to music? Try using your music skills to enhance your memory. Take the information to be remembered and put it to music. Take, for example, the major components of a computer. In trying to remember the components of a computer, put the words to a tune and sing it to yourself. To the tune of "Twinkle Twinkle Little Star": "Monitor, keyboard, mouse, and speakers, video card, sound card, RAM and CD. Motherboard, printer, scanner, and microphone . . ." Okay, you get the idea. Now let's see how many of those names you can remember.

✐ ✗ Exercise: Name Association

Match the list of first names to the last names provided (the last names are not it order).

1. John _____ Miller (_____)

2. Lillie _____ Smart (_____)

3. Marge _____ Marshall (_____)

4. Harry _____ Waters (_____)

5. Sam _____ Fields (_____)

6. Mike _____ Hill (_____)

7. Sandy _____ Hammer (_____)

8. Dedrick _____ Filling (_____)

Compare your answers to the original list in the preceding exercise. How did you do? Let's examine how you remembered each name. Next to each last name in the parentheses, list the method that you used to associate the first and last names. Examples might include the use of humor, repetition, or visualization. Which ones did you do better on? Use the methods that were successful to help you remember names in the future. As you learn new strategies for encoding, you can review this list and find out what is working for you and what to build upon for later use.

🔑 Memory Tip: Chunking

Chunking is a technique wherein multiple pieces of information are collapsed into a central unit. Through collapsed units, large pieces of information are broken down into smaller pieces of information for better organization and management of information. Phone numbers are routinely put into two manageable chunks to lessen the demands of having to remember seven individual bits of information. Although typically done with numbers (phone numbers, social security number), anything with commonality can be chunked. For instance, you can mentally chunk grocery items by common categories to assist you in remembering them. With just a little bit of creativity, even otherwise distinct information can be made common and then collapsed. For instance, if you had to remember several items with nothing in common, you could take the first letter of each item and try to make a word, an acronym, so that you would only have to remember one word, and then through association the acronym may elicit the items. We have dubbed this strategy acronym chunking. RARE-DREAM owes its name to acronym chunking.

✐ ✗ Exercise: Using Acronym Chunking

We'll take the first letter of each item below and make a word out of it. Your objective is to remember your acronym and the associated words. Be sure and scan the original list a couple of times so that you can later transcribe the acronym back into the original list. The items are: a camera, a rake, anchovies, dishes, lipstick, and envelopes. This list can be represented by the acronym CRADLE.

🔑 Memory Tip: Remembering to Remember

If you find yourself in a hurry and need to remember to do something, give yourself a reminder to remember it later. This is similar to tying a string around your finger. You may want to place your watch on the opposite wrist or place a rubber band around your wrist. Whatever method works best, you will find this to be an effective tool for remembering to remember.

✏️ ✗ *Exercise: Acronym Chunking*

Next to each letter list the item associated with the first letter.

C _____

R _____

A _____

D _____

L _____

E _____

Check the previous page to see how well you did. Try this on a real list that you have to remember. Give it a couple of tries and see how it works for you.

As a final exercise to examine your long-term verbal and visual memory, we will ask you to copy the following figures and words. Later on we'll ask you to recall these figures and words and compare your performance on each to gain a sense of where your strengths lie.

✏️ ✗ *Exercise: Long-Term Visual and Verbal Memory*

Review each figure and copy them in the space provided.

1.

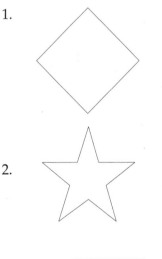

2.

3.

Now let's do the same with words. Examine the following words and write them in the space provided.

1. Paper   _____

2. Rug   _____

3. Camera   _____

We will ask you about these later. Now that we've examined your visual and verbal memory, go back and review your performances on each of the exercises in this chapter. Did any patterns emerge? Are you stronger with verbal or visual information? You can now use this newfound knowledge to adopt and implement the strategies that reflect your strengths.

Now let's take a look at rehearsal.

> *Our limited perspective, our hopes and fears become our measure of life,*
> *And when circumstances don't fit our ideas, they become our difficulties.*
> —Benjamin Franklin

⋆ 10 ⋆

Rehearsal

In this chapter, we will examine the use of rehearsal as a technique to encode information into memory. Rehearsal represents the second "R" in RARE. One difference between this model and that of many others is the focus placed on rehearsal as a unique extension of attention. Rehearsal is a way to place something deep within multiple memory systems by utilizing different memory and sensory modalities. Rehearsal is a hierarchical component of effective attention and an intuitive skill that all of us have utilized at one time or another (like when we're studying for a test). Rehearsal is a method to sustain information in the working memory long enough for the information to be encoded into long-term memory (Parente and Stapleton 1993). Remember in school, memorizing the alphabet, the multiplication tables, or the pledge of allegiance? By repeating the information over and over, you were eventually able to commit it to memory.

Consider the following phone number.

724-9650

Phone numbers are often challenging to remember, especially if you have come to rely on the auto-dial function on modern phones. Some phone numbers seem easier to remember than others. This is partially due to some containing more repetition of numbers or containing series of numbers that occur in consecutive order. When Edgar first moved to his new home, he was given a phone number that was somewhat difficult to remember. The phone number listed above was his number. Take a look at it. That's a tricky one to commit to memory.

✎ ✗ Exercise: Numerical Processing

You know, there's something that we wanted to do earlier but we forgot. See, everyone forgets. But we will not beat ourselves up over it. Let's do the exercise now. It's a simple math exercise. All we want you to do is count backward by three. Let's start with thirty-nine. In your head count backwards from thirty-nine by threes (thirty-nine, thirty-six, thirty-three . . .). Time yourself and see how long it takes you to get to three. Write in your time below. Ready—go!

Time: _____

This was a simple attention exercise, and repetition is an extension of attention. We would expect that you did this within twenty-five seconds with few errors. If you found this exercise to be difficult or if you made multiple mistakes, then we recommend that you undergo a formal memory evaluation from a neuropsychologist or neurologist. Consult your physician for a referral.

Transferring Information from Short-Term to Long-Term Memory

Okay, do you still remember the phone number without looking? We don't expect that many of you still remember it, because we distracted you away from it. You also did not have adequate time to encode it. Lastly, you may have not been prepared to remember a useless phone number because we provided no instruction to do so. However, had we asked you to remember the phone number, rehearsal would have likely been the instinctive strategy employed by most. Rehearsal is a simple but effective technique for helping you to remember. It's a natural strategy that most of us would use to commit a phone number to memory. Traditional rehearsal usually involves verbal repetition. We will expand rehearsal to include the other senses and memory systems, creating cross references to the traditional verbal mode of rehearsal.

Rehearsal simply means to repeat something over and over to yourself in order to learn the information. The effectiveness of rehearsal is better enhanced if you're able to repeat the information aloud. If you look up a phone number in the phone book and simply repeat the number over and over to yourself until you've got the phone in your hand, ready to dial, you're almost guaranteed not to forget the number. If you repeat something enough times with the proper amount of attention, you can effectively transfer the information from your working memory into your long-term memory. Remember, according to the literature, the problem experienced with memory in aging is due to changes in attention span.

It's a Matter of Attention

Rehearsal instills attention on the information to be remembered. Rehearsal is a great method for remembering phone numbers, names, facts, and even appointments. Through repetition, your attention is focused in a purposeful manner that results in better retention and recall. By the way, when you're in the process of committing that information to memory, make a mental note of where you are and the time and store that information with the memory. This will create a backup route by which to recall the information via episodic memory (time-oriented memory).

🔑 Memory Tip: Effective Rehearsal

When utilizing rehearsal to commit data to memory, repeat the information using different memory systems (WEPPS, visual and verbal). In essence, this creates alternative backup routes and facilitates deeper encoding. For example, using the phone number, rehearse the sequence of numbers aloud and mentally picture yourself punching the number into the phone's keypad. This will provide both a numerical sequence memory trace and a visual-spatial memory trace. Performing a preparatory set of imagining yourself dialing the phone will also activate memory traces within your motor system. The simple seven-digit phone number is now encoded in three distinct memory systems.

Who's in Control Here?

Is efficient memory just a matter of rehearsal? Then why are we so easily distracted in our daily activities? What if a million dollars was on the table and all you had to do was remember a large number for thirty seconds to make the money yours? Would you naturally use rehearsal to hang on to that memory? What would keep you from becoming a millionaire? Who's in control here? Every time you're distracted while using rehearsal, gently refocus your attention by thinking of that million dollars.

What's happening when you rehearse a phone number but then forget the number when you get to the phone? You are in some way being distracted! Whether it's the phone ringing or that nagging self-talk constantly repeating how bad your memory is. It's happening all around you and within you, those lousy distractions. The solution lies in awareness.

Work toward greater awareness of the distractions that interrupt your rehearsal. Be most aware of internal distractions (interfering thoughts, conflicting emotions) as opposed to external distractions (the phone suddenly ringing). Internal distractions are far more subtle and therefore far more devious.

🔑 Memory Tip: Spaced Retrieval

Landauer and Bjork (1978) developed a technique involving rehearsal called "spaced retrieval." Essentially, the goal is to repeat the information back to yourself at increasingly longer intervals of time. Begin by repeating the information to yourself immediately and then after one minute. Double the time on each attempt for four or five successions. After an unsuccessful recall attempt, decrease the time by one half and then work your way back up by again doubling the time. This technique will help you to encode information through the use of rehearsal.

Let's Try it Again

Let's try another phone number, this time using rehearsal to assist in remembering it. We're going to show the phone number within the text. Remember what we've learned so far—relaxation will maximize attention, and attention will maximize the encoding of memory. Rehearsal is an active method to keep your attention focused. Relax and attend, and once you read past the number, repeat the number over and over to yourself. Then we're going to ask you to repeat the attention exercise by subtracting thirty-nine by threes. Repeat the phone number as you count, perhaps after every second or third subtraction. As you've learned from the divided attention exercise from chapter 5, you'll be able to continually repeat the phone number while allowing just enough attention to conduct the calculations. We won't focus on how long it takes you this time. Your goal is to remember the phone number. Unfortunately, we don't have a million dollars to give you—but healthy memory is priceless.

✎ ✗ *Exercise: Repetition*

The phone number is 724-9876. This number may be more easily retained via visual-spatial orientation. Picture yourself punching this number into the phone's keypad. Now repeat it back to yourself aloud: 724-9876. Using both methods will better enhance the memory.

Now count backwards by threes from thirty-nine (thirty-six, thirty-three, thirty . . .) while continuing to repeat the phone number to yourself. Establish a rhythm as you go along.

Now write the phone number down: _____

Did you successfully retain the phone number? If you repeated the number enough times and really focused, it's likely that the number has begun to etch itself in your long-term memory. In addition, writing things down, creating a memory note, is not only a good external aid to jog your memory, but will also serve to further encode information across multiple memory systems as you are using your motor and visual memory when writing.

What was that phone number again? _____

Did the phone number make its way into your long-term memory? Knowing your strengths will lead to a reliable memory.

🔑 Memory Tip: Organization Through External Aids

External aids (also called "memory prostheses") are basically tools to compensate for memory. These include lists, calendars, recorders, and so on. If you have gotten in the habit of using external aids, then we encourage you to continue their use. We also recommend that you utilize external aids to help with organization. For example, when creating a grocery list, write down the items in the order that you will encounter them in the store. If you are making a "to-do" list, correlate the tasks in the list in the order that you plan to complete them. This type of preplanning will not only serve as a record of items to be remembered but will also free up your memory while accomplishing the task.

You have now done some work with the first R (relax), the A (attend), and the second R (rehearse), and you've started to DREAM. Before discussing the E (envisioning or visualization skills), let's complete the DREAM component of the program and then examine some recall strategies.

Staying in the Race in Spite of Obstacles

When your crinkles turn to wrinkles
And your wrinkles turn to seams,
When your nicely rounded bottom
Is a widely flattened beam,
When you see your outsides changing
While your insides stay the same,
So old age won't overtake you
Keep on running! That's the game!

—E. Noland and J. T. Fischer

★ 11 ★

A Final Interpretation of DREAM

In this chapter, we will examine the entries from your memory journal and expand on them in order to further streamline any negative beliefs about memory. We will assist you in flushing out some of your individual beliefs that may be getting in the way of your memory. Let's start with a review of DREAM.

✎ ✗ *Exercise: DREAM Review*

List the concepts associated with DREAM.

D _____

R _____

E _____

A _____

M _____

Do you remember what mindsets are? *Mindsets* are essentially our overall belief systems. Our beliefs are composed of many factors, including our thoughts and feelings. Our beliefs can help us or hamper us. Let's use your journal to further examine your mindsets.

Review Your Journals

Shortly, we will review your memory journal and look for patterns. We will take five entries from your journal and break them down into the format on the worksheets contained in the exercise at the end of the chapter. The format that we will use includes the categories of:

Memory Lapse	Feelings	Negative Thoughts	Cognitive Distortions	Positive Response

Before conducting this exercise, let's look at these categories in a little more detail.

Column 1—Memory Lapse

In the first column, you will list the specific memory lapse from your journal. Examples might include forgetting your keys in your car, forgetting an appointment, or leaving your wallet at home on the way to the store. We've all done it, and we usually beat up on ourselves afterward. In the next column, we're going to focus on the feeling associated with the memory lapse.

Column 2—Feelings

Feelings are based on thoughts. You must first think the thought before a feeling can develop. You can, therefore, alter negative feelings by paying attention to the type of thought that precedes the feeling. For example, while sitting on your front porch you see your new neighbor walking out to his car. You say "hello," but he doesn't respond. You could say to yourself, "I had the feeling that guy didn't like me when we met. And to think I took the time out to initially introduce myself." As a result of these types of thoughts you might experience anger or perhaps you just feel slighted. Now imagine engaging in different thoughts. "He probably didn't hear me. Just moving in, he probably has a lot on his mind." With this frame of mind, the feeling you might experience is compassion. Two very different feelings stemming from the same situation. Each feeling is guided by different thoughts and overall beliefs.

We all have an internal commentary continually running through our minds. This self-talk is the verbal portion of your mind and is the conscious thought that guides you from day to day. This self-talk dictates the feeling you'll experience based on your perceptions of external events. Your internal commentary is also your window of opportunity to intervene. Once something is experienced at the feeling level, the autonomic nervous system and the limbic system within the brain takes over. At this point, your rational mind shuts down. The fight or flight response is triggered and normal reactions to fear and stress are activated. In other words, once the feeling is experienced, it is too late to intervene. Here's another way to look at this:

Opportunity for Perceptual Change

Situation → Thoughts About the Situation → Feelings → Beliefs

Complex Feelings

Feelings can be primary or secondary. Fear is a primary feeling, but we may react to it through anger. Anger, therefore, is a secondary emotion in this scenario. Depression is also often a secondary emotion. Depression may occur when we feel overwhelmed. For example, you may feel a loss of control and therefore a sense of helplessness as a primary emotion becomes manifest with a secondary experience of depression. If this example, there is not clear alternative present to alleviate the primary feeling of helplessness. in this example, we often can feel several feelings simultaneously (fear, anger, sadness). Sometimes we can even feel conflicting feelings simultaneously (hate and love). Extreme conflicting feelings are referred to as *ambivalence*. No feeling is ever right or wrong, they just are. When left unacknowledged, we can carry our feelings over to other situations. The perfect example of this is going home and kicking the cat because you are angry with your boss.

In the second column of the worksheet, you will list the feeling that was associated with the memory lapse (like anger, fear, and so on). Rate the emotion on a scale of 1 to 10, with 1 being a minor level of feeling and 10 being the strongest feeling. Negative emotions might include feeling: angry, miserable, frightened, muddled, panicky, ashamed, bitter, confused, defeated, troubled, depressed, threatened, devastated, useless, sorry, discouraged, embarrassed, frantic, uptight, frustrated, dejected, hopeless, hostile, humiliated, impatient, inadequate, incompetent, insecure, irritated, outraged, pessimistic, fearful, pressured, regretful, foolish, remorseful, sad, desperate, self-conscious, stupid, furious, terrified, despairing, tired, disappointed, trapped, uneasy, violated, disgusted, vulnerable, or worried. Positive feelings might include feeling: silly, amused, calm, happy, satisfied, content, optimistic, peaceful, rested, loving, excited, joyful, forgiving, playful, concerned, relaxed, secure, or worthwhile. In the next column you will list negative thoughts.

Column 3—Negative Thoughts

Our thinking process is essentially a running commentary that we have within ourselves. It is the subtle way in which we think. It is so ingrained that we usually don't even notice it. This self-talk defines our feelings. Self-talk is often perceived in the form of an image or even a single word, which can make it more difficult to detect. Self-talk is often developed in your younger, more primitive developmental years. It is associated with and may trigger other primitive thoughts and feelings stored at the same time.

Negative self-talk is almost always irrational, unquestioned and yet perceived as the truth. It's often driven by fear, with its roots in our *feeling*-based belief system. It not only happens automatically but is usually automatically accepted. It tends to force us to avoid situations it's associated with, never allowing us to challenge the irrational belief system on which it is based. For instance, if your negative self-talk tells you that you're terrible at remembering people's names at parties, you probably feel pretty reluctant to attend parties, fearing that you may forget someone's name and feel embarrassed. Negative self-talk also activates the body's natural physiological responses to stress (increased heart rate, release of adrenaline) and can be the root of anxiety and depression (depression is anxiety turned inward). To assist you in noting your negative self-talk in column 3, let's take a closer look at your negative self-talk.

✎ ✗ Exercise: What Kind of Self-Talk Are You Using?

Often we can be our own worst enemy. "Boy, am I stupid!" "Why do I always do that?" Negative self-talk is a learned behavior and can be unlearned. To do this, we must first learn to identify it. How do you treat yourself in your personal commentary? Here are some common examples of negative self-talk. Rank yourself on a scale of 1 to -5 on your tendency to use the following forms of self-talk. Can you identify yourself anywhere in here?

Critical Self-Talk. Are you always judging yourself? Do you jump at the chance to point out your faults to yourself? "I sure am a failure." Critical self-talk continually - belittles you for always falling short of the mark. This is like Samantha in *Bewitched* with her mother Endora constantly looking over her shoulder to remind her of how she should have done things. "I should have done better," "I should not have gotten myself involved" are common self-critical thoughts. When engaging in critical self-talk, we tend to "should" all over ourselves. Critical self-talk ignores your positive characteristics and highlights your negative ones. The critic is often the internalized voice of a parent, boss, or teacher. **Rank yourself on this characteristic on a scale from 1 to 5 (5 being the worst)** _____ .

Helpless Self-Talk. Do you remember the Bad Luck Schlep Rock character from the *Flintstones* or Eeyore from *Winnie the Pooh*? Always the victim, they always had everything that could go wrong actually go wrong. This is Murphy's Law at its worst. Like these characters, helpless self-talk will make you feel like you'll always be the victim. "I don't have the ability to change my circumstances." "My lot in life is to just helplessly flow with the current and to let myself drift wherever the powerful forces in nature take me." Through this internal self-talk, depression and anxiety are promoted. The road to happiness feels uphill all the way, and you fall two steps back for each step taken forward. You are unworthy and may as well not even try because you are sure to fail. **Rank yourself on this characteristic on a scale from 1 to 5 (5 being the worst)** _____ .

Anxious Self-Talk: This form of self-talk means that you're constantly worrying about every detail. The running commentary is always scanning for the worst-case scenario. "I know my memory will fail me; it never seems to work right." This is probably best illustrated by the lion in *The Wizard of Oz*, who is searching for his courage. He fears everything and believes that everything will prove to be a catastrophe sooner or later. Panic symptoms are often escalated, as the first physical symptoms of the stress response experienced continue to feed upon themselves. Vigilance is the guiding force in anxious self-talk. Potential failure is the object of constant fear. **Rank yourself on this characteristic on a scale from 1 to 5 (5 being the worst)** _____ .

Perfectionist Self-Talk: The perfectionist always lives by the rules of "should," "would," and "could." "I should be doing better." "Maybe I could have done it this way." This style is similar to critical self-talk, except that it allows the provision of possibly doing better next time. This form of self-talk is always setting you up for failure, thus promoting anxiety and even depression. Driven to desperation, the perfectionist will never seem to do things quite well enough. The perfectionist strives to measure themselves through external means. The job, promotion, money, and social status are all means to measure self-worth. **Rank yourself on this characteristic on a scale from 1 to 5 (5 being the worst)** _____ .

We all tend to use these internal running commentaries at different times. If you find that this is a central part of your daily thought patterns, then this may be an area for you to work on as it may very well be getting in the way of your memory functioning. Tally up your total score. If you received a score of 10 or above, this is an area that you probably need to work on it. If you received a 3 or higher in any single column, focus on altering that particular form of self-talk first.

These internal thoughts can negatively influence your memory. Each of these thought patterns represent functioning that is irrational and maladaptive. The first step in change is always identification of the problem. Once you identify maladaptive thoughts, you can begin to consciously change them and thus change the resulting negative emotion. Be alert in your daily life. The next time you catch yourself engaging in similar thoughts, stop the thought. Distract yourself away and let it go. Or, take a moment to consider what makes the thought irrational. Think about the advice you'd give to a friend if he or she explained the situation and his or her thoughts that occurred in the situation. Replace the maladaptive thought with an adaptive one and alter your beliefs.

* Reprinted, by permission, from Albert Ellis, *The Essence of Rational Psychotherapy: A Comprehensive Approach to Treatment.* 1970. Institute for Rational Living.

In the third column of the worksheet, you will list the negative thoughts (self-talk) associated with the memory lapse ("I'm always forgetting," "Boy, am I stupid"). Rate the degree of severity of the negative thought from 1 to 10 (again, 10 being the worst). In the next column, we will look at cognitive distortions.

Column 4—Cognitive Distortions

Beck (1967, 1979) and Ellis (1962, 1970) identify cognitive distortions as a series of thought patterns that are based on multiple self-commentaries. Cognitive distortions often serve to distort perception in some way. They are a kind of pigeonhole where negative self-talk grows into unchallenged, subjective fact. There are many cognitive distortions. Let's identify some of them.

★ *Overgeneralization:* Seeing a single incident as a too-often recurring event. Predicting from a single incident that this is the way things are and the way things will always be. Overgeneralization involves ignoring all the positives and focusing on the single negative event.

★ *All-or-nothing thinking:* This is black-and-white thinking. If you perform less than perfectly, then you see yourself as a failure (like forgetting to pack a toothbrush but remembering the other twenty-four items that were packed).

★ *Jumping to conclusions:* Making a negative interpretation of a situation, even though there are no facts to support this ("I'll probably mess this up, too").

★ *Emotional reasoning:* Assuming that your negative feelings reflect the way things are. If you feel it, it must be true.

★ *Catastrophizing:* Exaggerating mistakes or small incidences that begin to take on a life of their own.

★ *Minimizing:* Not giving yourself the credit you deserve for your positive qualities.

★ *Shoulds:* Whenever you use the word "should," you are probably setting yourself up for failure ("I should have done it the other way"). Shoulds are full of demoralizing ruminations.

★ *Personalization:* Attributing a negative circumstance to yourself when there is really no connection.

★ *Labeling:* Extreme overgeneralization! Instead of saying, "I failed," you say, "I'm a failure."

In the fourth column of the worksheet, you will identify the cognitive distortion associated with the negative thoughts. In the final column, we will list positive response.

Column 5—Positive Response

Positive thoughts are based on positive beliefs. After all, the ultimate goal of the DREAM portion of this training is to adjust your beliefs about memory, aging, and yourself and to develop a positive foundation on which to build healthy memory functioning. There are many healthy positive beliefs and the list that follows is certainly not all-inclusive. Can you see yourself with some of these beliefs? This is a list to get you started, who knows where these beliefs could take you.

Positive Beliefs and Memory

1. *I can change.* I don't have to remain a certain way and hold on to qualities in myself that limit my happiness. I can change anything I choose about myself. I can change my belief that memory is an entity that I have no control over. I am learning that my memory, although imperfect, works pretty well if I strategically utilize the energy to attend and strategically encode.

2. *I can accept when things go wrong.* If something goes wrong, I do not have to engage in negative self-talk or in negative thoughts. I do not have to limit myself with the anticipation that things might go wrong and that my memory may not work like I want it to.

3. *I don't have to make everyone happy.* I do not have to try to make everyone accept me. If I mistakenly slight someone by forgetting his or her name, I will offer the appropriate social graces and forget it.

4. *I do not have to control everything.* I can remain content in my day even though things do not go the way I want them to. I can accept myself, others, and things the way they are, imperfect with imperfect attributes and imperfect memories.

5. *It's okay if I make mistakes.* I am a good person even if I make mistakes. I am only human, with human thoughts and feelings and a human memory. Of course my memory does not always serve me perfectly.

6. *I can remain flexible.* Flexibility in my thinking will add to my memory performance and overall well-being. I will always choose to try to view things from different perspectives and to remain open to other alternatives.

7. *It is essential that I try.* Even if I fail at something, it is more important that I tried. Avoidance will hinder my growth as a person and in improving my memory.

8. *I am responsible.* I am responsible for my feelings and my actions. I can only feel or behave in a certain way if I choose to. If I feel demoralized about my memory, it is because I chose to. I also have the power not to feel demoralized or helpless.

9. *I am able.* I am able to take care of myself and make the improvements in myself that I choose. I do not have to depend on someone else for my memory. I am able to remember if I choose!

Finally, in column 5 of the worksheet, let's put in place a more adaptive positive response. Write three positive thoughts for every negative thought (column 3) that you identified. Rate your belief in the positive response from 1 to 10 (with 10 being the strongest).

Example of Positive Responses to Negative Thoughts

An example of three positive responses replacing a negative thought based on a cognitive distortion might be:

Negative Thoughts (Column 3)	Positive Responses (Column 5)
1. "I'm always forgetting things." (7)	1. I would have liked to remember, but I can't remember everything. (8)
	2. I'll be more content if I'm realistic about my expectations of my memory. (9)
	3. My memory is all right, even if it doesn't always perform perfectly. (7)

✎ ✗ Exercise: Examining Your Beliefs

Choose five entries from your journal that reflect an episode of forgetfulness. Apply them one at a time to the above analysis using the worksheets on the next few pages (Beck et al. 1979). Don't forget to rate your emotions, negative thoughts, and positive responses on a scale from 1 to 10. This will help you to identify patterns and to develop alternative positive responses to these patterns.

Now that we've done this analysis with five entries from your journal, it's time to begin to do this in everyday life. Apply this line of thinking to your future lapses in memory. Replace negative thoughts with alternative positive responses, with the enthusiam that will effect change. Next time you forget something, identify the thought that is leading toward negative feelings. Actively seek to change the mindset by putting in place a more adaptive thought. Everyone forgets, so in the process of improving your memory remember to be fair to yourself. In the next chapter, we will complete the RARE presentation with envisioning, which is the E in RARE.

Memory Lapse	Feelings	Negative Thoughts	Cognitive Distortions	Positive Response

Memory Lapse	Feelings	Negative Thoughts	Cognitive Distortions	Positive Response

Memory Lapse	Feelings	Negative Thoughts	Cognitive Distortions	Positive Response

Memory Lapse	Feelings	Negative Thoughts	Cognitive Distortions	Positive Response

Memory Lapse	Feelings	Negative Thoughts	Cognitive Distortions	Positive Response

* 12 *

Envision—Sensory Elaboration

Why Envision

In this chapter, we will present techniques to enhance memory functioning through the use of sensory elaboration. The focus on visual mnemonics is warranted by the proven success of imagery techniques in the literature. Although visual imagery is the most common technique utilized, we want to emphasize that all of your senses can be used to elaborate potential memories. West (1995)* states that memory specialists have treated visual imagery as the single most important memory-training technique over the past twenty years. Numerous studies have demonstrated the success of interactive imagery in improving memory skills for older adults (West and Crook 1992; Yesavage et al. 1983; Zarit et al. 1981). In interactive imagery, the items to be remembered are pictured interacting in some way. In a study of various factors involved with memory training, Verhaeghen and associates (1992) found that only two memory-training groups out of forty-nine did not use visual imagery as part of their training.

Imagery Leads to Elaboration

The use of imagery instills elaboration thereby enhancing encoding. And, as you've learned, using multiple senses results in the use of multiple memory systems. Elaboration relates to the level of processing involved when learning information. With increased elaboration, a deeper level of processing will occur. Therefore, attaching a visual image or sound or smell to information will make the information more memorable (Robertson-Tchabo 1980). For example, placing the scented cotton ball in your memory spot serves to reinforce retention by creating connections to the memories in olfactory pathways. In the use of imagery, the goal is to create a sensory experience (a mental picture) of the information that is to be remembered.

What Is Interactive Imagery?

Interactive imagery consists of a mental picture that is vivid and distinctive, with at least two objects interconnected or interacting in some way (West 1995). If you wanted to

---

* Reprinted, with permission, from Alan D. Baddeley, Barbara A. Wilson, and Fraser N. Watts, *Handbook of Memory Disorders*. 1995. John Wiley and Sons, Ltd.

remember to go to the store to buy carrots and eggs, you may visualize a group of eggs with little feet carrying carrots down the aisle of the grocery store. The effects of interactive imagery on recall have been found to be roughly twice as efficient as noninteractive imagery (Poon et al. 1980).*

🔑 Memory Tip: Face-Name Memory

Yesavage (1983) and his associates conducted a series of studies utilizing visual imagery to improve face-name learning in seniors. In face-name learning, the goal is to identify a prominent facial feature of a person and then transfer the person's name to a visual image by combining the facial feature with the visually altered name (for instance, Dr. VanSchnozen is the Dr. with the big nose). The next time you're struggling to remember someone's name, pick a feature that is unique in the person and associate his or her name to it. The more creative you become, the better the reliability of your memory will be for names.

The Impact of Imagery

Soon we will begin to teach you how to use some simple memory-enhancement techniques involving mental visualization and imagery. These techniques involve visualizing things that you want to remember. Imagery adds more impact and detail to information that you want to remember. In essence, it adds quality to information resulting in enhanced recall. If we wanted you to remember what a car looked like, which method would result in better recall? If we just described the car to you, or if we described the car to you and then showed you a picture of the car? Right. You'd be more likely to remember the car if we described it and then showed you a picture.

There's more impact on your brain if an image is included with the description. You are activating both the visual and verbal processors within your working memory and utilizing both sides of the brain rather than just one. Essentially, that's what we're going to do now—create a mental picture or other sensory experience for information that is presented to you. We will focus primarily on visual techniques, but remember to also apply imagery to smell, hearing, taste, and touch.

We will begin with a simple imagery exercise. When this is completed, we will move into more advanced techniques. For the first exercise, we want you to imagine the face of someone whom you know well.

✎ ✗ Exercise: Visualizing a Familiar Face

For this exercise, a spouse or a child would work best. Close your eyes and mentally imagine the face of a loved one. Make it someone with whom you are very familiar. Slowly work to make the image more and more clear. Imagine the person's hair, eyes, and mouth—all the details of the face. Allow yourself several minutes to do this. Is the person smiling? Do they look happy? Are they looking at you or at something else? Once this image is clear, think of someone else whose face you know well. Allow yourself to imagine this face in perfect clarity.

Continue to practice this until you are able to form the image in your mind. The next step in visualization will build on this skill. Make sure you are comfortable with this first exercise. When you're ready, move on to the next phase of visualization.

---

* Reprinted, by permission, from L. W. Poon, *Handbook of Psychology of Aging.* 1985. Harcourt, Inc.

✎ ✗ *Exercise: Visualizing a Famous Face*

Next, we want you to try to imagine something less familiar to you. Let's pick somebody famous. How about a former president like George Bush, Sr.? Again, close your eyes and mentally imagine George Bush, working to make the image more and more clear and remembering as many details as possible. Take a few minutes to let the image grow in clarity. Allow yourself to read his lips. Continue to practice until you are comfortable with the quality of the generated image. Now try it with: Bill Clinton, Richard Nixon, JFK, Winston Churchill, Elmer Fudd.

Did it get easier? Were you able to produce the images in your mind's eye? Remember to relax first and don't get discouraged. With practice you will begin to refine this skill. Visualization is a skill that needs to be practiced like any other skill. You start with the basics and move on. After you feel comfortable with this exercise, we will move on to an exercise that is just a little more difficult.

✎ ✗ *Exercise: Visualizing Objects*

Okay, now let's try to imagine some objects. For each object that we name, take a few seconds to form a mental image of the object. Don't move on to the next object until you feel comfortable with the last one. Allow yourself a few minutes to adequately get a mental picture for each item. Ready?

★ rose

★ pen

★ shirt

★ hammer

★ plane

★ light bulb

Good! Now let's lay some context and tie the images together.

An Introduction to Interaction

Let's take the hammer, the plane, and a light bulb. Picture a hammer falling from a plane and landing on a light bulb, smashing it to pieces. Try it—a hammer falling from a plane and landing on a light bulb, smashing it to pieces. Were you able to develop the picture? We'll ask you to recall these words in just a minute. First, let's look at a mnemonic technique called "pegging."

🔑 Memory Tip: Pegging

If you find that you are more verbally oriented, the pegging technique might be for you. It's a form of association that helps you to organize the items to be remembered. Choose a series of words that you will always remember in the same order. We will give an example of five words that rhyme with the numbers one through five.

1 = gun

2 = shoe

3 = tree

4 = door

5 = hive

You can now associate the items to be remembered to the set list of words. In other words, you can hang the words to be remembered on the peg words. This method can also enhance memory for names by simply choosing a word or words to associate with the new name. With some practice you can take this method a step further by visualizing the items to be remembered interacting with the pegwords. With creativity, this method will help you to solidify retention and enhance recall.

Interaction Leads to Better Attention

Can you tell us what those last three words were that you visualized interacting from page 115? Exactly! And your interactive mental images helped you to remember. The point is that the more vivid the mental image is, the more likely you are to remember it. For example, you're more likely to remember an image of a hammer falling from the air than you are to remember just the image of a hammer. That's because there's more detail involved with a hammer falling through the air, and therefore there's more for your brain to grasp. The first image has meaning and is more entertaining. "More entertaining" leads to better quality attention. Better attention results in better encoding and effortless retrieval.

If you're trying to remember more than one thing, it helps for you to tie two detailed images together to create a vivid image. For example you're more likely to remember a hammer falling through the air and smashing a light bulb than you are just trying to remember a hammer and light bulb separately. Let's practice doing this in steps. Mentally add some detail to objects. Remember, the more ridiculous the better.

✎ ✗ *Exercise: Single Item Interactions*

Let's imagine a rose again. Take a minute or two and allow the image of the rose to crystallize in your mind. See the color, examine the texture of the petals and the leaves. Notice the thorns. Smell the sweet fragrance.

★ Now imagine the rose extremely small. Allow the rose to actually shrink in your mind.

★ Now visualize the rose growing until it becomes very large.

★ Now imagine a pen. What color is the pen? Does it have writing on it?

★ Now imagine a huge pen.

★ Now imagine a pen flying through the air.

★ Now visualize a shirt.

★ Now the shirt hanging from a flagpole.

★ Now a shirt swimming in the ocean.

★ Now a plane.

★ Now a plane driving down the street.

★ Now a plane flying backwards.

You see? Items that are in action are easier to remember. How much detail did you incorporate into your image? What color was the shirt? Was it a shirt that you are familiar with? What were the markings on the plane? Was it a large jet plane or a small propeller-driven plane? If you take only a moment to create a ridiculous visual image (like a shirt swimming in the ocean), the memory trace will be much more accessible for later recall. Now we will move to the next level of complexity in visualization.

✎ ✗ Exercise: Multiple Item Interactive Visualizations

Now let's link two objects together with interactive imagery. We are going to give you two objects, and we want you to try to come up with your own vivid interactive images. Just like we did with the hammer smashing the light bulb. Remember to take all the time you need until you feel comfortable with visualizing the two objects interacting together. Be creative and grab a laugh or two while you do this.

Okay, how about a rose and a pen? Give it some time while you imagine. Were you able to come up with an image of the two?

Now let's try a shirt and a plane. Remember, give yourself plenty of time to dream up some inventive interaction. Good! Now let's try three words.

Try a piece of bread, a ruler, and a stop sign. Take a few minutes to try to visually connect the three words in some creative way. Make up a story of how they interact. This will allow you to further incorporate your verbal memory into the overall memory trace.

All right, how was that? With more and more practice, it becomes easier to do. During the course of this exercise, we've given you seven objects to remember. Let's see how many you can remember right now.

✎ ✗ Exercise: Recall of Multiple Interactive Items

Write down the objects that we just had you link up in the preceding exercise. Use the interactions that were presented and that you created to assist your recall. When using this method, if you can remember one object, then you will usually remember the other items that were interacting with that object. It provides another safety net for remembering.

1. _____

2. _____

3. _____

4. _____

5. _____

6. _____

7. _____

Check above for answers. Compare the success of this exercise with the success of others. Throughout the book there are multiple lists that we ask you to remember using different techniques. Do any stand out as areas of strength for you? Begin to review the exercises that we have already covered. Utilize the strategies that work for you in real life memory challenges.

Most Importantly, Have Fun

The main point of the previous exercise is to demonstrate that when you take a moment to visualize what you want to remember, it will be easier to recall. If you have more than one item to remember, try to visually connect the various items together. In either case, place some action into the visualization. Animate the object or objects in some creative way. Imagine vivid colors and unusual scenarios. The human brain contains wonderfully complex structures dedicated to the processing of where an object is and what it is doing. And remember, the more elaborate and the more ridiculous or silly, the more likely you will be to remember it. The test of a good memory is not if you can remember—it is how effortlessly you can remember. An ounce of prevention is worth a pound of cure. Prevent poor recall through good encoding. Most importantly, make remembering creative and fun!

Attending Only to Specifics

Next we want you to think only about the following subject. Take several minutes to visualize the scene. Remember to first relax and prepare for the visual exercise.

✎ ✗ *Exercise: Magnify Your Senses*

Visualize a weeping willow tree. Notice how the branches hang from the tall tree and touch the ground. See the moss hanging from the tree. Notice the cool, dark green grass growing underneath the tree. You might even smell the scent of fresh air combined with the mild, sweet scent of wild flowers. You may hear the sound of birds singing in the background or just the gentle breeze rustling the leaves. Notice the different textures of the bark. Perhaps the bark is a little coarser on the trunk and smooths out on the branches. How does the bark feel? Notice all of the different colors and textures in the picture. Focus all of your senses on the tree. See the shadows and the different colors, the different hues. Hear the tree. Smell the tree. Taste the tree. Feel the tree.

Incorporating your senses is like focusing a lens. It allows you to magnify the experience. Attention to detail while visualizing allows you to better encode the subject to memory. Try to open a memory trace for each sense that can potentially experience the object. If your mind wanders, it's okay. Just place your attention on some other aspect of the tree. Would you be better able to remember the tree after seeing it or touching it?

Sensory Elaboration Leads to Efficient Recall

You may recall the study we discussed earlier about how older adults are able to remember objects equally as well as younger adults when the objects naturally involved all the senses. This study illustrates the importance for older adults to involve all their senses in order to remember. When all the senses were involved, older adults encoded and recalled information as well as younger adults!

How Do You Involve All the Senses?

To involve the senses, you relax to maximize the capacity of your senses. You actively apply your attention so that your senses are focused on your environment. Being aware of the attentional demands that exist in your environment will further prepare you. Forming a preparatory set will prepare you for the attentional demands that you are about to encounter. Examine the object to be remembered from multiple angles. Ask yourself what it might smell like, what it might taste like, how it sounds, or how it feels. Picture the object to be remembered engaged in some activity. Apply this technique when actually confronted with the things that you want to remember. Begin to generalize this knowledge to your life outside of the pages of this book.

Generalization

Generalization is the ability to transfer knowledge learned in one context to other contexts. Generalization is the ability to transfer what we learn in this book to the real world. It is essential that you apply these new strategies and skills to your everyday life. The level of your success in improving your memory is dependent upon your ability to take what you have learned from the pages of this book and apply it to your everyday life. Focus first on the skills in the book that stand out as areas of strength for you. Try the strategies on real things that you must commit to memory. Utilize the retrieval techniques to assist you in remembering—and don't forget to have fun. Remember, with fun comes enjoyment, and with enjoyment comes good attention.

How does one learn to generalize? How does one get to Carnegie Hall? Practice, practice, practice! The best jazz musicians practice and practice so that music becomes natural. Once music becomes second nature for them, they can improvise. They can create their own music, because it is very natural for them. Memory is an improvisation, so utilize your new skills whenever possible by practicing. *Use your skills daily—use your imagination—generalize your skills—have fun!*

Method of Loci

The next technique we're going to learn continues to build upon the imaging skills that we've been developing. It's called the "method of loci" technique, and it consists of remembering things by visually placing what you want to remember in places that are familiar to you. The method of loci (MOL) is a well-established technique and was known and used in ancient Greece as a memory strategy. It is also an excellent way of remembering things in a specific order, such as things to do within a specific time sequence (like to-do lists). To utilize the MOL, you first visualize very familiar places in a specific order, and then you visually place the things that you want to remember in these places. To retrieve the information, you imagine yourself walking through the familiar place, retrieving each image as you come to its location. In this strategy, you always use the same locations and simply place new items to be remembered within them.

Establishing Your MOL

One of the best places to visualize and utilize as your MOL is your house or apartment. The first step is to establish about ten rooms or places in your house that you will visually walk through in the exact same order each time. With the MOL, you create a context in which to anchor the content of memory. As an example, we'll go through Edgar's house and map out ten places. Then we will visualize the places and subsequently place one thing that we want to remember in each place.

When Edgar opens the door to his house, the first thing that he sees is his foyer. That'll be place #1. Then he walks into his guest bedroom and that'll be place #2. After entering the guest bedroom, he walks over and opens the closet in the guest bedroom, that'll be place #3. He then walks out of the guest bedroom and into the kitchen, which is place #4. He then leaves the kitchen and enters the dining room, which will be place #5.

The next place he will visit is his den, place #6. He then walks into the bathroom, place #7. While in the bathroom, he opens the shower curtain and looks into the tub. That's place #8. Next, he enters the master bedroom, and that's place #9. Finally, he walks onto the porch, and that's place #10. Edgar has his places identified and memorized, and he will always think of them in this order when he visualizes walking through his home. Let's watch as Edgar fills these places with errands.

Placing Items to Be Remembered within Edgar's Locations

We realize this seems awkward at first, but once the places are established and memorized it will become much easier and even routine. The next step is placing the image of the item that you want to remember in the memorized spots. Be creative and entertain yourself in the process. Take the time and effort to actually visualize the item in its location (one item per location). For instance, a car in your kitchen to remember to get your car tuned up.

Let's say that on a particular day Edgar has five things that he wants to remember. First he has to remember to go to the library to drop off some books. He then needs to speak to Mr. Jones from the library. Next he needs to go to the store to pick up milk, and then get gas for his car. Finally he has to visit the doctor's office. All in that order.

The next step is to take a few minutes to place each of the images in the preestablished locations within Edgar's house. Edgar's foyer is the first location and the library is the first place that he needs to go. So Edgar imagines a pile of books lying in his foyer as he walks in. In fact, there are so many books, that he visualizes himself almost losing his balance while stepping between the piles of books. His second location is the guest bedroom, and the second thing he needs to remember is to speak to Mr. Jones. To do this, he imagines Mr. Jones lying on the bed in the guest bedroom as he walks in. His third location is the closet, and his next errand is to get milk. So, Edgar imagines opening the closet and seeing a quart of milk hanging from a hanger in the closet (remember, the more unusual the image, the easier it is to remember). His fourth location is the kitchen, and he next has to remember to get gas for his car. So he creates a memorable image of his car sitting on the oven. His fifth location is his dining room, and he next has to remember his doctor's appointment. To do this, he imagines his doctor eating in the dining room. He then goes over all of these images a couple of times in his head to rehearse them. Throughout the day he continues to reinforce the memory of his errands by visualizing himself walking through the locations. This helps to maintain all the things that Edgar has to remember. You will find that once you have your locations firmly established, it doesn't take much effort to actually place your images in the locations. This is a wonderful way in which to incorporate traditional left brain function (verbal memory) with right brain function (visual and spatial orientation). Remember, utilizing multiple memory systems results in improved retention and recall. Now let's work on getting your locations established.

✎ ✗ Exercise: Establishing Your Method of Loci

Develop your own personal method of loci. The most important part is establishing ten locations that you'll visually walk through, always in the same order. You may want to use many of the locations that Edgar used. Just make sure to place them in the order that you'd come upon them if you were walking through your house. Imagine yourself walking through your home, establish ten locations, and write them down below. Again, if necessary break up the room into smaller components (like the oven, closet, or refrigerator). Write down the ten places that you wish to use as your MOL in the order that you will use them.

1. _____
2. _____
3. _____
4. _____
5. _____
6. _____
7. _____
8. _____
9. _____
10. _____

Now take this list and memorize it. Write it on a piece of paper so that you can take it with you the first few times. Put a copy in your car and wherever else you think you may need it. Repetition through writing is another way to help you encode information.

✎ ✗ *Exercise: Using Your Method of Loci*

Now we'll give you some everyday errands that you might encounter. Place an image that represents the errand into your established locations. The five errands are:

1. First you need to drop some letters in the mailbox.

2. Then you need to go to the store to buy a loaf of bread.

3. Now it's time to put air in your car tires.

4. Next let's stop at the bank and deposit your check.

5. Finally, it's time to go home and water the plants.

Use your list of locations if necessary to make sure you're placing the images in the appropriate rooms. Take a few minutes to tie each errand to its location through visualization. Remember, make them unique and creative.

Creativity—The Key to Effective Memory

Incorporate your individual personality style into your memory techniques. Tailor the suggestions to fit *you*. For example, a good sense of humor can go a long way toward finding something unique about an individual to associate with his or her name. Go beyond your mind's natural limits and plug in a detail that you may not have initially observed until you took the time and effort to do so. Good memory starts with the quality of the information that is taken in through your senses and the creativity involved in establishing and encoding unique personally meaningful and even ridiculous retrieval methods.

✎ ✗ *Exercise: Recall for Method of Loci*

Now write all the items that you placed in your method of loci. Let's see how many of the errands you remember.

1. _____

2. _____

3. _____

4. _____

5. _____

✎ ✗ *Exercise: MOL in the Grocery Aisle*

Now let's try it with a list of items that you want to get at the grocery store. This time we want you to try to do it without having to look at the written locations. Place each grocery item within one of your locations. The grocery list is:

milk

bread

cookies

potatoes

coffee

aspirin

peanut butter

This will be a little tougher because the items aren't distinctive, so therefore try to make the images as vivid as possible. Concentrate. Remember to relax, attend, rehearse, and envision. It should take you several minutes to adequately review your individual places and to imagine one item in each place.

Before we come back to method of loci, let's look at another memory tip.

🔑 Memory Tip: Organizational Strategy PQ3RST

To better organize information that you read, watch, or hear, try the PQ3RST method (Glasgow et al. 1977; Sandman 1993). PQ3RST stands for Preview, Question, Read-Rehearse-Review, Summarize, and Test. Before being presented with information, mentally preview what will be involved. Then ask yourself some questions about things that may be important to look for. This helps to clarify and expand the information within your memory. Then read, rehearse, and review the information you've been presented with. Repetition is an important element in the strategy of memorization. Then, mentally summarize all the main points found in the information. Finally, test yourself. This technique is especially useful if you are attempting to memorize lengthy data such as a poem or a long list (like the capitals of all the states). Remember to grade with a curve, and maintain those healthy beliefs!

✎ ✗ Exercise: MOL in the Grocery Aisle, Continued

Now write the items from the grocery store in your book.

1. _____
2. _____
3. _____
4. _____
5. _____
6. _____
7. _____

Review the exercise from page 122 for the answers. This technique will become more and more familiar as you continue to practice. Take it out for a test drive and try it during your next visit to the store. If this is information that you need to retain for a long period, remember to do periodic reviews of the items throughout the day.

The next exercise will require a combination of interactive visual imagery and method of loci. Combining the two is a useful technique if you need to manage and remember detailed information. For example, when having to run multiple errands over the course of a day.

Advanced Method of Loci

Imagine the following scenario: You have blocked out an entire day to take care of several errands that have gone neglected. For reasons of efficiency and necessity, the errands must be accomplished in a specific order. Therefore, you have a dual burden: remembering specific details as well as the order of events. In the next exercise we will ask just that of you. We will give you ten detailed errands that you must remember in order. To accomplish the dual task, try combining interactive visual imagery with the method of loci technique. For example, imagine two errands that must be accomplished in order. Errand #1 is to place the aluminum cans in the recycling bin. Errand #2 is to call Tom Middleton at the recycling plant to tell him your recyclables need to be picked up at 8:00 A.M. To remember the errands, you start the method of loci in the first room of your residence and add interactive imagery. If your first room is a living room, you might imagine a line of cans diving from your TV into the recycling bin sitting on the couch. If the second room is a dining room, errand #2 could be represented as a colorful map of your town covering the table. In the dead *middle* of the map of your *town*, you imagine a tomcat waving the number *8* at the end of pole (Tom Middleton, 8 A.M.). It takes a little effort, but the memories will be embedded deep within your mind.

✎ ✗ Exercise: Advanced Method of Loci

We will now give you ten errands that you are to remember in order. It will be a busy day for you, particularly because you plan on having a barbecue that night. Take ten or fifteen minutes to incorporate the errands into an interactive-imagery method of loci combination. Shortly we will check your success. Compare your results then with the list that follows.

Things To Do List

1. Right after waking up, check the weather channel (channel 24), to make sure they're not calling for rain until after midnight.

2. Check the garage to make sure there's enough charcoal.

3. Call Dr. Greenberg to make sure she called in the prescription to Pharm-Mart Pharmacy.

4. Go next door to ask Ms. Coppley if she can lend you her punchbowl.

5. Fill in the birthday card for Peggy, and don't forget to include the memory-improvement article you clipped from DREAM magazine in the envelope.

6. Go by Pharm-Mart to get the prescription and buy a book of stamps while there.

7. Stop by Ridgley's Market to buy mayonnaise, lettuce, and charcoal.

8. Stop by the mailbox in the store parking lot and mail Peggy's birthday card.

9. After coming home, preheat the oven to 450 degrees for the cheese casserole and take out four steaks to defrost.

10. Start up the barbecue.

Take the time necessary to create unique images of the errands on the list. Link these images into your preestablished locations. We will check your success shortly.

Verbal Repetition Verses Repetitious Writing

Let's compare a couple of other encoding strategies to determine which might be more beneficial for you to use in the future. First, we are going to examine your ability to encode a list by repeating it to yourself several times. This is a good test of your verbal memory. We will then give you another list and ask you write it down several times. This not only includes verbal memory but also incorporates visual and motor memory. We will give you two sets of ten words to remember. For the first set of ten words, repeat them out loud to yourself. For the second set of ten words, write them down the number of times indicated.

✎ ✗ Exercise: Verbal Repetition

Repeat the following ten words aloud to yourself five times, going over them carefully and committing them to memory. Memorize the list as a whole and do not repeat the first word five times and then move on to the second word. Do not utilize other mnemonics that we have learned, only rely on the verbal repetition.

1. Bird

2. Camp

3. Key

4. Paper

5. Iron

6. Book

7. Bear

8. Hook

9. Shirt

10. Radio

Again, repeat these words to yourself aloud five times. Wait three minutes (time yourself) and write down the words you remember in the following spaces.

1. _____   2. _____

3. _____   4. _____

5. _____   6. _____

7. _____   8. _____

9. _____   10. _____

How did you do? Let's try it again, plugging in a couple of other memory systems (visual and motor).

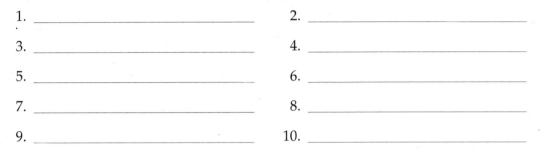 ## Exercise: Writing Repetition

On a scrap piece of paper, write the following ten words five times each. Write the words as a whole list rather than writing each separate word five times in a row. The ten words are:

1. Cat

2. Fork

3. Phone

4. Staple

5. Carpet

6. Picture

7. Mirror

8. Table

9. Lamp

10. Tree

After writing the list down five times on scrap paper, place the list out of sight. Again, take a three-minute break before proceeding to the next portion of the exercise.

Now write the words on the following lines.

1. _____   2. _____

3. _____   4. _____

5. _____   6. _____

7. _____   8. _____

9. _____   10. _____

What Were the Results of the Writing Verses Verbal Repetition?

How did you do? Compare the number correct between the verbally memorized list and the list memorized through writing. If you got more than a two-word difference on either the verbal or written list, then you're probably stronger in utilizing repetition in that form. Our hunch is that most people will find they did better on the writing portion. Again, the memory trace laid down through this means involves multiple memory systems, thus a deeper level of encoding.

✎ ✗ Exercise: Advanced Method of Loci

Write down the errands from the advanced method of loci exercise. Compare your answers with the original list.

1. _____
2. _____
3. _____
4. _____
5. _____
6. _____
7. _____
8. _____
9. _____
10. _____

That was probably the most difficult exercise thus far. How did you do? Grade yourself on a curve—if you were able to remember more than half of the errands, then you are doing well. With that said, let's do a quick review of the ten places that you chose for your method of loci.

✎ ✗ Exercise: Method of Loci Review

As a final review of the method of loci, write down the ten areas that you chose for you method of loci below.

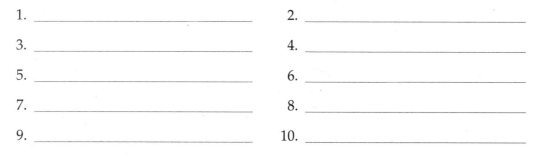

1. _____   2. _____

3. _____   4. _____

5. _____   6. _____

7. _____   8. _____

9. _____   10. _____

✎ ✗ Exercise: Delayed Verbal and Writing Repetition

In the space provided below, list all of the twenty items that you can remember from the prior word repetition and writing exercise. Remember, there were two lists of ten items each? Don't worry about which word went with which list. Just write down as many of the total twenty words as you can remember.

1. _____
2. _____
3. _____
4. _____
5. _____
6. _____
7. _____
8. _____
9. _____
10. _____

11. _____
12. _____
13. _____
14. _____
15. _____
16. _____
17. _____
18. _____
19. _____
20. _____

Now go back to the original exercises where the words were first introduced. Count the number of words that you remembered using verbal repetition and write it in the space provided below. Now count the words that you encoded through writing and mark the number in the space below.

_____ Number of words remembered by verbal repetition

_____ Number of words remembered by writing repetition

Do you see a difference between the two encoding methods? Were the results similar to the immediate recall exercise? If the numbers were within one or two points, then you have strengths in both areas. If one stood out with three or more points over the other, then you're stronger in that area. Use this to your advantage and experiment with different ways of utilizing the method that works best for you.

✎ ✗ Exercise: Review of RARE-DREAM

Now that we have presented the major components of the program, let's take this opportunity to review the steps of the program represented by the acronym RARE-DREAM. What does each letter stand for? What does each letter (step) help us to accomplish? Take your time and use the review provided below to confirm to yourself that you have a good working knowledge of what each letter represents, when and how to use it, and what each stage is designed to do. After reviewing the following information, if you feel that you might need additional work in any of the areas, take whatever time is necessary to gain a sense of comfort with corresponding chapters that have been presented thus far. Once you are comfortable with your familiarity with RARE-DREAM, proceed to chapter 13 ("Recall").

RARE-DREAM Recap

Relaxation techniques

Designed to maximize the receptiveness of your senses

Designed to help in the encoding and retrieval processes

Attention techniques

Designed to maximize the receptiveness of your senses

Opens the door of your working memory to allow the data in

Rehearsal techniques

Maintains data within conscious awareness

Helps in the transfer of data from working memory into long-term memory

Envisioning or visualization techniques

Designed to help in the deeper storage of information

Helps to create an anchor to enhance recall

DREAM
(Develop Rational and Emotionally Adaptive Mindsets)

Portion of program designed to assess and adjust cognitive belief systems (mindsets) and emotional components that serve to negatively influence memory functioning.

The next chapter is dedicated to recall or retrieval. In that chapter we will offer specific strategies to help you retrieve information more effectively. We will also help you to determine whether you may be experiencing marked difficulty with either encoding or recall stages of memory.

★ 13 ★

Recall

We have spent a great deal of time so far discussing the encoding process in memory. But there is another side of memory that we wish to address more directly. Memory can be subdivided into two broad classifications. These categories are retention (encoding) and recall (retrieval). In essence, recall is the process of pulling information from memory. In this chapter, we will address some of the concerns directly related to recall and offer some guidelines as to how to make your recall work better for you. We will also take a look at your memory functioning and help you to determine if you're stronger in retention or recall.

A journey of a thousand miles always begins with one step.

—Ancient Chinese proverb

Retrieval Frustrations

Remember the diagram of memory presented earlier?

Information → Senses → Storage = (Memory Consolidation) ← Information ← Retrieval

Information enters your mind through your senses into your working memory. It's then transferred to and retained in your long-term memory for later use. Most of the strategies presented up to now have been related to encoding information effectively. After all, this is the area where we can effect the most change. But what about the retrieval process? This stage is where we most notice our difficulties with memory. This is where we often find ourselves frustrated.

Conscious Encoding and Retrieval

Retrieval tends to be a conscious process. It becomes even more conscious if we are unable to remember the information that we desire. Encoding tends to be subconscious. Through the construction of the RARE-DREAM model, we have attempted to reverse this process. The simple formula for improving your memory is to place as much conscious effort in encoding a memory as you do in retrieving a memory. But there are some effective strategies that can be utilized in the retrieval process to further enhance your memory functioning.

With Good Encoding, Retrieval Takes Care of Itself

Now it is time to explore how you can better retrieve the expanded, rich information that you have strategically placed in your memory. The good news is most of the strategies presented so far can be applied not only to retention but also to recall. Recall should be naturally less effortful if we place the emphasis on encoding the information. If good information goes in and the information is strategically encoded, then less effort is needed to recall that information. Let's explore some specific strategies to enhance recall.

🔑 Memory Tip: State-Dependent Memory

State-dependent memory (Goodwin et al. 1969) refers to long-term memory where the recall of that memory is dependent upon being in the same state of mind as when the memory was formed. For example, if you were very happy during the encoding of a memory, the memory may be more accessible when you are happy. If you have difficulty remembering something, try to recall the state of mind that you were in when the memory was formed. If you can return to that mindframe, you might find that the item to be remembered comes back to you.

Relax Again

Let's go back to the foundation of RARE-DREAM—relaxation. Relaxation applies as much to the retrieval process as it does to encoding. As a matter of fact, the concept of state-dependent learning (Goodwin et al. 1969) also emphasizes the importance of relaxation. Again, the theory states that we are more likely to remember something if we're in the same emotional state as when the memory was originally encoded. So relax when you acquire information, and relax when you retrieve information. Use relaxation skills when trying to remember something. Remember, the more anxious you get in not being able to retrieve a memory, the less likely it is that you will succeed. So relax—the item to be remembered will eventually come to you. You may need to purposely place yourself into a greater state of relaxation, but the memory will come to you in good time.

In Through the Back Door

Often we have difficulty getting the exact information we want right when we want it. How many times have you experienced being in a conversation and feeling unable to remember a name? As hard as you try, you just can't get it. It's frustrating, because it's right on the proverbial tip of your temporal lobe. You can almost feel it there, waiting to jump out. The harder you try, the further it seems to slip away. Try a less-direct method. You have learned how memory works. Information is stored according to many themes. A few of these include: time, sound, category, property, sight, feel, smell, and taste. Try to tap into the memory using a secondary network.

Perhaps you're trying to remember the name of a restaurant that you and your spouse want to revisit. Obviously you can't look up the phone number without knowing the name of the restaurant. If you are unable to access the memory under the general network of "restaurant," try another network. Use your envisioning skills. Picture yourself at that restaurant. Walking in, you look up and see the sign above the door. Picture yourself paying the bill the last time you were there. Perhaps there were business cards next to the cash register that had the name of the restaurant. Taste the food that you had the last time you were there. What did the waiter who waited on you look like? What was his name? We guarantee that the name of the restaurant is contained in these memories somewhere. Remember, relax and try to enter memories of the restaurant through the back door. The point is that the concepts of RARE can also be applied to recall, so don't be discouraged.

Talking Through the Problem

If you find yourself with only a memory trace or a vague notion of a memory, a good technique to use is to talk through the problem. Try to verbalize the notion or image that exists in your memory. Keep working at articulating this trace until it becomes solidified. Essentially you're excavating your memory and attempting to unearth the buried information. This technique is interesting to utilize or observe because it can lead you down some silly places as you search all over your memory and verbalize all the junk that comes out before the valuable information is uncovered.

Before examining more retrieval strategies, let's take a look at recognition and free recall.

Recognition Versus Free Recall

Free recall refers to the ability to spontaneously recall previously learned information. *Recognition* is the ability to recognize and select previously learned information amongst other potential choices. A good example of the difference between the two is eyewitness identification. An eyewitness who is capable of providing accurate detail of a criminal such that a sketch artist could draw a good likeness would be an example of free recall. In contrast, an eyewitness making identification through a police lineup would be an example of recognition. With the sketch artist example, the eyewitness's facial memory is provided without cues or choices, straight from memory onto the artist's paper. In a police lineup, the eyewitness is choosing among an array of people to pinpoint a specific person. This eyewitness makes recognition of the right face and then selects that face as being the guilty among the innocent.

By examining any performance difference between free recall ability and recognition ability, information may be gleaned about your memory functioning. If you are unable to recall new information by either free recall or recognition, the conclusion can be drawn that problems occurred at the encoding stage of memory functioning. The information could not be accessed even when given clues or different items to choose from, indicating that the information never entered your long-term memory. However, if you discover that your free recall ability is less than optimum but your recognition ability is good, the problem may be more of a retrieval memory compromise. A substantially better recognition memory may suggest that the information entered, but not in a deep or organized fashion necessary for effective free recall. Conversely, the problems may occur at the retrieval stage with the possibility that the information was encoded effectively, but something hindered the ability to access the information from memory. Recognition versus free recall ability is critical diagnostic information for distinguishing between normal memory changes associated with healthy aging and dementia. With Alzheimer's disease, for example, new information is not usually properly encoded, so people with Alzheimer's are unable to adequately recall or recognize recently presented information. In general, memory changes associated with healthy aging tend to have a pattern of reduced, delayed recall, with stronger recognition (Welsh-Bohmer and Ogrocki 1998). Next we will take a look at your delayed recall and recognition memory.

Revisiting and Recalling Edgar's Garage

The time has come again to revisit Edgar's garage. You have now learned several techniques to assist your recall skills (going in through the back door, talking through a problem, relaxation). Let's see if any of these techniques facilitates your recall. But don't forget your previously learned skills of relaxing, attending, rehearsal, envisioning, and "DREAMing." Assume a relaxed state, implement your attention skills (form a preparatory set and review), elaborate on the items through rehearsal and envisioning, and most importantly, maintain a positive mindset. We will present a partial list of items found in Edgar's garage.

✎ ✗ *Exercise: Edgar's Garage*

Review the list of items that Edgar found in his garage. Take about five minutes and memorize the following list.

1. Some lamps

2. An old radio

3. A stack of newspapers

4. Some hubcaps

5. An unusable barbecue grill

6. Some old phone books

7. A power drill

8. A hammer

9. An old television set

10. A checkers game

🔑 Memory Tip: Word-Finding Difficulties

Do you ever find that you have trouble finding the word or phrase that you want to use in a conversation? This can be terribly irritating. It often results in a complete halt in midsentence and an acute feeling of confusion as you focus your efforts on finding the word that seems to be on the tip of your tongue. Because of frustration, you may find yourself engaging in spoken or unspoken self-degrading thoughts or statements. The secret is to *let it go*. The English language is rich in a multitude of words that serve to identify and describe the same thing as the lost word. Choose another word and go on. Don't beat up on yourself and become overly focused on your "poor memory." Simply tell yourself that you will get it next time. We all have this difficulty at some time or another.

If it is absolutely necessary that you retrieve that specific word, then try to relax. Try a mini relaxation and attempt to access the word indirectly. In your mind, describe the word. Visualize the word in writing. What letter does it start with? How many syllables does the word contain? What might the word rhyme with? When was the last time you heard or used the word? Think about where you were, whom you were with, and what it was you were discussing. Try to identify what might be getting in the way of remembering the word. Is there some emotions the word brings up? These emotions could be acting as a blockage. What other words are coming to mind as you try to recall this word? What might their connections be to the word that you are trying to recall? If nothing else works, go on and allow the word to seep into your consciousness on its own.

Now let's look at your ability to recall those items from Edgar's garage.

✎ ✗ Exercise: Recall the Items from Edgar's Garage

List the items from Edgar's garage that you can remember from the list on page 132.

1. _____
2. _____
3. _____
4. _____
5. _____
6. _____
7. _____
8. _____
9. _____
10. _____

Check your answers against the original list on page 132. Convert the number you got correct into a percentage by dividing the number correct by ten (the total number of items). So, if you got five correct, you would divide that by ten to arrive at 50 percent. You therefore would have remembered 50 percent of the information that was presented to you. Put the percentage that you obtained in the space below.

Number correct _____ ÷ 10 = _____ %

After we review another tip for recall, we will look at you performance on recognition.

🔑 Memory Tip: Alphabetical Associative Recall

If you find that you're having difficulty remembering an item, a name, or a place, try slowly going through the alphabet to jog your memory. After repeating each letter to yourself either out loud or in your head, pause and consider if the thing that you are trying to remember starts with that letter. This strategy is simply a way of transferring what was a demanding free recall task into a less burdensome recognition task.

Now that you've listed all the items that you remember from Edgar's garage, let's see how many you can recognize.

✎ ✗ Exercise: Recognition of the Items from Edgar's Garage

In the list of items below, circle "yes" or "no" according to whether each item presented was in the list of ten items taken from Edgar's garage (page 132).

1. *yes / no* Some lamps

2. *yes / no* An old stereo

3. *yes / no* A stack of newspapers

4. *yes / no* Navy discharge certificate

5. *yes / no* Some hubcaps

6. *yes / no* A beautiful pink satin jumpsuit

7. *yes / no* A small and unusable barbecue grill

8. *yes / no* A power drill

9. *yes / no* An old computer

10. *yes / no* A saw

11. *yes / no* An old radio

12. *yes / no* A can of sardines

13. *yes / no* A checkers game

14. *yes / no* A worn-out set of auto tires

15. *yes / no* A chess game

16. *yes / no* A large seashell

17. *yes / no* Some old phone books

18. *yes / no* A pile of 8-track tapes

19. *yes / no* A hammer

20. *yes / no* An old television set

Now score the number of correct responses by comparing your performance to the answers in appendix E. Write your results in the space below.

_____ Correct number of "yes" responses _____ Correct number of "no" responses

Now convert both correct "yes" and "no" responses into a percentage by dividing the number correct in each of the categories (yes and no) by ten.

Correct number of "yes" responses _____ ÷ 10 = _____ %

Correct number of "no" responses _____ ÷ 10 = _____ %

Below write down the percentage correct from the delayed recall exercise from page 133.

Correct number of free recall responses _____ ÷ 10 = _____ %

Recognition Versus Delayed Recall

Let's take a look at what these percentages mean. Keep in mind that this information has not been formally administered and should not take the place of a comprehensive neuropsychological evaluation. Essentially what we want to determine is that learning is taking place. The percentage on both the recognition tasks should be above chance. If you were to have guessed at the recognition task you probably would have gotten about 50 percent by chance since there were only two possible responses (yes and no). Therefore, recognition for both yes and no responses should exceed 50 percent and should exceed the delayed recall percentage. The normal pattern observed in aging is one where recognition memory is higher than free recall (Luh 1922; Postman and Rau 1957; Craik and McDowd 1987; Wheeler 2000). Therefore, it's expected that both the yes and no percentages would be higher than the free recall percentage.

If the percentage of either yes or no is substantially higher than the free recall percentage (more than 50 percent difference), then it may reflect difficulty with the retrieval process of memory. A professional memory evaluation would be recommended in this case. If both the free recall and recognition percentages are low (below 30 percent), it may indicate deficits in the memory consolidation process. In this scenario, we would also recommend a formal memory evaluation.

To give you a rough idea of how others in your age range might perform on this task, we will provide some numbers for comparison. Although these percentages were taken from the Consortium to Establish a Registry of Alzheimer's Disease (CERAD) on a different word-learning task, they can provide some general guidelines to get a feel for how you're doing (Morris et al. 1988; Morris et al. 1989; Welsh et al. 1991; Welsh et al. 1992; Welsh et al. 1994). Match your performance to the appropriate age, gender, and education.

	Education Greater than 12 Years				Education Less than 12 Years	
	Age 50–69		Age 70–89		Age 50–69	Age 70–89
	Men	Women	Men	Women	Men and Women	
Delay Recall	70%	79%	63%	69%	70%	67%
Recog Yes	97%	98%	95%	97%	93%	93%
Recog No	99%	99%	98%	99%	99%	99%

How did your performance compare with others? Keep in mind that these are rough estimates, but they can serve to give you some idea as to how well your memory is functioning and help you to identify potential problem areas.

Verbal or Visual Recall

As a final tip on recall, let's incorporate the findings from the visual and verbal memory chapter. As previously discussed, most of us have natural strengths and an inherent preference in how we remember. We can now utilize the findings from chapter 9 to streamline the recall process. If you have identified verbal memory as a strength then try the technique from the previous memory tip entitled "Alphabetical Associative Recall." If you find this to be an effective method then you probably have a tendency toward storing memories phonemically, or by the sound of the word. Another type of storage is categorical. With this type of storage information is stored verbally according to category or function (for example, tools, living things, clothes). Retrieval strategies for verbal memory might involve describing the function of the item or naming similar or related concepts.

If you have identified visual memory as an inherent strength then utilize your visualization skills to enhance recall. Picture the item or event that you wish to recall. Picture yourself the last time that you used the item and how you used it. Now let's do a quick review of the information covered thus far.

✏️ ✗ *Ready for a Pop Quiz?*

Let's see how you do in remembering what you read. How much of what you've read have you encoded into memory?

1. Define alternating attention and describe a recent situation where you alternated your attention.

_____

_____

_____

_____

2. Define selective attention and think of a recent situation where you selectively applied your senses.

_____

_____

_____

_____

3. Define generalization. How are you generalizing the information from this book into your personal life?

_____

_____

_____

_____

4. Define what a preparatory set and preparatory review are and how and when you use them.

_____

_____

_____

_____

5. What position are your hands in when relaxed? How about your mouth? Your legs?

_____

_____

_____

_____

6. What do you find to be relaxing (everybody gets this right) and how often do you engage or participate in these relaxing activities (many won't get this right)?

_____

_____

_____

7. Generate a maladaptive thought, then an adaptive thought regarding this situation: You get home and realize that you forgot to stop at the bank.

_____

_____

_____

8. What is the purpose of rehearsal and envisioning? What do they accomplish in the memory process?

_____

_____

_____

Review your answers and check them for accuracy in the areas of the book that you have read so far. If you were unsure of any of the responses, reread that section of the book. A great deal of information is presented throughout this book, and it may take a couple of reviews of some sections before you encode the information.

Our next chapter will explore association. Association is another type of encoding that can be used to your advantage. It involves pulling up an existing memory and linking the item to be remembered to that existing memory.

I usually remember by tomorrow what I need to do today.

—Mildred Jones, age 96

⋆ 14 ⋆

Association

In this next chapter we will explore association. Association involves anchoring the item to be remembered to an existing memory or idea that's in some way related. In the retrieval process, elaboration can be used to gain the specific knowledge contained within the associated memory. The advantage to association is that it allows you to piggyback the information to be remembered onto an existing memory trace, using less effort in the encoding process. Association is a quick, effective way to dump something into your memory when there is not sufficient time to undergo the encoding process necessary to establish a reliable, separate memory network. A potential problem with association is that, in order to retrieve the memory, you usually have to first recall the old memory that you linked it to. Therefore, you can be faced with a locked door searching for the correct key phrase to get in with during the recall phase. Association thus becomes a matter of remembering the original memory that the new memory is tied to.

The Brain Uses Associations to Manage Memory

Memory is composed of a series of associations tied together by related themes. Just like a series of words placed together in the correct manner to form a complete sentence, your mind forms complete memories through a series of associations. Smells associated to a visual memory are also tied to the memory of sound and texture for that item. Associations in the brain are intertwined in multiple, intricate ways. Once activated, they act to release a series of memories related in some way. Associations can enter the working memory and automatically trigger a sense of long-term memories. We will use this natural dynamic of memory to our advantage.

Free Association

Free association was an early psychiatric technique used to explore the complex workings of the mind. The technique would allow the subject to "say the first word that came to mind" as a response to a word provided. The psychiatrist would then throw in some loaded word like "mother." This would allow a window into the subject's thinking processes.

As an example, let's think of the word "cotton." This may trigger associated memories such as "soft," "white," "fluffy." It may make you think of something that is made of cotton, such as a Q-tip. After "Q-tip," you might think of "ears." "Ears" may lead you to thinking about that kid in the third grade who sat in front of you in English class with those big ears of his. You may relive the frustration of never being able to see the blackboard around him or his ears. Associations can also contain emotions that are tied to the memory. Frustration tied to cotton? "That's very interesting." The point is that you don't always have to memorize things. Sometimes you can just associate them. Be creative and allow association to work for you.

🔑 Memory Tip: Use Association as a Reminder

You can rely on association as a reminder and allow recognition to do the rest. If you have to buy milk tomorrow, don't worry about remembering it. Just place the empty milk jug in the front seat of your car. Association will take care of the rest. If you have to remember to take something with you to work, just lay it in front of the door. You're sure to remember it if you see it prior to walking out. After all, we can only ask our minds to remember so much. Association can serve to free up the energy needed for the memorization of more important things.

✎ ✗ *Exercise: The Power of Association*

Let's use another example. We will show you that we can take control of your memory. Yes, we can take control of your memory, and we don't even have to be there with you. If we can do it then you can certainly do it. We'll give you a series of five words. Take a moment to say them to yourself. Reflect on them for five seconds and then move on to the next. Absorb them into your memory and let your thoughts flow free. The list of words is:

1. JFK

2. Dallas

3. Convertible limo

4. Grassy knoll

5. Book depository

Lee Harvey Oswald

We would venture to guess that, at some point while reading the list above, you thought of Lee Harvey Oswald. We plucked Mr. Oswald from your memory, via association! More precisely, we pulled this entire historical tragedy from your mind by association. Furthermore, we may have triggered your episodic long-term memory and made you think of where you were when you heard JFK was shot, what you felt, the reactions of others, what you were wearing. This is a valuable tool that we can utilize in helping you to remember (encode and retrieve).

✎ ✗ *Exercise: Number-Letter Association*

Now we want you to associate a series of numbers with a series of letters. The exercise contains a series of numbers followed by a letter. Take your time and review them until you feel that you have them memorized. Remember, associate them in pairs so that if we say "6" you will think of "G." We will test you shortly.

1 = C	2 = A
3 = T	4 = D
5 = O	6 = G
7 = R	8 = U
9 = N	

✎ ✗ *Exercise: Number Letter Association Recall*

Write down the letters associated with the following numbers:

1 ___ 9 ___ 3 ___ 2 ___ 5 ___

7 ___ 4 ___ 6 ___ 8 ___ A ___

Did the "A" throw you? Remember, flexibility is important in good memory functioning. Did you happen to notice that the letters spelled the words "cat," "dog," and "run"? Did you utilize this pattern to help you remember? This is a form of "chunking" which we introduced earlier.

Let's try to remember three numbers to associate with letters. For example, the numbers 1 2 3. These numbers correspond to the letters C A T. We can therefore remember the single piece of information CAT to represent the numbers 1, 2, and 3. DOG = 4, 5, 6. RUN = 7, 8, 9. TORN = 3, 5, 7, 9. It's often easier to remember one word than four numbers. See above for the correct answers. Next we will also be looking at how association can be used as a tool in both retention and recall.

Association in Recall

Association can be a powerful tool to help recall forgotten information. Let's say you need to recall something and can't quite get it. Try fishing it out through association. Let's say you wanted to remember the word "watch." For some reason you can't pull it out, even though it's on the tip of your tongue. To utilize association in recall, think of the item in approximations. You might say to yourself "something to keep time with" (association by function); you might remember the first watch you owned (time association); you might say to yourself "small clock" (association by category). The point is that you can assist your recall through association. Plug in both episodic and semantic memory. Trying to directly recall a word that you can't remember is like watching (no pun intended) water boil. The harder you try, the longer it takes. But if you associate what you are looking for with something else that is similar, you can often get it with minimal frustration.

✎ ✗ *Exercise: Word Association*

Read the following list of words and associate each pair of words together. Remember to associate the words in pairs. The goal of the exercise is not to memorize the words but rather to associate each word with its paired word. Repeat the list of words three times to yourself.

1. Apple—Orange

2. Black—Red

3. Beans—Tooth

4. Cup—Shoe

5. Watch—Glass

6. Pencil—Shirt

7. Hand—Hammer

8. Hanger—Button

9. Paper—Eye

10. Flag—Meat

Remember, read through the list three times before moving on. Now list the word next to the word that corresponds to the previous associations.

1. Hanger— _____

2. Pencil— _____

3. Paper— _____

4. Apple— _____

5. Beans— _____

6. Flag— _____

7. Black— _____

8. Cup— _____

9. Hand— _____

10. Watch— _____

Check your answer above. If you got seven to ten correct, then you're doing well. If you got four to six correct, then you are doing about average. If you got zero to three correct, then you may need some work in associative memory tasks.

Let's try that list once again and see if you improve.

✎ ✗ *Exercise: Word Association, Again*

Read the following list of words through three times and associate each pair of words together.

1. Apple—Orange

2. Black—Red

3. Beans—Tooth

4. Cup—Shoe

5. Watch—Glass

6. Pencil—Shirt

7. Hand—Hammer

8. Hanger—Button

9. Paper—Eye

10. Flag—Meat

List the word next to the word that corresponds to the previous associations.

1. Watch— _____

2. Hanger— _____

3. Paper— _____

4. Apple— _____

5. Pencil— _____

6. Cup— _____

7. Flag— _____

8. Black— _____

9. Beans— _____

10. Hand— _____

Again, tally the number correct from the list provided in appendix E. We would expect to see some improvement after two trials on this exercise. Eight to ten correct = excellent. Five to seven correct = average. Zero to four correct = may need more work.

Association in Encoding

Association can also be strategically used to encode information. For example, if you need to remember someone's name you might want to purposely encode it in such a way as to have easy access later. It's actually fun after you do it for a while. The sky is the limit and creativity is your guide. Let's say, for example, that you meet someone named Lilly Fields. There are many options other than rote repetition to remember this name. For example, her name can be associated with the perfume that she wears. Let's say for example that she happens to be wearing a familiar fragrance that reminds you of flowers. This can be placed in an association between flowers and lilies in a field.

✎ ✗ *Exercise: Number Association*

Read through the following pairs of numbers three times. Remember to associate the numbers in pairs.

1. 5—9

2. 6—3

3. 8—4

4. 1—2

5. 11—22

6. 54—45

7. 67—83

8. 32—19

9. 27—75

10. 59—21

Now list the number that goes with each of the numbers below. Do you remember the pairs?

1. 5—____
2. 59—____
3. 6—____
4. 27—____
5. 8—____
6. 32—____
7. 1—____
8. 67—____
9. 54—____
10. 11—____

Check your answers above. If you got seven to ten right, than you're doing well. If you got four to six correct, then you are doing about average. If you got zero to three, then you may need some work in associative memory tasks. Now for a final association exercise using symbols.

✎ ✗ Exercise: Symbol Association

Review the following pairs of symbols. Remember to associate the symbols in pairs. Again, the goal of the exercise is not to memorize the symbols but rather to associate each symbol with its paired symbol.

1. ! +

_____

2. @ =

_____

3. # $

_____

4. % ^

_____

5. & *

_____

6. ( )

_____

7. < >

_____

8. ? /

_____

9. { ,

_____

10. [-

_____

List the symbol next to the previously shown corresponding symbol.

1. [_____

2. ? _____

3. { _____

4. (_____

5. & _____

6. < _____

7. @ _____

8. # _____

9. % _____

10. ! _____

Check your answers from the previous exercise. If you got seven to ten right, then you're doing well. If you got four to six correct, you are in the average range. If you got zero to three, you may need some more work in associative memory tasks. Whether strong, weak, or average, an analysis of any significant relative strengths or weaknesses may help you learn more about your personal capability.

✎ ✗ *Exercise: Are You Strongest in Word, Number, or Symbol Association?*

Compare the results from the first trial of word association and the results of number and symbol association. Write down the scores below:

Word Association Score _____

Number Association Score _____

Symbol Association Score _____

Does one stand out as a strength? You may want to incorporate associations into your daily memory functioning. Choose the area that you are strongest in and use it. You may want to associate things to be remembered with a set of memorized symbols or words. Or you may want to associate things to be remembered by numbers. Word association is more verbally oriented and symbol association is more visually oriented. Does your strength correspond to findings in the verbal/visual memory chapter? Let's now revisit chunking.

Using Chunking to Remember Phone Numbers

Another great way to use chunking is in remembering phone numbers. Most people chunk the numbers into two sets: XXX-XXXX. This allows them to remember two bits of information rather than seven.

We can also make up words using the number-letter associations on a phone keypad and use association to tie the made-up word with the phone number. 800 numbers are often marketed in this manner for ease in remembering, like (800) CALL-NOW for (800) 227-7669.

A Log in the Fields

Let's combine chunking with association. Going back to the party where you met Lilly Fields let's try to remember a few additional new names. At the party, Lilly Fields introduces you to her mother and father, who are named Orville and Georgette. To help remember their names, you could take the first letter of each and come up with the acronym LOG to represent Lilly, Orville, and Georgette. You can now store this information as a log in the field. Only a couple of pieces of information to remember, right? Six months from now, you meet the three of them at the shopping center. You immediately smell Lilly's familiar fragrance and remember Lilly Fields. Fields then reminds you of the associative encoding strategy of log in the field. Oh yeah, Orville and Georgette. Let's look at a final example of chunking.

✎ ✗ Exercise: Word-Letter Association

Memory functioning is only one of many cognitive domains. The domains of cognitive functioning include: reasoning, memory, language, spatial function, sensory functions, and motor functions. Take the first letter of each of the memory functions in order and make a silly sentence or phrase using each letter to represent a word in your sentence. For example, using the words "reasoning," "memory," "language," "spatial function," "sensory functions," and "motor functions," you would come up with the letters R, M, L, S, S, M. You could then allow these letters be the first letter in your new phrase (something like "Red mice love stirred sour margaritas). This single phrase can more easily be remembered and serves to provide some organization to the task. Take a few moments to associate the original words to the letters. We may ask you about it later.

A Final Word on Chunking

By chunking, you significantly reduce the amount of information you need to remember. Remember, the working memory is usually limited to holding seven to nine pieces of data at a time. By chunking the information you can still hold seven to nine bits of data, but you further code the data so that each bit represents several more bits of data. Next, let's take a final look at your memory journal.

✎ ✗ Exercise: Final Memory Journal Review

Let's take a final look at your memory journal. Again, look for patterns. Look for times that you might have unfairly beaten up on yourself. Look for times when anxiety may have influenced your memory functioning. Most importantly, determine strategies that you might have used to remember. Do you see different patterns from the initial patterns that you noticed in the beginning? If you feel it would help, return to the exercise that we did on negative self-talk (on page 103) and place some of the remaining entries in the format provided.

At this point, you should be developing some strategies for remembering that are working for you. Continue to use what you have learned from the memory journal, but try to do the analysis simply in your head. If you find that you're having an unexplained memory lapse, look for patterns in your thinking or feelings that might be getting in the way and take the steps to correct them.

In the next chapter we will take a look at medications.

We are made wise not by the recollection of our past,
But by the responsibility for our future.

—George Bernard Shaw

⋆ 15 ⋆

Drugs That Affect Memory Functioning

Talking to Your Doctor

In this chapter we will explore medications and their effect on memory functioning. We will provide information on medications that may help improve memory and medications thought to possibly impair memory. But before we get into that, we thought it might be helpful to start this chapter with some general suggestions about communicating with your doctor. Your physician is the person with whom you will address concerns about medications. It has been our experience that having to ask their doctor questions is a source of anxiety for some, and that people often leave their physician's office with unanswered questions. Different people have different relationships with their doctors. Some doctors are willing to form a more collaborative relationship and welcome your input into treatment and medication decisions. Others may become offended if you dare "question" their wisdom. It is important that you choose a physician who fits your preferred style. We recommend that you consider the following recommendations to assist you in getting the most out of your doctor visit.

Choose One Primary Physician

The first recommendation we would like to make is to choose one primary-care provider whom all other doctors report through. He or she must be willing to coordinate your overall care and monitor your medications. We know that it's easy to get involved with many health-care providers and to begin to lose track of specific details, such as who prescribed which medication for what purpose. Remember, you are the consumer and can negotiate specific components of your care. Don't hesitate to directly ask your primary-care physician if he or she is willing and able to take on the responsibility of coordinating your overall care. It is essential to your health that you hire one primary physician to coordinate your health care and your medications.

Prepare for Your Visit

A second recommendation is to prepare yourself for the visit. It often helps to write down your questions and to bring a list of medications and other health-care providers treating you. Be prepared to initially answer a large number of questions associated with your health concerns. It's best to reply as succinctly as possible and to take time to formulate an answer before responding. Write down what they say, and ask about alternative treatment methods.

If You Don't Know, Ask

Remember, don't be afraid to ask your doctor questions about your medications. You are the one placing the prescribed medication into your body. You therefore have the right to ask your doctor questions and learn as much as you can about the medications that are prescribed for you. Your physician is the expert on medications and it is therefore important to develop a trusting relationship with him or her. You are hiring him or her as a consultant in how to properly take medications and in obtaining the knowledge of what side effects you might encounter.

Have Your Primary-Care Physician Review Your Medications

Once you have chosen a primary-care physician that you trust to coordinate all of your care have them review your current medications. Make your doctor aware of any medications that you receive from other physicians or that you may be taking over the counter. Also make them aware of any allergies that you might have and what a typical allergic reaction involves. It's always a good idea to start by bringing in all of your current medications so that you can properly review them. Always ask about any side effects that a new medication may have. If you develop a new symptom after starting a new drug, it's probably a safe assumption that the drug may be causing the symptom. Report this to your doctor. Ask your physician about alternative medications that might be available, and always try to limit the number of medications that you are taking. If a new drug is added, ask if it can replace an existing drug. Gain an understanding of the typical dose of the medication and let your physician know that you would like to start on the lowest dose possible. It is always better to start low and go slow. As we age, our metabolism slows down and we usually need less of a medication to do the intended job. Don't take a drug any longer than is necessary. Make sure you have a clear understanding of how the medication is to be taken and the proper dose. Finally, get rid of any old drugs that you're not currently using.

🔑 Memory Tip: Are You Fighting an Infection?

If you are currently fighting an infection such as a urinary tract infection, the flu, or an ear infection, it can greatly impair your memory function. Consult your physician and get the appropriate medications to treat the infection, and you may see a dramatic difference in your memory functioning. Don't underestimate the effects of infection on your overall bodily function.

Medication Side Effects

All medications have side effects along with the intended effects that they are prescribed for. The question in taking medications really boils down to asking the question, "Do the desired effects outweigh the side effects?" Unfortunately, many of the medications prescribed and purchased over the counter have some effect on your memory functioning and it is important that you are aware of these potential risks. Educate yourself on the effects of your medications.

Edgar's Poor Memory

Before we get into specific medications and how they might affect your memory, we thought it might be beneficial to demonstrate the effect medications can have on your memory. We thought we could best accomplish this with an example. Edgar came to us complaining of general forgetfulness, losing things, and forgetting people's names for the last couple of years. We did a thorough neuropsychological exam on him, and his memory functioning was in the average range except for some noted slowing in cognitive processing speed, some mild naming difficulties, and some marginal impairment in verbal memory. The noted impairments were nowhere near the level that would warrant a diagnosis of a dementia. Upon reviewing his medications we discovered that he had been taking 50 mg of Benadryl at night for the last two years to help him sleep. He was advised to stop taking the Benadryl and was offered some alternative treatments for his sleep difficulties. Six months later he was reevaluated and his neuropsychological test results showed marked improvement. The Benadryl had been interfering with his memory functioning. So, you can see that even the most seemingly innocuous drug like Benadryl can have a significant effect on your memory.

Next let's compare your long-term verbal and visual memory.

✎ ✗ Exercise: Long-Term Visual and Verbal Memory

In the space provided below reproduce the three figures and words from the end of chapter 9.

1.

2.

3.

1. _____

2. _____

3. _____

Compare your performance on each by comparing your answers with the original exercise from chapter 9. Give yourself one point for each item correctly reproduced. Write your answers in the space provided below.

Visual memory score _____   Verbal memory score _____

If there was a one-point difference or more between long-term visual and verbal memory then you are probably stronger in that modality. Did one stand out as a strength? Were your results similar to the immediate recall exercises from chapter 9? Utilize this newfound strength in your day-to-day memory functioning. Let's now return to our review of medications.

There are many medications that can impair your memory. Shortly, we will review some of these. First let's start with medications and supplements that have been identified or are currently being studied to enhance memory functioning.

Medications That May Assist with Memory Functioning

There are many medications on the market that have been shown to have some limited effects on improving memory. We would like to stress the word "limited," as there have been no medications to date that have shown a strong ability to improve cognitive functioning or to reverse the damage sustained through a dementing illness. The most commonly used class of medications to treat memory problems are cholinesterase inhibitors.

Cholinesterase Inhibitors

Cholinesterase inhibitors are a class of medications that have been shown to help slow the process of cognitive deterioration in some cases. It should be noted however that studies have shown that the effectiveness of these medications is limited (The Medical Letter 1997).* But cholinesterase inhibitors are the best drug that we currently have to

---

* Reprinted, by permission, from The Medical Letter, Inc., *The Medical Letter on Drugs and Therapeutics*. 1997. The Medical Letter, Inc.

treat memory problems. Essentially, they act to preserve the neurotransmitter acetylcholine, which is a primary neurotransmitter in the brain involved in memory functioning.

As an individual progresses through the stages of Alzheimer's disease, the nerves that are responsible for memory functioning slowly die. Supplies of acetylcholine begin to dry up. Cholinesterase inhibitors act to keep acetylcholine at the receptor sites of these nerves longer, thereby increasing the odds that the nerve will have an adequate supply when needed.

The first of these types of medications came out in 1993 and is known as Tacrine or Cognex. It was the first FDA-approved drug for the treatment of Alzheimer's disease. Unfortunately, it had many side effects, such as nausea, diarrhea, and liver complications. Liver-function tests had to be gathered on a regular basis by the physician. Maltby et al. (1994) found no benefit of the medication in a double-blind study of patients with mild to moderate symptoms of Alzheimer's disease. Mayeux and Sano (1999) state that there is a 3 to 6 percent improvement in cognition following treatment with cholinesterase inhibitors. So as you can see, the benefits are limited at best.

In 1997 the second cholinesterase inhibitor, Donepezil or Aricept, came out. It allowed for a "cleaner" cholinesterase inhibitor that could be taken once daily rather than the four times daily required with Cognex. This medication is now widely used for mild to moderate stages of Alzheimer's disease and usually takes six to eight weeks to be effective. Its effects are believed to be similar to Cognex. One of the newest medications on the market is Exelon or Rivastigmine. It has recently been approved by the FDA and has similar actions to Aricept.

There are many new cholinesterase inhibitors coming out now or that will be available in the near future. Essentially effects are limited. Cholinesterase inhibitors should not be used in patients suffering from alcohol abuse, peptic ulcer disease, liver disease, severe COPD, asthma, bradycardia, or Parkinsonism.

Hydergine

Another medication that has been approved by the FDA for the treatment of cognitive impairment in older adults is called hydergine or ergoloid mesylates. Some studies have shown that this drug has limited success, has questionable physiological bases, and may actually further impair cognitive functioning in older adults (Larson 1991; Thompson et al. 1990). This medication has been available for several decades and is usually prescribed at about 1 mg three times daily. Some of the later studies have speculated that it may actually be toxic to the brain.

Muscarine and Nicotine Agonists

There are neurotransmitters in the brain that act on muscarine and nicotine. *Muscarine agonists* are another class of drugs being tested for use in memory improvement. They are cholinergic drugs that act directly on muscarinic receptors within the brain. They mimic the actions of acetylcholine (acetylcholine is the primary neurotransmitter involved in memory). This is exciting research because muscarinic receptors do not seem to be effected in Alzheimer's disease and therefore may prove to be an intact system to address acetylcholine defects.

Nicotinic agonists are also being studied in the treatment of Alzheimer's disease. These drugs are in the early phases of study. It is known that nicotinic receptors are among the type of nerve systems that sustain damage in Alzheimer's disease. It has also been postulated that smoking enhances attention and may have some protective cognitive effects in Alzheimer's diseased patients although the risk posed to other systems of the body are severe.

Nonsteroidal Anti-Inflammatory Drugs

Other studies have suggested that prolonged use of nonsteroidal anti-inflammatory drugs may play a role in helping to delay or prevent the onset of Alzheimer's disease. Inflammation within the brain is believed to be a key characteristic of the disease that leads to cognitive decline. Cholinergic neurons or neurons responsible for processing acetyleholine, are believed to be especially vulnerable to damage from inflammation. Epidemiological studies have shown that prolonged use of anti-inflammatory medications may be correlated with a lower prevalence of Alzheimer's disease (Stewart et al. 1977). Oxidative stress or the production of free radicals are terms given to the generation of normal waste byproduct in the brain's metabolic process. This process is believed to work in conjunction with the inflammatory process in damaging proteins, fats, DNA, and carbohydrates within the brain.

It is believed that rheumatoid arthritis patients may have a lower prevalence of Alzheimer's disease. This has been attributed to the sustained use of anti-inflammatory drugs. Studies using anti-inflammatory drugs show marginal improvement in memory functioning in patients with known dementias.

Unfortunately, side effects are severe. Patients on these medications are believed to show a higher prevalence of developing a life-threatening ulcer disease such as upper GI bleeding. Precautions are also taken for those suffering high blood pressure. Because of the severe side effects in this class of medications, it is not recommended that you try this without first consulting your physician.

There is a newer class of nonsteroidal drugs being studied that do not have these severe side effects. These drugs are COX-2 Inhibitors. They may prove to be an effective treatment for the cognitive defects in Alzheimer's disease, although it is more likely that at best they would probably have some protective qualities. This means that they may delay the onset but would probably not stop the disease all together.

Estrogen

Estrogen has both anti-inflammatory and antioxidant properties and may even stimulate the growth of neurons that release acetylcholine. Estrogen has been correlated with a lower incidence of Alzeheimer's disease in epidemiological studies (Yaffe et al. 1998) and as a possible preventative measure and treatment of dementia in women (Birge and Mortel 1996; Birge 1996). Other studies have shown no treatment benefit in using estrogen in patients with mild to moderate levels of Alzheimer's disease (Mulnard et al. 2000) or in preventing the later onset of cognitive decline (Barrett-Conner and Kritz-Silverstein 1993).

Estrogen may serve as a protective mechanism in delaying the onset of Alzheimer's disease. Some studies have estimated its protective effects to be twice that of women not treated with estrogen replacement therapy (Birge and Mortel 1997). It has been speculated that the reason the prevalence of the disease is higher in women is because of the falling levels of estrogen that women experience during menopause.

Estrogen is speculated to stabilize and enhance the brain's neurons involved in memory and learning (Verghese et al. 2000). It is also speculated that estrogen may act to improve blood circulation and the way the brain uses glucose. It may also help to form new connections between brain cells (synapses), and prevent the decay of neurons and buildup of beta-amyloid proteins, which are the primary components of neurofibrillary tangles and plaques (Henderson 1997). There is currently a multisite National Institute of Aging funded study that will provide more sound evidence on the use of estrogen and memory maintenance/enhancement. Results of this study are expected to be complete in the next few years.

Unfortunately, the side effects of estrogen are great. Estrogen has been associated with a higher prevalence of uterine and breast cancer. New drugs (called selective estrogen modulators) that counteract this side effect of estrogen are being examined. The first of these to be approved by the FDA is called Raloxifene. Many foods, such a tofu, contain high amounts of natural estrogen, although these natural forms of estrogen have yet to be studied.

🔑 Memory Tip: Menopause

Menopause can greatly impair your memory functioning. After the age of forty, a woman's normal levels of estrogen and progesterone begin to decline. As a result, menstrual cycles cease and other symptoms may become prevalent, such as memory loss, irritability, hot flashes, night sweats, bone loss, osteoporosis, increased cholesterol and increased risk of heart disease and colon cancer. Many of these symptoms can go on for years if left untreated. Whether menopause is caused by a hysterectomy or naturally through aging, it may be necessary to consult your physician. Symptoms can be treated effectively with estrogen replacement therapy. Many women notice improved memory functioning with effective treatment. Memory difficulties may also be more pronounced during or just prior to menstrual cycles.

Nerve Growth Factor

Nerve growth factor medications are currently not available for public use. The National Institute of Aging is currently studying a nerve growth factor medication simply called AIT-082. These medications have shown some potential to actually generate growth in nerve cells within the brain of animals. This is a new type of biochemical intervention and will not be widely available for several years.

Medications for Memory Are Limited

Those are the main medications that are now available for the treatment of memory disorders. As you can see we have a long way to go in the development of pharmaceutical interventions. The good news is that the work is well underway. There are multiple national studies being conducted that will assist us in better understanding the genetic workings of memory disorders. As we gain a deeper understanding about the causes of progressive memory impairment we can develop new medications to prevent or reverse the disease. New discoveries are being made every day.

Next we will examine some of the supplements that have been studied as potential memory enhancers. But before we do this there are a few things we thought you might want to know about supplements and vitamins.

Monitoring of Nutritional Supplements

Nutritional supplements represent a multibillion-dollar-a-year industry in the United States. Unfortunately, this industry is poorly monitored. The only legislation that regulates supplements is the 1994 Dietary Supplement Health and Education Act. It serves as the only regulatory mechanism for the sale and distribution of dietary supplements in the United States. By law, any claim can be made about the product as long as it is not "medical" in nature. Manufacturers do not have to provide proof of safety for their products and there is no mechanism in place that monitors injuries or deaths. Before a dangerous supplement can be removed from the market, the FDA must prove that the product is dangerous and harmful. This is the opposite of prescribed medications, which must undergo rigorous testing and scrutinizing analysis to prove their safety and effectiveness prior to introduction. Needless to say, supplements are not at the top of the priority list for the already overworked and short-staffed FDA. Manufacturing facilities are not inspected or monitored, and the labels on the bottle often do not reflect the actual contents.

Recommended Daily Allowance

Strategic propaganda and clever advertisement on the part of supplement companies have created the myth that more is better. The truth is that many of these supplements are dangerous, especially in high dosages. More is not necessarily better when it comes to vitamins and minerals. You can actually harm or even kill yourself if too much of some vitamins and minerals are taken. For example, if you take folic acid and are deficient in Vitamin B12, you may develop some serious neurological symptoms. If you do decide to try a supplement, it is important to follow the recommended daily allowance. Following is the National Academy of Sciences (1989; Russell 1997) Nutritional Recommendations for people over the age of fifty. This can serve as your guide to identify safe daily dosages of vitamins and supplements.

Iron	10 mg—men and women	
Calcium	800 mg—men and women	
Zinc	15 mg—men	12 mg—women
Phosphorus	800 mg—men and women	
Magnesium	350 mg—men	280 mg—women
Vitamin A		
Retinol	1,000 mcg—men	800 mcg—women
Beta-Carotene	6,000 mcg—men	4,800 mcg—women
Vitamin B		
B1 (Thiamine)	1.2 mg—men	1 mg—women
B2 (Riboflavin)	1.4 mg—men	1.2 mg—women
B3 (Niacin)	15 m.g—men	13 mg—women
B6	2 mg—men	1.6 mg—women
B12	2 mcg—men and women	
Folic Acid (Folate)	200 mcg—men	180 mcg—women
Vitamin C	60 mg—men and women	
Vitamin D	400 I.U.—men	200 I.U.—women
Vitamin E	10 mg—men	8 mg—women

* mg = milligrams
  mcg = micrograms
  IU = International Units

Our diet impacts our emotional and thought processes. Although nutritional neuroscience is in its infancy, scientists have already discovered that certain nutrients influence memory. These nutrients include:

Nutrient	Role	Sources
B Vitamins	optimize brain function	B12, B1, B6, and B3
Folic Acid	assists in maintaining choline	dark green, leafy vegetables, orange juice, strawberries, peas
Iron	transports oxygen in red blood cells	raisins, prunes, dried apricots, beef, pork
Choline	converts to acetylcholine to regulate memory and mental acuity	nuts, lecithin, red meat, eggs
Anti-Oxidants	fight damage from free radicals	dark green, red, yellow, or orange fruits and vegetables
Linolenic	helps develop new connections in brain cells	canola, soy, walnut, and flaxseed oils, seaweed
Calcium	improves concentration	broccoli, low-fat milk, yogurt, cheese

Supplements Currently Under Study (Snake Oil or Fountain of Youth?)

There are many vitamins, herbs, and supplements that are currently being studied for the treatment of dementia. We will briefly review ginkgo biloba, choline, lecithin, and vitamin E.

Ginkgo Biloba

Ginkgo biloba comes from a tree. It has been used in Chinese medicine for thousands of years for its alleged benefits in treating circulatory disorders and cerebral insufficiencies. It is one of the best-selling supplements in the U.S and Europe. Ginkgo biloba is thought to act as a free-radical scavenger. In essence, it is believed that ginkgo biloba removes the waste byproducts created within the cells of the brain. It may also have antioxidant, anticoagulant, and anti-inflammatory properties.

There have been a number of small studies that have examined the effects of ginkgo biloba on memory functioning. Results are mixed, but some studies have found moderate success in helping to improve memory functioning with patients diagnosed with dementia. Oken et al. (1998) examined available studies and found that clinical trials suggest a slight improvement in Alzheimer's disease patients. Results from these limited studies do not seem to be as promising as those from studies examining cholinesterase inhibitors. Unfortunately, supplements like ginkgo are poorly monitored and amounts contained in caplets or solutions vary greatly. Excessive bleeding can occur if ginkgo is taken in conjunction with coumadin (Warfarin) or aspirin. Because of its limited effects, poor monitoring and possible danger, it is not recommended for use in Alzheimer's disease.

Choline and Lecithin

Choline is a water-soluble vitamin that belongs to the vitamin B family. It is involved in the synthesis of acetylcholine, the neurotransmitter in memory functioning. Lecithin is a supplement that can be broken down by the body to form choline. Studies were conducted years ago on both elements and all studies found little to no improvement in memory and learning. Choline also has the side effect of producing a fishy odor in your sweat. Neither are recommended as a treatment for memory improvement.

🔑 Memory Tip: Avoid Alcohol

Alcohol can only serve to damage neurons in the brain as it is actually toxic to brain cells. Although some studies show some limited health benefits, it is not good for your memory. If you find that you are drinking excessive amounts, it is probably affecting your memory. Permanent memory damage can result with chronic alcohol abuse. Wernicke's syndrome is a neurological condition in alcoholics that results from thiamine deficiency. Korsakoff's syndrome (alcohol amnestic disorder) is the term given to severe memory deficits and cognitive impairment resulting from chronic alcohol abuse. The two are often used together to describe both processes (Wernicke-Korsakoff's syndrome).

Vitamin E

The production of free radicals during the processing of oxygen in the brain has been suggested as a cause of cognitive degeneration in Alzheimer's disease. This has prompted the study of vitamin E (alpha-tocopherol) for use in the treatment of dementia, as it is an antioxidant. Sano and associates (1997) demonstrated that vitamin E delayed by seven months the onset of severe memory impairment in patients believed to suffer from Alzheimer's disease. Studies suggest that vitamin E is effective in treating both Alzheimer's disease (Sano et al. 1997) and vascular disease (Losonczy et al. 1997). The National Institute of Aging is currently conducting a multisite study on the effects of vitamin E on mild cognitive impairment.

Antioxidants act in the brain to destroy oxygen free radicals (a metabolic byproduct). The recommended daily allowance of this vitamin is about 10 IU. It is common for people to take up to 400 IU daily as a supplement. Roberts (1981) found that doses exceeding the RDA can be harmful. He stated that individuals who have exceeded the RDA often suffer symptoms of fatigue, increased blood pressure, headaches, and nausea. If prescribed by a physician to treat memory complaints, it is usually started at a dose of 400 IU a day and is increased by 400 IU each week as tolerated until a maximum dosage of 2000 IU is given per day, at 1000 IU twice daily. Other studies suggest a lower dosage (ultimately, 400 IU three times daily). Vitamin E is known to possibly interact with some medications such as Warfarin. Vitamin K deficiency can be dangerous in conjunction with the use of vitamin E, so you should consult your physician before starting this treatment. Doses at this level can be damaging, so we don't recommend that you try these supplements without consulting your physician.

Nutrition

Before looking at medications that may cause memory impairment, let's review the importance of nutrition. Older adults are the cohort of the population that may need nutritional supplements most. The reason for that need can usually be identified by your physician and always should be, if possible. These reasons might include: medical conditions that interfere with the processing and uptake of nutritional substances; the need to take medications that interfere with nutritional balance; alcoholism; and unhealthy diets that lack nutritional balance and adequate caloric intake. If you suspect that you have a nutritional deficit, consult your physician. It is always better to treat the source than to try to compensate by taking more supplements.

Causes of Decreased Nutrition

As we age, we often lose some of our sense of taste and smell. As a result, we may find that we have less of an appetite. We may have limited finances, and physical limitations may make it more difficult to prepare meals. Dental problems may limit our selection of food. Finally, being alone can greatly influence the variety of foods that you prepare, as meals serve as much a social function as they do a nutritional one. "Many people don't like to eat alone." This is why it is important to eat more nutritional food and to continue to exercise as we age. For additional information on nutrition we recommend two publications that are available for one dollar. The first is *Nutrition and Your Health: Dietary Guidelines for Americans* and the second is the *USDA's Food Guide Pyramid Booklet H6249*, both available by writing to Superintendent of Documents, Consumer Information Center, Pueblo, Colorado 81009.

Alcohol and Drugs Can Diminish Nutrition

Alcohol and drugs (medications) can greatly suppress your body's ability to absorb nutrients. There are many good books on the market to help you to identify the specific substances to avoid. Remember, you can always ask your doctor or pharmacist. As an overview, these medications include but are not limited to: cancer-fighting drugs, some antibiotics, many stomach medications and laxatives, heart medications, and some antiseizure medications.

🔑 Memory Tip: Exercise

While it is true that, as you age, you need fewer calories to maintain the same weight, you still must consume the same amount of nutrients. In other words, calories do not equal nutrition. As you age, your metabolism changes and you carry more fat and less muscle. Your essential organs such as your liver and pancreas may become less efficient at processing nutrients. One of the best interventions for the natural change in your body's metabolism as you age is exercise. Exercise allows you to eat more food and not gain weight. It increases your metabolism so that food is processed by the body more quickly, thus absorbing more nutrients. This is also why any hospitalization or sustained illness requires a much longer recovery period now than when you were a little younger.

With that said, let's look at some general guidelines for healthy, nutritional living. Again, there are many good books for this on the market, so go out there and educate yourself. Remember to always eat a well-balanced diet with lots of vegetables, fruits, and grains. Limit fat and salt intake. If you have a sweet tooth, eat cookies, candies, ice cream, and cakes in moderation. Limit caffeine and alcohol, and drink several glasses of water daily. And don't forget to consult your physician.

🔑 Memory Tip: Make Sure You're Getting Adequate, Restful Sleep

Another important consideration for healthy memory functioning is sleep. Without proper sleep, it is difficult if not impossible to have a reliable memory. Do you have difficulty falling asleep? Do you wake up several times during the night? Sleep is a complex subject worthy of expert opinion if you think you might be having problems in this area. We recommend that you seek medical advice if you suspect that this is a problem for you. A formal sleep study may help to improve your memory.

Avoid sleep medications if at all possible. Regularly taking medications to help fall asleep may actually be doing more damage than good. Studies have shown that when we rely on prescribed or over-the-counter sleep medications, our bodies have difficulty entering deep or REM (rapid eye movement) sleep. This deep sleep is the stage of sleep that serves to restore your body and provide restful rejuvenation. For every night slept you only cycle into this final stage of sleep for a limited time. Remember, sleep is a linear process and you must first cycle through the three proceeding cycles before entering the stage that provides the essential rest that your body and mind needs. With any break in this process you must start over from stage one. Given enough interruptions within the sleep cycle, you may spend eight hours in bed and rarely enter REM sleep. Are you waking up tired? Improving the quality of your sleep may improve your memory. Consult your doctor about a sleep apnea study.

Medications That May Inhibit Memory Functioning

Next we will present medications that have been identified as possibly causing temporary or permanent memory impairment. If you find that you are taking some of these medications, it is best to consult your physician and ask about alternative medications that might be available.

Anticholinergics

There are many over-the-counter and prescription medications that can greatly impair memory functioning. Of special note are medications called anticholinergics. These medications are prescribed for other conditions (such as urinary incontinence) and act to inhibit acetylcholine, the neurotransmitter primarily responsible for learning and memory. Older adults are especially vulnerable to the effects of anticholinergic medications. Side effects include: acute confusion, poor attention, disorientation, and short-term memory problems. Remember, a sudden onset of memory impairment (acute confusional state) probably represents a delirium and not a dementia. Toxic effects of medication or illness most commonly cause delirium. If you suspect that you or a loved one is experiencing delirium, get to the hospital immediately.

In general, any medication that has a sedating side effect can impair memory. Shortly we will provide a list of some of these medications. It is a good idea to check with your physician or pharmacist to see if any of the medications that you are on may be affecting your memory.

Other Medications That Can Impair Memory Functioning

We will complete this chapter with a list of medications that have been identified as possibly causing memory impairment (Physician's Drug Reference 2001; Sabiston 1997;

Preston et al. 1999). They are listed alphabetically by trade name, but generic names are included in parenthesis. We have also broken down the drugs into broad categories of use (what they are used to treat). Remember, any type of tranquilizer or sleeping pill is probably going to have some direct effect on memory functioning. Also keep in mind that many other drugs can impair memory functioning indirectly by causing other symptoms that eventually lead to memory impairment. Medications that may cause depression, insomnia, or change in glucose levels are examples of such medications. Now let's look at some of the specific medications that have been identified as possibly causing memory impairment. Use the following lists to compare your current medications or new medications that you receive.

Blood Pressure Medications

Aldactazide (spironolactone) ✱ Aldoril (methyldopa) ✱ Aldomet (methyldopa) ✱ Apresazide (hydralazine) ✱ Blocadren (timolol) ✱ Bumex (bumetanide) ✱ Cartrol (carteolol) ✱ Combipres (clonidine) ✱ Coreg (carvedilol) ✱ Corgard (nadolol) ✱ Corzide (bendroflumethiazide) ✱ Demadex (torsemide) ✱ Diupres (reserpine) ✱ Diuril (chlorothiazide) ✱ Dyazide (triamterene) ✱ Enduronyl (deserpidine) ✱ Enduron (methyclothiazide) ✱ Esidrix (hydrochlorothiazide) ✱ Hydropres (reserpine) ✱ Hygroton (chlorthalidone) ✱ Inderal (propranolol) ✱ Inderide LA (propranolol) ✱ Kerlone (betaxolol) ✱ Levatol (penbutolol) ✱ Lopressor (metoprolol) ✱ Lozol (indapamide) ✱ Moduretic (amiloride) ✱ Metahydrin (trichlormethiazide) ✱ Normodyne (labetalol) ✱ Rogroton (reserpine) ✱ Salutensin (reserpine) ✱ Sectral (acebutolol) ✱ Ser-Ap-Es (reserpine) ✱ Tenoretic (atenolol) ✱ Tenormin (atenolol) ✱ Visken (pindolol) ✱ Zaroxolyn (metolazone) ✱ Zebeta (bisoprolol) ✱ Ziac (bisoprolol)

Psychiatric/Neurological Medications

Atarax/Vistaril (hydroxyzine) ✱ Ativan (lorazepam) ✱ BuSpar (buspirone) ✱ Butisol Sodium (butabarbital) ✱ Centrax (prazepam) ✱ Compazine (prochlorperazine) ✱ Dalmane (flurazepam) ✱ Doriden (glutethimide) ✱ Halcion (triazolam) ✱ Haldol (haloperidol) ✱ Klonopin (clonazepam) ✱ Librium (chlordiazepoxide) ✱ Luminal Sodium (phenobarbital) ✱ Mellaril (thioridazine) ✱ Miltown (meprobamate) ✱ Navane (thiothixene) ✱ Nembutal (pentobarbital) ✱ Noctec (chloral hydrate) ✱ Noludar (methyprylon) ✱ Prolixin (fluphenazine) ✱ Restoril (temazepam) ✱ Serax (oxazepam) ✱ Stelazine (trifluoperazine) ✱ Thorazine (chlorpromazine) ✱ Tranxene (clorazepate) ✱ Elavil (amitriptyline) ✱ Valium (diazepam) ✱ Xanax (alprazolam)

Stomach Medications

Axid (nizatidine) ✱ Pepcid (famotidine) ✱ Tagamet (cimetidine) ✱ Zantac (ranitidine)

Are You Currently Taking Any of These Medications?

If you are on one of the above medications and feel that you are having difficulty with your memory, then consult your physician. The medication may be at least partially responsible for your memory difficulties. We all have different tolerance levels to different substances. What might be toxic for you may be an adequate dose for another. It may not be necessary for you to stop taking the medication. A simple adjustment in your prescription may prove to greatly reduce its side effects.

Now we will look at some medications that have been identified as occasionally causing delirium. Delirium usually has a rapid onset and is characterized by severe confusion. One of the leading causes of delirium in older adults is adverse reactions to medications. Following is a list of medications that may cause delirium. Use this list now and in the future to troubleshoot potential difficulties. Again, they are listed in alphabetical order and according to use.

Medications That May Lead to Confusion

Cardiac Medications

Catapres (clonidine HCl) ★ Dura-Tabs (quinidine) ★ Duraquin (quinidine) ★ Lanoxicaps (digoxin) ★ Lanoxin (digoxin) ★ Norpace (disopyramide phosphate) ★ Tenex (guanfacine HCl)

Antibiotics

Chibroxin (norfloxacin) ★ Ciloxan/Cipro (ciprofloxacin) ★ Cytovene (ganciclovir) ★ Levaquin (levofloxacin) ★ Maxaquin (lomefloxacin) ★ Ocuflox/Floxin (ofloxacin) ★ Penetrex (enoxacin) ★ Raxar (grepafloxacin) ★ Symmetrel (amantadine HCl) ★ Urised (methenamine/methylene blue/salol) ★ Zagam (sparfloxacin) ★ Zovirax (acyclovir)

Drugs for Diabetes

Amaryl (glimepiride) ★ DiaBeta/Micronase (glyburide) ★ Diabinese (chlorpropamide) ★ Dymelor (acetohexamide) ★ Glucotrol (glipizide) ★ Humalog (insulin lispro) ★ Orinase (tolbutamide) ★ Tolinase (tolazamide)

Systemic Medications

Acthar (corticotropin) ★ Azmacort (triamcinolone) ★ Cortef (hydrocortisone) ★ Cortone Acetate (cortisone) ★ Decadron/Hexadrol (dexamethasone) ★ Deltasone/Meticorten (prednisone) ★ Diprolene/Valisone (betamethasone dipropionate/valerate) ★ Medrol (methylprednisolone) ★ Metreton/Pred Forte (prednisolone)

Cold and Allergy Medications

Atarax/Vistaril (hydroxyzine HCl/pamoate) ★ Benadryl (diphenhydramine) ★ Chlor-Trimeton (chlorpheniramine) ★ Dimetane (brompheniramine maleate) ★ Hismanal (astemizole) ★ Myidil (triprolidine) ★ Optimine (azatadine maleate) ★ Periactin (cyproheptadine HCl) ★ Seldane (terfenadine) ★ Tavist (clemastine fumarate)

Pain Medications

Advil/Motrin (ibuprofen) ★ Aleve/Naprosyn (naproxen) ★ Ansaid/Ocufen (flurbiprofen) ★ Arthropan (choline salicylate) ★ Ascriptin/Bufferin (aspirin) ★ Bayer/Ecotrin (aspirin) ★ Butazolidin (phenylbutazone) ★ Clinoril (sulindac) ★ Daypro (oxaprozin) ★ Disalcid (salsalate) ★ Doan's Pills (magnesium salicylate) ★ Dolobid (diflunisal) ★ Duract (bromfenac) ★ Feldene (piroxicam) ★ Indocin (indomethacin) ★ Lodine (etodolac) ★ Meclomen (meclofenamate sodium) ★ Nalfon (fenoprofen calcium) ★ Orudis (ketoprofen) ★ Relafen (nabumetone) ★ Talwin (pentazocine HCl/aspirin) ★ Tolectin (tolmetin sodium) ★ Toradol (ketorolac tromethamine) ★ Trilisate (choline or magnesium salicylate) ★ Voltaren (diclofenac sodium)

Stomach Medications

Antivert (meclizine HCl) ★ Atropine (atropine sulfate) ★ Axid (nizatidine) ★ Bentyl (dicyclomine HCl) ★ Compazine (prochlorperazine) ★ Ditropan (oxybutynin chloride)

✱ Donnatal (Belladonna Alkaloids/Phenobarbital) ✱ Librax (clidinium/chlordiazepoxide) ✱ Lomotil (diphenoxylate HCI/atropine sulfate) ✱ Pepcid (famotidine) ✱ Phenergan (promethazine HCI) ✱ Tagamet (cimetidine) ✱ Tigan (trimethobenzamide HCI) ✱ Zantac (ranitidine)

Antidepressants

Asendin (amoxapine) ✱ Aventyl/Pamelor (nortriptyline) ✱ Desyrel (trazodone) ✱ Elavil (amitriptyline) ✱ Lithobid/Lithonate (lithium carbonate) ✱ Ludiomil (maprotiline) ✱ Limbitrol (amitriptyline/chlordiazepoxide) ✱ Norpramin (desipramine) ✱ Prozac (fluoxetine) ✱ Sinequan (doxepin HCI) ✱ Tofranil (imipramine) ✱ Triavil (amitriptyline/perphenazine) ✱ Wellbutrin (bupropion HCI)

Sleeping Pills/Tranquilizers

Ativan (lorazepam) ✱ BuSpar (buspirone HCI) ✱ Centrax (prazepam) ✱ Dalmane (flurazepam) ✱ Doriden (glutethimide) ✱ Halcion (triazolam) ✱ Librium (chlordiazepoxide) ✱ Miltown/Equanil (meprobamate) ✱ Noctec (chloral hydrate) ✱ Noludar (meyhyprylon) ✱ Restoril (temazepam) ✱ Serax (oxazepam) ✱ Tranxene (clorazepate) ✱ Valium (diazepam) ✱ Vistaril/Atarax (hydroxyzine pamoate)

Barbiturates

Butisol (butabarbital) ✱ Luminal/Solfoton (phenobarbital) ✱ Nembutal (pentobarbital)

Antipsychotics

Clozaril (clozapine) ✱ Haldol (haloperidol) ✱ Mellaril (thioridazine) ✱ Navane (thiothixene) ✱ Prolixin (fluphenazine) ✱ Reglan (metoclopramide) ✱ Stelazine (trifluoperazine) ✱ Thorazine (chlorpromazine) ✱ Triavil (amitriptyline/Perphenazine)

Neurological Medications

Artane (trihexyphenidyl) ✱ Cogentin (benztropine) ✱ Dilantin (phenytoin sodium) ✱ Klonopin (clonazepam) ✱ Larodopa (levodopa) ✱ Parlodel (bromocriptine mesylate) ✱ Permax (pergolide mesylate) ✱ Sinemet (carbidopa/levodopa)

Other Medications

Amipaque (metrizamide) ✱ Bipenden (akineton) ✱ Anafranil (clomipramine HCI) ✱ Cytosar-U (cytarabine) ✱ Elspar (asparaginase) ✱ Lioresal (baclofen) ✱ Mesoridazine (serentil) ✱ Oxybutin (oxybutin chloride) ✱ Trihexyphenidyl (trihexyphenidyl HCI)

🔑 Memory Tip: Medical Conditions That Affect Memory

As we grow older we can begin to accumulate many medical complications. Many of these medical conditions can greatly impact your memory. These include diabetes, heart conditions, restrictive airway diseases such as chronic obstructive pulmonary disease (COPD), problems with your kidneys, infections, hormone imbalances, cancer, degenerative eye conditions, vitamin and nutritional deficits (especially vitamin B12), and the buildup of ammonia in your system secondary to liver problems. Changes in your vision and hearing can also effect your memory. The list is endless. It is essential that you consult your physician on any of these conditions or other conditions that you suspect may be affecting your memory. You should have regular checkups with your physician and not allow yourself to be negligent in keeping an eye on certain bodily systems (for instance, prostrate exam for men, breast exam for women, cancer check if you have had cancer in the past).

Chronic pain is another condition that can greatly influence your memory functioning. When you are in pain, endorphins are released that can interfere with the neurotransmitters that guide memory. With pain, your attention tends to be on the pain and not on your environment. Let's complete this chapter with a review of some of the factors that may be getting in the way of your healthy memory functioning.

✎ ✗ Exercise: Evaluation of Factors Affecting Your Memory

Circle the answer that applies to you.

1. I am currently taking medications that may impair my memory. — Yes/No

2. My memory sometimes fails me because of difficulty sustaining my attention. — Yes/No

3. Anxiety sometimes gets in the way of my memory. — Yes/No

4. At times I feel my memory fails me because I feel depressed. — Yes/No

5. I suspect I have trouble remembering because of lack of sleep. — Yes/No

6. Too much alcohol may be getting in the way of my memory functioning. — Yes/No

7. Poor nutrition may be hampering my memory. — Yes/No

8. My memory may be giving me trouble because of past or present exposure to chemicals. — Yes/No

9. I have a grandparent, parent, or sibling with progressive memory problems. — Yes/No

10. I have medical conditions that contribute to memory difficulties. These include: cardiac problems, lung disease, cancer, diabetes, seizures, pregnancy, etc. — Yes/No

11. I feel my memory is poor and that there is little that I can do to improve it. — Yes/No

12. My poor vision may be contributing to my poor memory. — Yes/No

13. My inability to hear may be contributing to failures in my memory functioning. — Yes/No

14. My lack of organization often contributes to failures in my memory. — Yes/No

15. Lack of motivation often contributes to poor memory functioning. — Yes/No

16. I view memory loss as a normal part of the aging process. — Yes/No

17. Stress often gets in the way of my memory working correctly. — Yes/No

18. Unrealistic expectations often cause me to have memory difficulties. — Yes/No

19. Goals that I set up for my memory often go unmet. — Yes/No

20. Obsessive thinking sometimes affects my memory. — Yes/No

21. I suspect that carbon monoxide exposure may be affecting my memory. — Yes/No

22. I have an infection that may be causing memory difficulties. — Yes/No

23. I often use negative self-talk that interferes with my memory functioning.   Yes/No

24. I have great difficulty visualizing things that I want to remember.   Yes/No

25. I exercise at least three times a week.   Yes/No

26. I am taking estrogen, vitamin E, ginkgo biloba, steroids, nonsteroid anti-inflammatories, Cognex, Exelon, or Aricept.   Yes/No

Review the questions to which you answered "yes." Many of these questions mean that you probably need to see your physician. These include a yes response to questions: 1 through 13, 15, 17, 20 to 23, and 26. Others may require that you review applicable chapters in this book. These include a "yes" response to questions: 2 through 4, 11, 14 to 20, and 23 to 24. Finally, an evaluation by a qualified psychologist, psychiatrist, or social worker might be a good idea if you responded "yes" to questions: 3 to 6, 11, 15 through 20, and 23. Use this questionnaire to troubleshoot your difficulties and take action toward improvement.

Next we will review specific memory disorders.

⋆ 16 ⋆

Memory Disorders

This next chapter is intended to help you to further differentiate between changes in memory due to aging and more severe memory disorders. It can also serve as a reference for later use. We wanted to include this chapter to help you review a little bit about some of the more prevalent memory disorders. The following information is technical in nature, so don't be surprised if it's a bit slower going. We may throw in a test or two to evaluate your learning and memory of written information. Our description of memory disorders is not comprehensive by any means. Volumes have been dedicated to this topic. This chapter is only meant as a passing reference, as we know that many of you have had neurological work-ups and may have been or know someone who has been diagnosed with some type of identifiable memory problem. We will start off with some general conditions to look out for and then discuss what a good neurological exam might consist of. We will then present some of the dynamics of dementia and outline reversible causes of dementia. The remainder of this chapter is intended to educate you on some of the more common neurological disorders and to provide definitive examples of severe cognitive compromise. This section is not intended to be a means of self-diagnosis. Appendix A, "Glossary of Terms," can help you decipher some of the language that is commonly used by physicians and psychologists. Appendix C is a quick reference to some agencies that might be able to assist you with concerns that you may have. Appendix D is a brief review of major areas of the brain and the functions associated with them.

Beyond Normal Aging

We've already addressed what to expect in your memory functioning with normal aging. This chapter will present information on memory problems that represent impairment beyond normal aging. Don't forget, if you are concerned that you may be suffering from one of the following disorders we strongly urge you to get a comprehensive neurological examination. Symptoms that might warrant a neurological work-up include: memory dysfunction that influences your daily functioning, periods of confusion, getting lost in familiar places, apathy or a loss of motivation, severe symptoms of depression with no apparent cause, difficulty with motor skills, tremors, paralysis, difficulty speaking or poor articulation, comprehension impairments, difficulty with reading or writing, acute changes in personality, visual problems, and dizziness.

Conditions That Impair Memory Beyond Normal Aging

Crook et al. (1986) provide some guidelines to consider if you are having difficulties with your memory. Review the following conditions. If any apply to you, then we recommend that you consult your physician. The presence of any of these conditions may indicate that your memory functioning is being influenced beyond the normal aging process.

1. Current use of psychiatric drugs

2. Current struggle with a psychiatric disorder (like depression or anxiety)

3. Alcohol or drug dependency

4. Medical conditions that impair memory functioning

5. Delirium or an acute confusional state

6. Neurological disorder that impairs memory functioning (like Parkinson's disease, stroke, Alzheimer's disease)

7. History of significant head injury resulting in unconsciousness or multiple minor head injuries

8. Exposure to toxins with noted cognitive decline afterwards

9. History of inflammatory or infectious disease (syphilitic, viral)

10. History of significant vascular disease

What Should a Good Neurological Evaluation Consist Of?

A thorough neurological evaluation should involve a comprehensive history, including a family history of neurological disorders so that genetic influences can be considered. It should also include: an examination of current medications, a review of current symptoms, a comprehensive medical work-up, and a comprehensive neurological work-up. The medical and neurological work-up might include:

* ✴ Neuropsychological testing

* ✴ X-rays

* ✴ Neurological imaging (Computer Tomography Scans (CT), Magnetic Resonance Imaging (MRI), a Single Photon Emission Computed Tomography (SPECT), Positron Emission Tomography (PET)

* ✴ Electroencephalogram (EEG) to look at the electrical activity of the brain

* ✴ Electromyogram (EMG) to measure activities of muscles

* ✴ Blood work-up (often to check thyroid functioning, vitamin levels such as B12, electrolytes, glucose level, liver function test, and heavy metals screen to name a few)

* ✴ A lumbar puncture to check for infections within the CNS

* ✴ A cranial nerve examination

* ✴ A motor system examination

* ✴ A mental status examination, and

* ✴ A sensory examination

What Is Dementia?

Let's look in more detail at what dementia is. After that we will examine specific memory problems. Again, the following information is not meant to be a means to diagnose yourself. You may find that you think that you have a good number of the symptoms contained within the next few pages. This is common. It is a well-known fact that medical students often develop many of the symptoms of the disorders that they are currently studying. The question to ask yourself is, "Are these symptoms affecting my day-to-day functioning?" Use the following information to help you better comprehend what your neurologist has to say. Let your neurologist make the diagnosis and let this information serve as some background reading to better educate you.

Dementia

The *Psychiatric Dictionary* (Campbell 1989, 185)* defines dementia as "an acquired, persistent, or irreversible reduction in intellectual functioning that occurs after the brain has matured (around 15 years of age). It is manifested by impaired: language (aphasia), memory (amnesia), orientation, motor skills (apraxia), visuospatial skills, and cognition (e.g., abstraction, reasoning, attention)." It also includes loss of perception (agnosia), poor judgment and impulse control, changes in emotion or personality, loss of ability to recognize memory loss (anosognosia), loss of organizational and planning abilities, loss of ability to concentrate, disorientation, and apathy. These impairments must be to the degree to interfere with daily social or occupational functioning. Most memory disorders fall under the general heading of dementia.

Dementia Is a Matter of Severity

Dementia ranges in severity from marginal to severe cognitive compromise (Petersen et al. 1999). For a dementia to be diagnosed, it must impair your day-to-day functioning. This level of impairment is characteristic of "... deterioration of previously acquired intellectual abilities of sufficient severity to interfere with social or occupational functioning and to impair [one's] capacity to meet the ordinary demands of living" (Campbell 1989, 185). There are more than sixty forms of dementia, and the type is usually identified by the cause (Haase 1977). For a dementia to be present it must render you or be capable of rendering you incapable of independent functioning.

Categories of Dementia

Dementia can be broken down into four categories. These include: amnestic disorders, cognitive disorders, attention disorders, and motivation disorders (Heilman et al. 1995).*

Amnesia

Amnesia is the medical term associated with forgetting. Memory loss is the most common problem associated with dementia, but not all dementias have memory loss as part of their initial or overall progression. Memory loss is closely associated with

---

* Reprinted, by permission, from R. J. Campbell, *Psychiatric Dictionary*. 1989. Oxford University Press.

---

* Adapted with permission, from Heilman et al., *Helping People with Progressive Memory Disorder*. 1995. University of Florida Health Science Center.

structural changes in the basal forebrain and the temporal lobes in the brain (see appendix D for help with terms). These areas are responsible for the production of the neurotransmitter acetylcholine. There are two types of amnesia: *anterograde amnesia* is the inability to remember new information and is usually the first type of amnesia seen in progressive dementias; *retrograde amnesia* is the inability to recall old memories from long-term memory.

Cognitive Disorders

Cognitive disorders are essentially a loss of knowledge and are usually the result of damage to the temporal and/or parietal lobes of either the right or left hemispheres. Cognitive disorders include: language impairment, reading and writing impairment, loss of math skills, inability to draw, loss of ability to use objects, getting lost, and loss of the ability to recognize familiar faces or things.

Attention Disorders

In *attention disorders* (often seen in delirium) people are unable to sustain their attention long enough to complete a task and are easily distracted. This type of disorder is often acute, with a sudden onset. It is often the result of an infection, abnormal pressure on the brain, or a reaction to medications. Attention disorders are often reversible with treatment.

Motivation Disorders

Motivation disorders are exhibited by a severe lack of motivation. Patients often lose interest in doing things to the point of not taking care of themselves or not being able to express emotions. These behaviors are often related to depression or to abnormalities in the frontal lobes or major relay centers within the brain, such as the basal ganglia or thalamus.

✎ ✗ Exercise: Flexibility in Thinking

Now for a guessing game. We're thinking of an animal that can be one of many colors. Some are multicolored, and some are single colors. It lays eggs and flies but is not a bird. What is this animal? Think about it. The answer is forthcoming.

Cognitive Flexibility

The answer to the animal question is a butterfly. Did you have some difficulty with that? When my (D.M.) little girl asked me that question, I had difficulty because all I could think about was birds. But the question clearly states that it is not a bird. I was stuck on birds! Flexibility in thinking is very important in good memory functioning. Adults tend to think in more black-and-white terms and neglect the gray. The ability to see things from different perspectives and to remain flexible in your thinking is referred to as cognitive flexibility.

Progressive Verses Static Dementia

Dementia can be divided into two broad classifications: progressive and static. *Progressive dementias* are related to an ongoing disease process such as Alzheimer's disease and tend to get progressively worse. *Static dementias* are usually associated with an injury, stroke, or some reversible condition such as a vitamin deficiency. Static dementias tend to remain the same if no other injury or medical complication occurs.

Most dementias are progressive and usually involve a gradual change in baseline functioning that takes place over months to years. If the progression of symptoms takes place in a matter of days or weeks, it's probably delirium (Kaye 1998). Progressive dementias involve progressive neuronal dysfunction and loss of neurons in certain areas of the brain (Cummings et al. 1998). Although specific areas of the brain can be identified as being structurally affected by a progressive dementia, symptoms such as memory loss and behavioral change are usually more global in nature. Shortly we will review some of the specific types of dementia that fall under the general heading of progressive dementias.

Dementia Can Be Focal or Global

Dementias can also be focal (localized) or global. In *focal dementias,* the cause of the problems and the symptoms are limited to specific areas of the brain (such as the damage done by a single stroke). In *global dementias,* the problem cluster and damage are located in several areas within the brain. Many dementias affect frontal lobe functions involving judgment, social conduct, and behavioral inhibition.

Reversible Causes of Dementia

The prevalence of potentially reversible dementia is around 20 percent (Freter et al. 1998). There are many causes of dementia that are reversible. If a dementia is suspected, these potential causes should always be ruled out:

- ★ Vitamin B1 (thiamin) deficiency (often caused by alcohol abuse)
- ★ Liver or kidney failure
- ★ Thyroid gland malfunction
- ★ Normal pressure hydrocephalus
- ★ Medication reactions
- ★ Vitamin B12 deficiency
- ★ Hypercalcemia
- ★ Hyper- or hypoglycemia
- ★ Tumors
- ★ Salt or water imbalance (Hyper and hypoatremia)
- ★ Depression/anxiety
- ★ Infections
- ★ Lyme disease
- ★ Herpes simplex
- ★ Cryptococcus Infection
- ★ Syphilis
- ★ Heart and lung disease

- ★ Exposure to toxins (heavy metals, carbon monoxide, etc.)
- ★ Infections of the CNS
- ★ Communication problems (poor vision, hearing, etc.)

✎ ✗ Exercise: Memorize Categories of Reversible Dementia

Now let's see if we can commit some of the reversible causes of dementia to memory. We will utilize a mnemonic technique of acronym association to assist you. Remember reversible dementia categories with the word "dementia" (Sabiston 1997).

Categories of Potentially Reversible Dementia

Drugs and alcohol toxicity

Ear and eye problems

Metabolic and endocrine abnormalities

Emotional problems

Nutritional deficiencies

Traumas or tumors

Infection processes

Atherosclerotic complications

Notice that the beginning letter of each word makes up the word "dementia." Take some time to memorize this list using other strategies presented throughout the book, and we will test you on it later.

🗝 Memory Tip: Are You Drinking Enough Water?

Older adults are more prone to dehydration and should therefore make the effort to drink plenty of water. Water helps balance the sodium in the body and also assists in maintaining mental alertness, improving digestion and kidney function, assisting in absorbing medications, and helping the body to absorb nutrients. Therefore, to help your body and mind, it is recommended that you drink six to eight glasses of water daily.

Cortical Verses Subcortical Dementias

Dementias can be roughly broken down into two types depending on where in the brain degeneration is initially seen. These include cortical and subcortical disease processes (Koltai and Welsh-Bohmer 2000). Deterioration that involves cortical structures within the brain includes disorders such as Alzheimer's disease or frontotemporal dementia. They are referred to as *cortical dementias* because they initially affect the outer layers of the brain (cortical). This classification of disorders is often marked by deterioration in memory, language, and disturbances in motor functions and perception. Areas of the brain affected with cortical dementias include the medial temporal lobes and the association cortices in the temporal, parietal, and frontal lobes (Welsh-Bohmer and Ogrocki 1998).

The second type of dementia involves deterioration of the subcortical portions of the brain. These are disorders such as Parkinson's disease, Binswanger's disease, normal pressure hydrocephalus, Huntington's disease, and supranuclear palsy, among others.

Subcortical dementias are marked by the initial deterioration of the deeper structures of the brain (subcortical) and are often first detected by motor abnormalities. There are often milder memory deficits, slowed information processing, more intact language functions, impairments in executive functioning (decision making and quick thinking), motor slowing, and changes in behavior and mood (Welsh-Bohmer and Ogrocki 1998). Specific areas often initially affected include: the brain stem, midbrain, diencephalon, and basal ganglia (Welsh-Bohmer and Ogrocki 1998). Let's first examine some of the cortical disorders.

Alzheimer's Disease

Alzheimer's disease (AD) was named after its discoverer Alois Alzheimer (1864–1915) who first described the pathology of the disease in 1906. AD is the most common form of progressive dementia affecting people today and accounts for 50 to 60 percent of all dementias (Smith and Kiloh 1981). It is suspected that both genetic and environmentalfactors contribute to the disease. To date, we know of two types of Alzheimer's disease.

1. The first type is *familial AD*. It is genetically based and is inherited through genes from our parents.

2. The second type is *sporadic*. In this type, there is no known genetic component. Environmental factors are suspected to play a key role in sporadic Alzheimer's disease.

Most cases of Alzheimer's disease carry a strong genetic component. The risk within the general population of developing Alzheimer's disease is about 1 percent but moves up to 4 percent for first degree relatives of those who have been diagnosed with the disease (Campbell 1989). Of all diagnosed cases of Alzheimer's disease, about 80 percent are estimated to be genetically based (Plassman and Breitner 1996). Environmental factors are believed to contribute to both familial and sporadic types of AD.

Early Versus Late Onset

Alzheimer's disease is further broken down into early and late onset types. In *early onset,* the disease occurs before the age of sixty-five. This type is rare, usually progresses faster, and accounts for about 10 percent of Alzheimer's disease cases. In the *late onset* type, the disease occurs after the age of sixty-five (National Institute of Aging, National Institutes of Health 1999). This type is much more common and makes up the remainder of cases.

Prevalence

Alzheimer's disease is the fourth leading cause of death in the U.S. and is believed to occur in 1 to 2 percent of the general population. It is estimated to occur in about 10 percent of individuals over the age of sixty-five and to affect about four million Americans (Brookmeyer et al. 1998). We know of a genetic component to the disease as first degree relatives of people with confirmed Alzheimer's disease stand a slightly greater risk of developing the disease than does the general population. To date there is no treatment for this disease.

There are 360,000 new Alzheimer's cases each year (Brookmeyer et al. 1998). The current prevalence rate doubles every five years after the age of sixty. This equals 1 percent for sixty to sixty-four-year-olds, 2 percent for sixty-five- to sixty-nine-year-olds, 4 percent for seventy- to seventy-four-year-olds, 8 percent for seventy-five- to seventy-nine-year-olds, and 16 percent for eighty- to eighty-five-year-olds (Campbell 1989). In short, the prevalence doubles roughly every five years beyond the age of sixty-five (Hebert et al. 1995). The prevalence increases up to 35 to 40 percent for those over the age of eighty-five. The overall prevalence is about 10 percent after the age of sixty-five (Cummings et al. 1998). These odds are not all that bad, as you probably have an equal or greater chance of being involved in a fatal or debilitating auto accident.

Diagnosis of Alzheimer's Disease

Alzheimer's disease can only be diagnosed with certainty upon autopsy or by a biopsy of the brain. This is done by the detection of the two hallmark structures within the brain. These are called amyloid plaques and neurofibrillary tangles. At more sophisticated medical centers, the disease can be diagnosed with up to a 90 percent certainty prior to death (Gearing et al. 1995). Unfortunately this diagnosis is often given out erroneously and made prematurely upon the first onset of minor short-term memory deficits. This creates an unimaginable burden for the patient and their families. If you have been told that you have AD and question the accuracy of the diagnosis, we recommend that you get a second opinion.

For a definite diagnosis there must be both structural changes within the brain and behavioral symptoms present before death. Identifiable pathologic changes include: neuronal plaques, neurofibrillary tangles, amyloid angiopathy, loss of synapses and neurons, granuovacuolar degeneration of the hippocampus, and neuronal loss (Cummings et al. 1998). *Plaques* are protein deposits of beta-amyloid (toxic substance) that form on the outside of the individual neurons. *Tangles* are abnormalities within the cell structure where cell fibers become tangled and cease to function. Tangles consist of a protein called "tau." *Tau* is involved in the structural integrity of nerve cells. In Alzheimer's disease, the tau proteins break down, which creates malformations in the structural framework of the neuron. It is unknown whether AD is caused by these abnormalities or whether the cellular abnormalities are a byproduct of the disease process. As both progress, malfunction in key structures within the brain occur. The National Institute on Aging and the Reagan Institute of the Alzheimer's Association have worked jointly to establish new criteria for the diagnosis of Alzheimer's disease. The new criteria have placed emphasis on the appearance of both neurofibrillary tangles and neuronal plaques in the neurocortex (Cummings et al. 1998). It should be noted that neuronal plaques are more specific to Alzheimer's disease, whereas neurofibrillary tangles are also associated with other progressive central nervous system (CNS) diseases. Neuronal plaques are also found in normal aging but to a much lesser degree.

Affected Chromosomes

Research has linked Alzheimer's disease to multiple chromosomes including: 1, 6, 12, 14, 19, and 21. Chromosome 21 is also associated with Down's syndrome and Down's syndrome patients almost always develop symptoms similar to Alzheimer's disease. It is speculated that the amyloid precursor protein gene on chromosome 21 accounts for a few cases of familial Alzheimer's disease. Familial cases, which often have an early onset, have been linked to abnormalities on chromosomes 1, 14, and 21. Abnormalities on chromosomes 1 and 14 make up the large majority of familial cases of Alzheimer's disease (Sherrington et al. 1995). Susceptibility genes in themselves do not cause the disease. Rather, it is believed to be a combination of multiple factors that influence the age of onset and increase the chances of developing the disease. Amongst suspected genes related to the sporadic form of the disease, the influence of apolipoprotein E (ApoE) on chromosome 19 has been identified (Strittmatter et al. 1993).

Protective Factors Against Alzheimer's Disease

Research has demonstrated that there are several protective factors that seem to prevent or delay the onset of AD. These include: higher intelligence, larger head size, lack of past head injuries, male gender, ApoE-2 genotype verses ApoE-4 genotype, higher educational level, history of use of nonsteroidal anti-inflammatory medications, and use of estrogen replacement therapy in postmenopausal women (Cummings et al. 1998).

Snowdon and colleagues (1996) have demonstrated an example of the protective factor of intelligence and education in delaying or preventing the disease. The group of researchers has been following a group of nuns for several years. They provide yearly examinations and the nuns have agreed to donate their brains for study upon death. Snowdon and his associates found a correlation in the "Nun Studies" between the nuns' complexity of writing styles in early adulthood and the later onset of AD. Nuns who had more complex writing styles were less likely to develop the disease.

Destructive Aspects of Alzheimer's Disease

The average range from onset to death in this progressive disease is five years, with a range of one to ten years. Alzheimer's disease accounts for about 100,000 deaths per year in the United States with 360,000 new cases diagnosed per year (Brookmeyer et al. 1998). Alzheimer's disease affects three main processes within the brain.

1. The first process involves the *repair of damaged cells*. When most nerve cells within the brain die, they are not replaced. Therefore they must have the capacity to repair and restructure themselves if they are to last throughout our lifetime. Alzheimer's disease is, at least in part, related to the breakdown of this normal repair process. Recent studies (Xu et al. 1999) have supported the theory that AD may result in part from inappropriate activation of *apoptosis* (programmed death of cells) and its relation to tumor suppressor proteins.

2. Another process known to break down in Alzheimer's disease is the normal communication between nerve cells. This process is dependent upon the integrity of the nerve cell and its interconnections to other nerve cells. It is also dependent upon the availability of neurotransmitters.

3. The final process involves *metabolism* or the feeding of the nerve cell. Alzheimer's disease greatly interferes with the neuron's ability to receive adequate energy and nutrients. Because the cells lose their ability to obtain nutrition, they eventually starve to death.

Behavioral Changes in Alzheimer's Disease

Although the progression of the disease has unique features for each individual, certain patterns can usually be identified. The disruption of degenerative processes eventually leads to cell death that usually begins in the memory-encoding portion of the brain known as the hippocampus. This leads to an initial impairment in recent memory marked by rapid forgetting. This is often marked by patterns of denial of forgetting by the patient. Initial changes also involve naming and word fluency (Murdoch et al. 1987). Often we see the patient use *circumlocution* (substituting other words for words that are lost to memory impairment) with minimal awareness given to the word-finding difficulties. The ability to form cohesive sentences, procedural memory, and general comprehension usually remain intact early in the disease (Hier et al. 1985).

Cueing and other memory strategies usually remain ineffective, and afflicted individuals usually do poorly on both free recall and recognition tasks when tested. As the disease progresses upward into the cerebral hemispheres, disruptions in expressive language, personality, and judgment begin to occur. Patients lose their ability to distinguish between left and right, and there are profound disturbances in visuospatial abilities (Eslinger et al. 1985). In the final stages the brain deteriorates to the point that the afflicted individual becomes completely helpless and reliant on others for their day-to-day functioning. These represent the 4 "A's" of Alzheimer's disease: amnesia, aphasia, apraxia, and agnosia. There is also a high prevalence of depression in Alzheimer's patients.

Oxidative Stress

Damage through oxidative stress is a current topic of research and is considered a nongenetic factor. Through aging we receive damage to nerve cells through the buildup of free radicals. Free radicals are a normal byproduct of the oxidative process within brain cells but can also modify the structure of proteins or molecules within nerve cell structure. Free radicals have been linked to both AD and cancer (National Institute of Aging, National Institutes of Health 1999).

Stages of Alzheimer's Disease

Alzheimer's disease usually progresses through three distinct phases. Early in the disease process the patient often has limited awareness of his or her deficits. One of the first notable deficits is difficulty with short-term memory. Patients become more forgetful, have difficulty recalling words they wish to use in a conversation (*anomia*), and begin losing things. *Disorientation* quickly sets in, and they begin to get lost in familiar places and lose track of time. *Apraxia* is another cardinal sign of the disease process and involves the person forgetting how to use a familiar tool or an appliance. Personality changes begin to be noticed and personal hygiene begins to be neglected. The middle stage of Alzheimer's disease is marked by an increased severity of the above symptoms. Those afflicted may begin to experience more pronounced expressive and receptive language difficulties. They may forget when they ate their last meal and become more noticeably disoriented to time. Often they have difficulty identifying people they have known for years and become increasingly more withdrawn. Inappropriate behaviors become more prevalent. Frustration leads to greater episodes of agitation, especially in the evening (referred to as *sun downing*). Eating and sleep disturbances become more frequent. In the final stages of the disease, both short-term and long-term memory are severely impaired. Illusions, delusions, and hallucinations begin to be prevalent. There ceases to be recognition of others and communication becomes almost impossible. Bladder and bowel control are greatly impaired and constant assistance is needed for daily functioning. The patient becomes increasingly more frail and more susceptible to infections and diseases.

Current Treatments

According to the Alzheimer's Association, the current annual cost for treatment of Alzheimer's disease in the United States is in excess of 60 billion dollars (Cummings 1998). Research is producing new progressive treatments including: a variety of cholinesterase inhibitors, antioxidants such as vitamin E, estrogen, non-steroidal inflammatory drugs, psychotropic agents, free radical inhibitors, transmitter replacement therapies, nerve growth factors, and prevention of amyloid formations through drugs (Cummings 1998). Although treatment options are limited, goals of current treatments are to improve cognition and behavioral symptoms, slow the progression of the disease, and to delay or prevent the onset of the disease (Farlow and Evans 1998).

Current treatments are mostly palliative in nature and seek to delay the progression of the disease. Future interventions will focus on drugs designed to attack the underlying mechanisms associated with the disease (and Evans 1998). As an example of this, Soto and associates (1998) demonstrated that injection of a small peptide similar to beta-amyloid actually reduced the size of beta-amyloid deposits in rats. This has strong implications for future treatment strategies for multiple neurodegenerative diseases.

Vaccine for Alzheimer's Disease

and colleagues (1999) are testing a treatment for AD in humans that is designed to treat the underlying cause of the disease. The group has shown that mice injected with beta-amyloid proteins seem to both clear existing plaques and prevent the onset of new plaques. The vaccine is also being tested in a nasally administered form. It stimulates the immune system to produce antibodies that bind to amyloid fragments and remove them from the brain. Limited studies have been started in the U.S. and England, and results look promising. Clinical trials are expected to be conducted soon.

How We Can Predict the Presence of Alzheimer's Disease

The proper diagnosis of Alzheimer's disease usually involves several visits to your physician. He or she may also want you to get additional testing that will assist in the diagnosis. Often a baseline has to be established, and exams such as neuropsychological testing or imaging need to be repeated so that a measure of deterioration can be obtained. New advances in the early diagnosis of possible or probable AD allows patients and their families to better prepare for the future and allows for some autonomy on the part of the patient in the decision-making process.

Alzheimer's disease may be present for many years before symptoms become noticeable. Studies with neuroimaging have shown that structural changes within the brain are often present many years before symptoms of dementia set in (Cummings et al. 1998). Although no diagnosis is definitive in itself, an MRI can set one's mind at ease if no significant structural abnormalities are found.

Neuropsychological Testing

Neuropsychological testing is an inferential process that compares cognitive behavioral domains of function against established norms (Lezak 1995)*. It can help to rule out the presence of Alzheimer's disease. Although there are some atypical presentations of

---

* Reprinted, by permission, from M. D. Lezak, *Neurological Assessment*, 3d. ed. 1995. Oxford University Press.

the disease, we can usually differentiate on behavioral tests between Alzheimer's disease, other dementias, and normal aging.

Genetic Risk Factors

What is a genetic risk factor? Within the nucleus of most cells within your body is the genetic code that makes you who you are. This genetic code is known as DNA. Chromosomes make up the DNA in the form of two parallel strands (double helix) of twenty-three pairs. You inherit one side of the helix from each parent. Portions of the genetic code arranged in specific sequence patterns make up genes. Genes produce various proteins based on their individual sequence patterns. These proteins determine your physical characteristics and dictate the physical functioning of your body. Sometimes malformed proteins are created that can lead to disease or a predisposition to a disease. These changes or malformations in the gene's codes are called *mutations*. We all have numerous polymorphisms (genetic mutations) that do not directly result in disease. When one of these mutations increases an individual's chance of developing a disease, it is referred to as a *risk factor*.

Genotyping

Currently there are no reliable tests that will predict who will develop Alzheimer's disease (Roses 1995). Genotype testing can help to predict the chances of the current or future onset of the disease. We know that those who have a family history of the disease and present with one or two copies of the apolipoprotein epsilon 4 (ApoE-4) genotype on chromosome 19 stand a better chance of developing the late onset form of the disease. Strittmatter and associates at Duke University (1993) showed that the ApoE allele accounted for up to 50 percent of genetic causes of the late onset form of AD. Hyman et al. (1996) estimates that 60 to 75 percent of sporadic cases carry the ApoE 4 gene. It is speculated that this is due to excessive beta-amyloid buildup. Other studies have confirmed these findings. Holzman and associates (1999) demonstrated in mice that the ApoE protein influenced plaque formation. Buttini et al. (1999) also showed that ApoE 3 proteins protected mice from injury to brain cells where ApoE 4 proteins did not. We also know that those with an ApoE 2 genotype are better protected against the disease or tend to develop the disease much later. Currently it is believed that the ApoE3 variation has a neutral effect in the onset of AD. This is the most common variation of ApoE.

Keep in mind that possessing an ApoE 4 genotype does not mean that you will develop the disease. We know of many people with this genotype who never develop Alzheimer's disease and those without the genotype who do. Neuroscientists believe that the ApoE protein helps to coordinate the processing of cholesterol throughout the body. The discovery of the relation of the ApoE 2, 3, or 4 pairs has helped us to gain greater understanding in the variations in age of onset of the disease. ApoE testing can also aid in diagnostic certainty in cases of atypical presentation involving visuospatial abnormalities or circumscribed language disturbances (Welsh-Bohmer et al. 1997).

✎ ✗ Exercise: Remembering Reversible Causes of Dementia

Let's review that list of classifications of potentially reversible dementias. Let's see how many you can remember using the memory tool of the word DEMENTIA.

Potentially Reversible Dementia

D _____

E _____

M _____

E _____

N _____

T _____

I _____

A _____

Check appendix E for answers. How many were you able to recall? If you recalled at least half, then you're doing well. Refer back to the beginning of chapter 17 to refresh your memory, focusing on the ones that you missed. Think of a new mnemonic to remember them with, or use your method of loci technique.

Frontotemporal Dementia

This type of dementia occurs at about one-fourth the rate of Alzheimer's disease (Lezak 1995). It is referred to by this name because the frontal and anterior temporal lobes show localized *atrophy* (wasting) and upon autopsy reveal a loss of neurons, astrocytosis (small tumors) with intraneuronal inclusions (Pick bodies), and inflated neurons. Mutations in the tau gene on chromosome 17 have been associated with a frontotemporal dementia with parkinsonism (Poorkaj et al. 1998).

Key Features of Frontotemporal Dementia

The frontal lobe (forehead region of the brain) is responsible for the control of a number of behaviors that are referred to as "executive functioning." Ogrocki and Welsh-Bohmer identify several features of executive functioning that can be affected in disorders involving the frontal lobes. These include: attention, planning, self-awareness, abstraction, flexibility in thinking, self-regulation, behavior execution and inhibition, decision making, changes in personality, and creativity (2000, 23). In frontal-lobe dementias these functions are severe enough to impair daily functioning.

Kaye (1998) identifies a number of characteristics that are unique to frontotemporal dementia. These include:

- ★ Insidious onset with slow progression
- ★ Conduct and behavioral deficits appearing early in the disease process
- ★ Neglect of hygiene (Loss of personal awareness)
- ★ Inappropriate social behavior
- ★ Disinhibition, impulsivity, and distractibility
- ★ Excessive eating, smoking, or alcohol consumption
- ★ Pica (compulsive eating of items that are not considered eatable)
- ★ Changes in speech patterns
- ★ Social withdrawal

- ★ Perseverative (repetitious) or ritualistic behaviors
- ★ Changes in speech output
- ★ Echolalia (repeating what they have recently heard)
- ★ Stereotyped speech (constant repetition of phrases)
- ★ Late mutism (progressive reduction of speech)
- ★ Physical changes
- ★ Incontinence
- ★ Early or prominent primitive "frontal" reflexes
- ★ Late akinesia, rigidity, tremor*

Ogrocki and Welsh-Bohmer (2000) note that some of these functions can slow as we age (attention and abstraction) thus requiring more conscious effort to execute, but not to the degree seen in dementias affecting the frontal lobes. Welsh-Bohmer and Hoffman (1996) also note reductions in frontal lobe blood flow with advanced age that might explain some of this slowing.

Typical Order of Symptom Presentation

Frontotemporal dementia usually presents with deficits in social grace, judgment, and appropriate behavior or language that are inproportional to memory deficits and usually present prior to the onset of more severe memory problems. Noted deficits are often coupled with preoccupations with bodily functions, depression, anxiety, and delusions (Kaye 1998). The disease often ends in a terminal vegetative state. Recent memory, visuospatial skills, and mathematical skills may remain relatively intact, which is a clear distinction from Alzheimer's disease (Welsh-Bohmer and Ogrocki 1998).

Pick's Disease

Pick's disease (also known as circumscribed cortical atrophy) is named after the psychiatrist Arnold Pick (1851-1924) (Campbell 1989). This disease is the most widely known subtype of frontotemporal dementia. Its presentation is unique in that the first symptoms usually center on strange behaviors, lack of judgment, and impulsiveness rather than the memory problems seen in many other forms of dementia. Pick's disease is relatively rare, comprising only about 2 percent of dementia patients, or less than one tenth of 1 percent of the general population (Lezak 1995). Because cognitive functions are usually preserved early in the illness, psychosis usually needs to be ruled out as a differential diagnosis (Kaye 1998). The duration of the disease is usually between two to seventeen years (Lezak 1995, 220).

In this progressive dementia involving the temporal and frontal lobes, symptoms are similar to other disease processes involving the same anatomy. Early symptoms may involve difficulties with attention, significant changes in personality and emotion, and lack of motivation. Language disturbances usually involve impaired verbal fluency and reduced conversational speech (Moss et al. 1992). Personality and emotional changes are usually more pronounced than seen in Alzheimer's disease, although the severity of dementia is usually not as prevalent.

---

* Reprinted, by permission, from K. A. Welsh-Bohmer and J. M. Hoffman, *Neuroimaging II: Clinical Applications,* edited by E. Bigler. 1996. Plenum Press.

Who Does It Affect and What Can We Do?

The average age of onset for Pick's disease is fifty-five years old (Campbell 1989). It affects more women than men, and there is a strong correlation between developing Pick's disease and having a blood relative with the disease. Up to 60 percent of patients with a frontotemporal dementia have a family history of the disease (Kaye 1998). Frontotemporal dementia has been linked to chromosome 17 and is usually revealed in neuroimaging by atrophy (wasting) in the frontal and anterior temporal lobes. SPECT scanning may reveal decreased cerebral blood flow over the frontal lobes, which is a distinct finding for this type of dementia (Kaye 1998). Treatment options are limited but include cholinesterase inhibitors coupled with behavior modulating medications, such as benzodiazepines, antidepressants, and/or neuroleptics.

Diffuse Lewy Body Disease

Diffuse lewy body disease is marked by lewy body degeneration throughout the neocortex, limbic system, hypothalamus, and brainstem. Lewy bodies are found in nerve cells and are more prevalent in pigmented brain stem neurons. Lewy bodies are found in 5 to 10 percent of normal brains of people over the age of sixty and in 10 percent of brains of people diagnosed with Alzheimer's disease (Ayd 1995). They are also found in the brains of virtually all cases of people diagnosed with Parkinsonism and lewy body dementia. The presence of lewy bodies does not indicate the presence of the disease and the number present in the brain does not correlate with the severity or duration of the disease (Ayd 1995).

Symptoms of dementia with lewy bodies include progressive dementia coupled with severe rigidity and moderate Parkinson's symptoms. It has been postulated that the neurological findings may be associated with degeneration in the areas where lewy bodies form. Diffuse lewy body disease should be suspected if a rapidly progressive dementia is present followed by rigidity, visual hallucinations, and other features of Parkinson's (Burkhardt et al. 1988).

Diagnosis of the Disorder

Diffuse lewy body dementia affects both outer-brain (cortical) and inner-brain (subcortical) structures. There seems to be pathology within the brain that is similar to Alzheimer's disease in some cases (Katzman et al. 1995). Therefore, there are currently two subtypes of the disorder identified. The first is called lewy body variant of AD and the second is diffuse lewy body disease (Welsh-Bohmer and Ogrocki 1998). Both types are marked by progressive cognitive decline that interferes with normal social or occupational functioning. Memory impairment may not be evident in the early stages of the disease but becomes more apparent as the disease progresses. There is often impairment in attention, visuospatial abilities, and other skills that are dependent upon frontal-subcortical structures (Kaye 1998).

Symptoms Associated with the Disease

Symptoms associated with diffuse lewy body disease include:

★ Fluctuating cognition with pronounced variations in attention and alertness

★ Spontaneous motor features of parkinsonism

★ Recurrent detailed and elaborate visual hallucinations (Kaye 1998; Perry et al. 1996). Frontal lobe impairments

★ Slowing of motor functions

★ Forgetfulness (Wagner and Bachman 1996).

★ Syncope (fainting)

★ Repeated falls

★ Transient loss of consciousness

★ Systematic delusions

★ Sensitivity to neuroleptic medications

★ Hallucinations (Kaye 1998).

Kaye also notes that the diagnosis of dementia with lewy bodies is less likely if there is history of strokes, focal neurologic signs on imaging, or evidence that another physical illness or brain disorder may be attributable to the symptom cluster.

Now let's check your retention of the reversible causes of dementia.

✎ ✗ Exercise: Remembering *DEMENTIA*

Let's review that list of classifications of potentially reversible dementias one more time. Let's see if you can get some of the ones that you missed last time. Take your time and remember to try to recall through approximations rather than direct routes for the ones you can't seem to remember.

Potentially Reversible Dementia

D _____

E _____

M _____

E _____

N _____

T _____

I _____

A _____

How many were you able to recall? Did you recall more than last time? Were you able to recall the same ones as last time? Give yourself a hand for remembering—or, more precisely, for associating! Next we will look at vascular dementia.

Vascular Dementia

Vascular dementia can affect either the cortical or subcortical areas of the brain. Its progression is fluctuating (step-like) rather than steady (hill-like) like some of the more progressive dementias. It was formerly referred to as "multi-infarct dementia" and is often associated with *cerebral arteriosclerosis* (thickening or hardening of the arterial wall). It is the result of a series of strokes, which have produced enough brain tissue damage to cause the onset of cognitive impairment. *Infarct* refers to an area of dead or dying brain tissue resulting from obstruction or destruction of the blood vessels that normally supply blood to that area. Vascular dementia accounts for about one fourth of progressive dementias (Tomlinson et al. 1970). Vascular findings are frequently seen with Alzheimer's disease related cortical pathology (Welsh et al. 1996). There has been a correlation found between some forms of vascular dementia, AD, and the ApoE gene, which suggests possible shared physiology (Saunders et al. 1993).

Types of Vessel Disease

There are two types of strokes (also called cerebral vascular accidents or CVAs).

1. An *embolism* is a clot or other obstruction that is carried from a larger vessel into a smaller one. It obstructs the circulation of blood and results in damaged tissue. A *thrombosis* is a formed clot that remains at the point at which it formed. A thrombosis typically involves a much slower progression than an embolism. Damage can also be in the form of softening of the brain tissue (*encephalomalacia*).

2. *Cerebral hemorrhage* is a massive bleeding into the brain. This bleeding results in abrupt tissue damage and is often fatal. It is often the result of hypertension (high blood pressure). An *aneurysm* is a vascular dilation or swelling of blood vessels, which results from defects in the elasticity of the vessel wall (Kolb and Whishaw 1995).

Single strokes usually result in much more localized or specific deficits than the more global vascular dementia, although a single stroke placed in the right area, such as the angular gyrus or anterior or paramedian thalamus, can mimic a multi-infarct's dementing process (Kaye 1998). Strokes can also be transient and fleeting in nature. These small strokes are referred to as *transient ischemic attacks* ("mini-strokes"). Lateralized motor dysfunction (weakness, lack of coordination, or paralysis on one side of the body) and acute speech impairments are cardinal symptoms of vascular involvement. If this occurs to you or someone you know, seek medical help immediately.

Symptoms of Vascular Dementia

Symptoms are variable but can include: memory impairment, lateralized motor impairment, difficulties in walking, urinary incontinence, deficits in judgment, personality changes, and changes in impulse control (Campbell 1989). A common pattern seen in subcortical vascular dementias is language impairments marked by broken fluency in speech (Barr et al. 1992). In this type of symptom presentation, comprehension usually remains intact, as does the ability to name objects (Villardita 1993). Inefficient information processing and motor slowing are also common hallmarks of the disorder (Welsh-Bohmer and Ogrocki 1998). For a diagnosis of vascular dementia to be given, there is usually a noted deficit in memory and a deficit in one or two other cognitive domains.

Researchers at the University of Kentucky are currently following over 600 nuns from the School Sisters of Notre Dame. The nuns undergo annual evaluations and have agreed to donate their brains for investigation upon death. Studies have shown a correlation between brain infarcts and the number of plaques and tangles within the brain (Snowdon et al. 1997). Heyman and associates (1998) demonstrated that patients with both a history of infarcts and AD showed more severe dementia than those patients with AD alone.

🔑 Memory Tip: Medical Conditions Unique to Men

There are several medical conditions that are unique to men that can affect memory functioning. Vascular disease is the leading cause of erectile dysfunction with atherosclerosis of the penile artery being the primary cause in most cases in men over the age of fifty (Kaiser 1999). Other neurological disorders such as temporal lobe epilepsy, strokes, tremors, and multiple sclerosis can also lead to erectile dysfunction (Morley 1993). There are many other causes of erectile dysfunction such as medication side effects, thyroid problems, and diabetes. So if you are experiencing erectile dysfunction, it may be indicative of a serious condition that can be diagnosed and treated. These problems warrant further investigation by your physician.

Testosterone (androgen) deficiency in older men has been linked to multiple symptoms including decreased cognitive functioning and visuospatial memory impairment (Morley and Perry 1999; Cherrier et al. 1998). This may prove to be a viable line of investigation by your physician if you are experiencing memory difficulties. Finally, prostate cancer affects one in five men in the United States (Walsh 1995). Both the treatment and the disease can lead to memory impairments. All of these conditions can greatly impair memory functioning. It is important to get a thorough medical exam annually. If you suspect that you are experiencing difficulties in any of these areas, consult your physician. Next we will take a look at some of the diseases that first affect the deeper regions of the brain.

Binswanger's Disease

Let's begin examining the subcortical diseases with a brief overview of Binswanger's disease (also called subcortical atherosclerotic encephalopathy). Otto Binswanger first described the disease in 1894, and it is the result of decreased blood flow to the brain, usually occurring between the ages of fifty and sixty. It is associated with hypertension and arterial wall thickening. The disease is associated with axonal loss, lacunar infarcts, dilation of perivascular spaces and loss of myelin (Welsh-Bohmer and Ogrocki 1998).

Symptoms of the Disease

Multiple symptoms associated with the disease include: amnesia, cognitive deficits, episodes of stroke or seizure, apathy, changes in personality and mood, language deficits, and gait and motor difficulties (Ayd 1995). Symptoms are usually gradually progressive.

Parkinson's Disease

James Parkinson discovered the disease that now bears his name in 1817. Parkinson's disease is the fourth most common neurodegenerative disorder seen in older adults (Berkow and Fletcher 1992). It involves a progressive deterioration of the nigrostriatal dopaminergic system (motor system) and is associated with the depletion of dopamine (neurotransmitter involved with motor functions) in the basal ganglia (part of the brain associated with the control and coordination of movement). The disease also involves the erosion of the limbic system, cortical projections, and midbrain.

It is believed that Parkinson's disease may be partially the result of environmental toxins. It is estimated that around .02 percent of the general population develops this disease with as high as 25 percent for those over the age of seventy-five (Lezak 1995). It affects more men than women, rarely sets in before the age of thirty, and is more prevalent in minority groups (Lezak 1995).

A gene has been linked to the disease. This gene is believed to be responsible for the regulation of a protein called "synuclein." This protein is also found in the plaques of patients with Alzheimer's disease.

Symptoms of Parkinson's Disease

Symptoms of the disease may initially be *lateralized* (on one side of the body) and include: hand tremors that resemble pill rolling movements, drooling, lack of facial expression, rapid onset of a *resting tremor* (tremor involving several muscle groups that is apparent during rest but tends to disappear during purposeful movement), and *cogwheel rigidity* (continual rhythmical interruption of passive movement that presents as a slight catch with each movement). Other symptoms include: *akinesia* (partial loss of voluntary muscle movement, or slowed initiation of motor movement), poor handwriting, *bradykinesia* (loss of voluntary muscle movement), absence of arm swing when walking, postural abnormalities (stooped posture or stiffness), joint pain, *gait disturbances* (disturbances in the ability to walk, often using small shuffling steps), and *retropulsion* (tendency to fall backwards) (Ayd 1995). The presence of dementia is estimated to occur in 20 to 40 percent of Parkinson's patients (Snyder and Nussbaum 1998).*

Cognitive Deficits Often Mimic Frontal Symptoms

Cognitive deficits associated with Parkinson's tend to mimic frontal lobe damage. This is in part due to the wiring of the frontal lobe. Our brains have five separate circuits or "loops" that run subcortically between the frontal lobes and other major cortical structures. In subcortical diseases such as Parkinson's, the frontal lobes and other cortical structures are damaged at the subcortical level via these five circuits. As the disease progresses, frontal symptoms such as poor executive planning and mental flexibility begin to be more prevalent. The degeneration of these circuits would impair the person's ability to form a preparatory set or concentrate and would result in rigid thinking. Attentional deficits are common, as are deficits in working memory and verbal fluency. Immediate verbal memory tends to diminish but can usually be triggered through association. Visual memory, vocabulary, syntax, reasoning, and grammar tend to remain intact (Cooper et al. 1991).

Depression Is Common in Parkinson's Disease

Depression is common in Parkinson's patients, with a higher incidence in patients suffering symptoms of pain associated with the disease (Lezak 1995). Dopamine replacement therapy is almost the universal treatment of the disease and patients are now surviving ten to fifteen years with proper treatment (Lezak 1995). This still brings to the forefront the realization of one's mortality. A Parkinson's patient and many other patients suffering neurological disease must negotiate thoughts of death on a daily basis. Existential therapy or a strong spiritual faith can greatly assist the person suffering from Parkinson's disease in finding meaning in their lives and in the disease process.

---

* Reprinted, by permission, from P. J. Snyder and P. D. Nussbaum, *Clinical Neuropsychology: A Pocket Handbook for Assessment.* 1998. American Psychological Association.

🔑 Memory Tip: Check Your Furnace

It's not uncommon for people to come to their doctor's office complaining of intermittent memory complaints and later find out that their old furnace was leaking gas. This is especially true in the colder months when we have to keep the house warm. Carbon monoxide exposure can greatly impair your memory functioning. It may be worth your effort to have a professional check your furnace and gas lines for leaks, especially if there is a seasonal pattern to your memory difficulties.

Parkinson-Plus Syndrome

Parkinson-plus syndromes are difficult to distinguish from Parkinson's disease. This is a class of disorders that tend to mimic some of the symptoms of Parkinson's disease with a few minor distinctions. These symptoms include: progressive supranuclear palsy (Steele-Richardson-Olszewski syndrome), the multiple system atrophies (olivopontocerebellar atrophy), striatonigral degeneration, Shy-Drager syndrome, and possibly corticobasal ganglionic degeneration. The prevalence rates for these disorders are low and are usually initially marked by disturbances in motor functions. Most are not responsive to dopamine therapies, which helps distinguish Parkinson-plus syndrome from Parkinson's disease.

Progressive Supranuclear Palsy Symptoms

This rare disorder is a subtype of a Parkinson-plus syndrome. Symptoms often begin around the age of sixty and are usually symmetrical at onset. Resting tremor usually occurs later in the disease process (Snyder and Nussbaum 1989). Symptoms are similar to other symptoms that characterize subcortical dementias but begin to mimic cortical dementias as symptoms progress. Symptoms include motor dysfunction, emotional disturbances, cognitive slowing, memory impairment, and executive dysfunction. *Dysarthria* (difficulty in articulation) is often present earlier than normally seen in Parkinson's disease. Gait disturbance is also prevalent early in the disease and negotiating stairs becomes difficult (Berkow and Fletcher 1992). Other symptoms that are characteristics of the disease include: difficulty looking straight up or down, facial spasticity, and difficulty maintaining posture (Johnson et al. 1992). Dementia usually occurs later in the disease. Although drastic drops in dopamine levels mark the disease, symptoms usually respond poorly to dopaminergic medications (medications that replace dopamine) and usually progress faster than seen in Parkinson's disease.

There is significant slowing in all mental processing, although accuracy usually remains relatively intact early in the disease (Campbell 1989). Therefore it has been postulated that memory is not as impaired as the timing mechanism of memory (Lezak 1995). Deficits can also be noted in visual-spatial abilities, visual tracking and scanning, hand-eye coordination, word finding, and visual field discrimination. Falls are common, and there is usually trouble in writing and eating. Blurring and double vision are also common.

Short-term memory difficulties are common but not to the degree seen in dementia of the Alzheimer's type. Apathy is often present and irritability and depression are common (Lezak 1995).

As the disease progresses, movement rigidity, defective control of mouth and neck muscles, drooling, and impassive facial expression become prevalent. Treatment is limited to medications to ease the symptoms and discomfort.

Parkinsonism

Parkinsonism is not the same as Parkinson's disease. Parkinson's disease refers to a specific disease entity, whereas parkinsonism refers to a syndrome that consists of four motor signs. These four motor signs are rigidity, tremor, postural abnormalities, and bradykinesia (slowing in the execution of movements) (Snyder and Nussbaum 1998). Parkinsonism is seen in Parkinson's disease but is also seen in several other disease processes.

Huntington's Disease

Huntington's disease is an inherited disease that begins in middle adulthood. Erratic, involuntary muscle movements and progressive memory and emotional deterioration mark the disease. It was originally called Huntington's chorea for the Greek word "chorea," meaning dance. This is a reference to the twisting, spastic movements associated with the disease. This progressive disorder has been localized to a genetic deficit on chromosome 4 (Huntington's Disease Collaborative Research Group 1993).

Areas of the Brain Affected

The basal ganglia is usually the first structure affected by the disease. Later the disease progresses to the frontal lobes where symptoms of inattention and lack of motivation appear. Huntington's disease is classified as a frontal-subcortical disease (Joynt and Shoulson in Heilman and Valenstein, eds. 1985). The disease goes largely untreatable except for measures taken to ease the symptoms and discomfort.

Diagnosis

The disease is easily diagnosed and even predictable with blood tests, given its genetic etiology. It is believed that the malformed Huntington's protein is formed into fibrils that represent the beta-amyloid plaques seen in Alzheimer's disease. Huntington's disease affects an estimated four to eight people in 100,000 and 50 percent of the children of a parent with the disease will inherit it (Harper 1992). Symptoms usually manifest themselves in adults between the ages of forty and fifty and can last as long as twenty to thirty years. If the disease is inherited from the mother, it tends to progress more slowly and appear later in life than when it is inherited from the father.

Symptoms

Symptoms are variable but often mimic the progression of Parkinson's disease in their initial motor effects and eventual effects on frontal lobe functioning. Cognitive deficits implicate the caudate nucleus in its mental rather than its motor functions. Eye movements slow down and become jerky (*nystagmus*). Other manifestations include slowed mental processing, shortened attention span, poor concentration, inflexibility in thinking, and slowed motor performance with the nondominant hand. Motor learning is impaired and working memory becomes especially susceptible to interference. Retrieval deteriorates as the disease progresses and visuospatial functions remain impaired throughout the disease process. Verbal functions (like speech comprehension, language processing) tend to remain preserved until the later stages of the disease with the exception of speech production (Welsh-Bohmer and Ogrocki 1998). Depression is likely to accompany

Huntington's disease. Some initial presentations initially involve psychiatric symptoms such as depression or symptoms that mimic schizophrenia (Folstein et al. 1979).

Wilson's Disease

Wilson's disease (hepatolenticular degeneration) is a rare, inherited disorder. It affects the body's ability to metabolize copper. Wilson's disease manifests itself as toxic levels of copper are deposited in the brain tissue, liver, and other organs. Prevalence rates are estimated at three in 100,000 individuals (Ayd 1995, 676). The disease is transferred to offspring through a recessive gene on chromosome 13 and usually becomes symptomatic between the ages of five and fifty, although it's more common between the ages of ten and twenty-five (Snyder and Nussbaum 1998).

Symptoms

Definitive symptoms of Wilson's disease are the *Kayser-Fleischer ring* (a greenish-brown pigmentation around the cornea of the eye) and cirrhosis of the liver (Ayd 1995). Other symptoms include a mix of psychiatric and neurological abnormalities including: emotional and personality changes, parkinsonian symptoms, tremors, rigidity, postural instability, cognitive deterioration, and *dysarthria* (slowness or incoordination of speech-related muscles). Treatment focuses on limiting the intake of copper and in taking measures to eliminate copper from the system (Snyder and Nussbaum 1998).

Creutzfeldt-Jakob Disease

Creutzfeldt-Jakob disease (spastic pseudosclerosis; cortico-striato-spinal degeneration) is an extremely rare, progressive dementia (occurs in one individual per one million per year worldwide) that is caused by the transmission of a prion (Tabrizi et al. 1996). *Prions* are infectious proteins that seem to lack DNA. In 1997 Dr. Stanley Prusiner won the Nobel Prize for his discovery of prions. Creutzfeldt-Jakob disease occurs two to three times more often in males and typically occurs in the mid fifties (Campbell 1989). In this extremely rapidly progressing disease, death usually occurs within a year after the onset of symptoms.

Symptoms

Symptoms include memory impairment, motor problems, *hemiparesis* (paralysis of one side of the body), *hemianopia* (visual-field deficits mimicking blind spots), *dysarthria* (speech impairment marked by weakness or slowness of speech musculature), *myoclonus* (brief repetitive muscle contractions stemming from the central nervous system), depression, seizures, and behavioral and emotional problems (Ayd 1995). Welsh-Bohmer and Ogrocki (1998) identify a triad of symptoms that aid in the diagnosis of the disorder. These include: myoclonus, acute onset of dementia, and electroencephalogram results showing general slowing of brain activity with occasional sharp spikes. The slowly progressive form of the disease can be distinguished from AD by noted changes in reflex and motor abnormalities (Tabrizi et al. 1996). The disease is highly contagious, especially with direct contact with infected brain tissue. There is no known treatment for this disease, and it usually first affects the cerebellum, or lower areas of the brain.

Acquired Immunodeficiency Syndrome Dementia Complex

AIDS dementia complex is progressive, with symptoms that mimic a subcortical dementia. Initial signs usually center around memory problems, neuromotor deficits such as tremor and ataxia, poor concentration, and impairment in psychomotor speed. As the disease progresses, behavioral and mood problems become prevalent and psychosis may set in (Ayd 1995). Symptoms of aphasia, agnosia, and apraxia are usually absent during the first stages of the disease (Welsh-Bohmer and Ogrocki 1998). This disorder is easily diagnosed, but treatments are limited.

Multiple Sclerosis

Multiple sclerosis or MS (disseminated sclerosis) is a common neurologic disorder that affects over 300,000 Americans (sixty to three hundred per 100,000 individuals). It usually affects people between the ages of fifteen and fifty, and the average life expectancy after onset is twenty to twenty-five years (Campbell 1989). It affects more women than men, occurs more in temperate zones, and is more common in people of Northern European heritage.

Relapsing Subtypes

There are several subtypes of the disorder. These include: Balo's sclerosis, Schilder's disease, Devic's disease, central pontine myelinolysis, and Marchiafava-Bignami disease. Multiple sclerosis is a relapsing disease (Campbell 1989). Symptoms often occur, clear up, and then reoccur. Symptoms may clear up for months or years before recurring. There is also a progressive pattern in which symptoms never completely clear up, but gradually or rapidly become worse.

Changes within the Brain

Swelling of the brain and central nervous system followed by demyelination marks multiple sclerosis. *Demyelination* is the loss of the protective coating (myelin) on nerve fibers that act to speed up nerve impulses. This results in scattering of well-demarcated sclerotic plaques throughout the brain and spinal cord (Campbell 1989).

Symptoms

The cause of the disease is unknown. Initial symptoms usually include loss of control of motor movements, weakness or numbness in one or more limbs, and visual deficits. Other symptoms include: sensory deficits, gait and balance difficulties, weakness, and cognitive changes. Only 20 to 30 percent of patients develop cognitive deficits sufficient to label them as demented (Snyder and Nussbaum 1998).

When dementia is present, patterns mimic those seen in subcortical dementias (movement disorders, cognitive slowing, executive dysfunction, memory impairment, and mood and personality changes). Treatment options include medications designed to treat the symptoms as they occur and medications designed to modify the disease activity.

✎ ✗ *Exercise: Reading Comprehension*

That was a lot of information to digest all at once. Let's take a quick quiz to review what we learned about memory disorders. Were you able to attend to the relevant data and screen out the minutia?

Circle the correct response.

1. Alzheimer's disease has a higher incidence in men than women.   True   False

2. After the age of sixty, the incidence of dementia doubles every five years.   True   False

3. Dopamine is the primary neurotransmitter associated with Parkinson's disease.   True   False

4. Symptoms to look for in determining if you should seek out a neurological exam includes: dizziness, poor memory, confusion, speech problems, depression, and problems with reading and writing.   True   False

5. Symptoms of dementia include impaired: language (aphasia), memory (amnesia), motor skills (apraxia), visuospatial skills, and cognition (abstraction, reasoning, attention), loss of sensory perception (agnosia), poor judgment and impulse control, changes in emotion or personality, loss of ability to recognize memory loss (anosognosia), loss of organizational and planning abilities, loss of ability to concentrate, disorientation, apathy, and difficulty with social and occupational tasks.   True   False

6. The four major categories associated with dementia include: amnestic disorders, cognitive disorders, attention disorders, and gastrointestinal discomfort.   True   False

7. Lyme disease, herpes simplex and cryptococcus infection are the leading causes of dementia.   True   False

8. Pseudodementia is a progressive dementia that currently has no cure.   True   False

9. Parkinsonism and Parkinson plus are other names for Parkinson's disease.   True   False

10. Pick's disease (Circumscribed cortical atrophy) is the most widely known subtype of diffuse Lewy body dementia.   True   False

11. The leading symptom in Parkinson's disease is memory deficits.   True   False

12. Parkinson-plus syndrome is different than Parkinson's disease.   True   False

13. Multi-infarct dementia is another term for vascular dementia.   True   False

14. Binswanger's disease is the result of decreased blood flow to the brain.   True   False

15. Huntington's disease is an inherited disease that is marked by erratic, involuntary muscle movements and progressive memory and emotional deterioration.   True   False

16. Wilson's disease is a rare inherited disorder of iron metabolism in which toxic levels of iron are deposited in the brain tissue, liver, and other organs.   True   False

17. Creutzfeldt-Jakob disease is a rare progressive dementia that is caused by the transmission of bacteria.   True   False

18. Swelling of the brain and central nervous system followed by demyelination marks multiple sclerosis.   True   False

19. AIDS dementia complex is similar to symptoms of subcortical dementia.   True   False

20. Apraxia is a symptom of many diseases where the person may forget how to use a familiar tool or forget how to use an appliance.   True   False

See appendix E for answers. How did you do? If you got fourteen or more correct then you were able to screen, comprehend, and retain some fairly technical information. Scores from 9 to 13 reflect fairly good comprehension. Even in reading through this information it is sometimes necessary to skim the unimportant details and to focus on the facts important to you.

⋆ 17 ⋆

Review of RARE-DREAM
and Congratulations

You've made it through this book, and that is no easy task. You have encoded and retrieved a great deal and your memory has definitely had a good workout. You have examined your strengths and your weaknesses. You have gained a good understanding of the general functions of the mind that guide the proverbial ins and outs of memory. You have made a commitment to improving your memory. Do you feel any different about your memory now than when you started the book? Let's put it in writing. Write down below what the differences are in your memory, what you know about it, and how you feel about it.

✎ ✗ *Exercise: Differences in Memory*

_____

_____

_____

_____

_____

_____

_____

_____

_____

Now, to help you fulfill the RARE-DREAM of a better memory, let's briefly review what these letters stand for.

Four small steps to memory improvement . . .

Relax

Attend

Rehearse

Envision

One giant leap for a kind mind!

Develop

Rational

and

Emotionally

Adaptive

Mindsets

The truth is that we can memorize just about anything that we choose, if we employ some simple tips to aid in the process. Again, remember the acronym RARE: relax, attend, rehearse, envision. These four components will maximize your memory performance. It's essential to relax so that you can attend to the material and commit it to memory. Use your attention as if it were radar gun. Purposely point it at the object to be placed in memory and shoot! Rehearse the material through sensory elaboration and visualization to enhance the encoding process. See it, smell it, taste it, feel it, and hear it—and don't be afraid to laugh at it. Combine the techniques in this book to make the information personally meaningful to you. But remember that your attitudes and beliefs are the foundation on which your memory functioning is built. As a general review of RARE-DREAM, let's look at the contents of the book in a little different way. After all, variety is the spice of life and the salt that enhances memory. Next, we will provide a summary of the workbook in the form of twenty memory tips to sustain effective memory functioning.

Twenty Tips to Maintain Your Memory

1. **Self-fulfilling prophecy:** If you view yourself as having a poor memory then you probably *will* have a poor memory. It will become a self-fulfilling prophecy. Tell yourself that you have a good memory and that it is improving every day. Focus on successes and actively navigate your mindset. Praise yourself for remembering, but never punish yourself for forgetting. Take charge! Approach your daily tasks with enthusiasm. Excitement fuels attention and concentration, which are the cornerstones of good memory.

2. **Organize:** Find a central location to place the things that you use in your daily routine. Keys, calendar, wallet, and purse can all be placed in your "memory spot." Find a scent that you like (such as an air freshener or a Glade "Plug In") and place it in that location. Smell enhances your memory. Being organized enhances your memory and decreases stress. Place things that are used together in one spot. Associate and simplify the components of daily routine. If you have to make a phone call in the morning, place a reminder next to your toothbrush, or place your toothbrush on top of the phone. Utilize a calendar to organize activities. If you make lists, centralize them in one location. Scattered notes instill stress and foster forgetfulness.

3. **Focus:** Pay attention to your attention. Use the strategies that you have learned to commit information to memory. Form a mental picture of the grocery items that you need, write them down, or use a tape recorder to jog your memory. Take the time necessary to rehearse the information immediately after hearing it in your mind. Utilize multiple memory systems to encode data. Repetition (either verbally or in writing) enhances encoding and reinforces the learned material. Concentrate on the task at hand.

4. **Relax:** Memory will be more efficient if you take the time needed to store and recall the information. Don't panic if you can't immediately recall something. Take your time, relax, and allow it to come to you rather than beating yourself up in the process of forcing it. Allow yourself the time necessary to complete a thought, to express yourself, or to complete a task. Examine any internal conflicts that may be hampering your memory and activating your stress response. Memory always works better when we are well rested. Take control and limit your responsibilities and expectations to a level that is comfortable for you. Make the relaxation techniques in this book an integral part of your everyday life.

5. **Limit distractions:** Chaos breeds confusion. It is much more difficult to access your memory when you are surrounded by contradictory stimuli. Find a quiet place, limit distractions, and allow your memory to work for you.

6. **Categorize:** Placing information into categories makes it easier to remember and simplifies the encoding and retrieval processes. Remember, everything that you know is contained in a series of associations. Link new memories to existing ones and organize through categorization.

7. **Sense it:** By using the different senses to aid in establishing a memory, you are physically utilizing different portions of the brain. Each side of your brain controls the sensory input from the opposite side of the body. Your sense of smell is much deeper in the brain than your vision. By utilizing the different senses to encode a memory, you can create memory traces at multiple levels and on both sides of the brain. Don't forget to use the unique functions within each sense to elaborate the item to be remembered and better establish the memory foundation. Visualizing the brightness of an object uses different cells and different areas of the brain than imagining the color of it. Actively utilize all of your senses to aid in the details of memory. The more effort put into the imaginary component of the task the greater will be the fruits of your labor.

8. **Attach it:** It's always easier to remember things if they carry some significant meaning. For example, if you hear on the television that a flood warning has been issued for your county, you will be more likely to remember it than if you hear about an actual flood somewhere across the globe. Try to decide why what you want to remember is important. Ask yourself how this applies to you and how it might impact your life later on. Attach the items to be remembered to an emotion.

9. **Preparatory set** (attention preparation): Prepare your mind in the same way an athlete prepares prior to engaging in sports. For example, if you have to give a presentation, do a mental warm-up before presenting. In your mind, rehearse everything that will be involved in making the presentation. Close your eyes and envision what the room will look like; do a mental inventory of all the materials that you will need and imagine some questions that might be asked of you. Doing a preparatory set or a preparatory review is not only empowering, it will help you to be better organized.

10. **Use humor:** Compose a humorous phrase, song, or mental image to assist in remembering. When humor is attached to the item to be remembered, it is both entertaining and more easily recalled. It naturally creates personal meaning for the information you need to remember. Humor will also serve to help you to relax, stay positive, and to become less burdened with stress and tension. Humor goes a long way toward remembering.

11. **Use it or lose it:** Memory is improved through practice. Doing puzzles, reading, or learning something new all serve to enhance your memory and aid in your confidence about yourself. Practicing drawing or doodling can also enhance your visual imagery skills. Simply drawing what ever comes to mind allows you to place a visual representation of what's in your mind on paper. Finally, find a way to teach others. By teaching you are enhancing your own memories. After all, isn't this why they make grandchildren?

12. **Label memory files:** By consciously choosing key word associations by which to store memories, you are saving space in the filing cabinet of your mind and enhancing accessibility. You are utilizing both active encoding and association and thus greatly enhancing your ability for later retrieval. Link your visual, auditory, and other sensory perceptions to future memories. Labeling memory files allows you to link one word with whole concepts. It allows you to utilize the natural encoding processes within the brain to your advantage.

13. **Memory prosthetics:** There are many external aids that can help your memory. Utilizing a calendar to guide you through your daily activities creates self-reliance and thus confidence and allows you to plan ahead and free up space in your mind for more pressing memories. Use one calendar to chronicle appointments, daily events, reminders, responsibilities, and goals. Write down anything that is important to you. Keep this calendar accessible in a central location and carry it with you. Leave yourself organized notes and/or carry a small recording device or Palm Pilot. Send yourself emails or set your computer up to prompt you to remember important dates such as anniversaries or birthdays. Get a watch with an alarm function to remind you of appointments throughout the day. Incorporate these external aids into your daily routine and free your memory for more important things.

14. **Mind-body connection:** It is essential that you take proper care of your body if your memory is to function at its fullest potential. Diet and exercise are an essential part of keeping your memory working for you. A well-balanced, healthy diet will provide your mind with the fuel it needs to function at its fullest potential. Exercise relieves stress, enhances blood flow, and provides needed nutrients to the brain. Avoidance of indulgence in too much alcohol, caffeine, and other drugs will also enhance your memory.

15. **Come in through the back door:** Everyone experiences blocks to his or her memory at times. Sometimes the more you try to recall a piece of data the further away it seems to get. This process is fueled by frustration and negative self-talk. Replace any negative self-talk with positive affirmations. If you practice positive thinking enough, it will become a habit. Avoid frustration by talking around the item to be recalled. Use words that are similar, express yourself in approximations, and keep the thought active. Attempt to recall the item through other memory systems. By doing so, you will often pull out the item to be remembered. Remember that the human brain

contains billions of nerve cells that are intricately connected to form memories. It is normal that we are sometimes unable to access a single pathway within this behemoth map of neural cells. Patience is a virtue, and sometimes we just have to let it go and gently embrace our imperfect human condition.

16. **Time is on your side:** Our brain uses the element of time to chunk memories together (episodic memory). When you have difficulty remembering something, try to reconstruct the time frame associated with that memory. By doing so, you are tapping into the general location within your brain where that memory is stored and activating the neural networks associated with that memory. For example, if you want to remember what you got for your birthday last year, reconstruct that time frame in your mind. Picture where you were, what you were wearing, how the day began, and whom you were with. Reconstruct the events of that day. As you link memories in this manner, other associated memories will gradually surface into your awareness.

17. **Chunk it:** Chunking is essentially conceptual association. It involves coding small portions of data into a larger, meaningful concept and later deconstructing the individual components of data back to its original form. The data is coded, stored, retrieved, and decoded. A good example of this is your social security number. Many of us remember three chunks or sets of numbers (like 123-45-6789). It is easier to remember three sets of numbers rather than nine individual numbers. Start with the main premise of an article that you are trying to remember. Then associate related themes back to the main premise by visualizing a representation of each. By breaking down the information we are checking the accuracy of the information and thus enhancing our memory. Finally, file this in your mental computer under one specific title.

18. **Associate it:** Memory begins and ends with association. Conscious awareness (working memory) serves to modulate our subconscious and unconscious memories and regulates the association of new memories with old ones. By knowing this, you can use this natural process to your advantage. Information is linked together according to an endless number of commonalties and stored in the brain according to these associations. When learning new words, utilize the knowledge base already contained in your memory and tie the new words with an existing similar word or category. Make a mental note under which heading this information is stored. Think about your thinking and use your mind's natural processes to your advantage.

19. **Creativity and flexibility:** Always ask yourself a simple question: "What is another way I can look at this situation?" Rigid thinking is often a precursor to poor memory. Examine the problem at hand. Turn it over and look at it from all angles. Put it down and do the same later. Examining things from different perspectives forms more reliable memory associations. Creativity and flexibility also allow you to find more ways to access the information to be recalled.

20. **Focus on your strengths:** Many of us learn better if we first view the whole concept; others do better by first learning the individual parts. Recognize your preference and start there. Use the strengths that you have identified through using this book and incorporate the mnemonics into your repertoire. Keep what has worked for you in the past and lose what no longer works. Review portions of this book occasionally to try on new memory techniques. Think positive, be creative, and challenge yourself in new ways.

✎ ✗ *Exercise: Crossword*

Let's have fun with another review, this time in the form of a crossword puzzle. Answers appear in the "Glossary of Terms" and in appendix E.

Down

1. Third phase of memory-training model which enhances encoding of information
2. Outer layer of the brain
3. A quantity measured in terms of another measured quantity
4. Mnemonic technique to remember to keep an open mind
5. Random-access memory
6. Name for not being able to remember a word
10. Term for discrimination based on age
11. Method of _____
12. Things you should always attend to when meeting people
14. Discarded clothing
15. Opposite of stop
16. Spanish for "is"
17. Read only memory
19. Organs for vision
20. Organ for hearing
22. Localized place to put important objects; memory _____
23. Short for network
26. Word suffix meaning condition or quality
28. A wrongful act, damage, or injury done willfully
29. Mnemonic technique to remember steps for enhancing memory
32. Magnetic resonance imaging
34. _____ , ego, and superego
37. Word used to indicate an alternative; this _____ that
38. Abbreviation for computed tomography
39. Symbol for Xenon
40. Opposite of beginning
42. Nutrients given intravenously or Roman numeral four
43. Repetitive, sudden, transient, and stereotyped movements, with limited distribution
45. A slender, bristle-like terminal process, as those found at the tips of the spikelets in many grasses
46. Human ant or wife of uncle
50. A dehiscent seed vessel or fruit of a leguminous plant (pea)
51. Abbreviation for Huntington's disease

54. The letter "n" or a space equal to half the width of an em in printed matter

56. To convert hide into leather or yellowish brown color

57. Unit of electrical resistance equal to current of one volt across terminals of a conductor

58. Oldest and most dangerous class of antidepressants due to its many interactions with foods (red wine, cheese)

59. An indefinitely long time period

Across

1. First step in our memory design that allows us to prepare our senses for reception of information

2. A mnemonic technique where several pieces of related information is placed in a central concept for ease in remembering; often used in remembering phone numbers

4. To sketch

9. Past tense of run

7. Another name for working memory

8. Final stage of memory program that adds richness to sensory experience

10. Most important concept involved in encoding and therefore memory

13. Modern carriage

16. _____ , id, and superego

18. Specific "techniques" and tips used to improve memory functioning

21. Impairment in speech production or reception

24. To consume

25. To put forth effort

27. An adult castrated bull

30. _____ West

31. Internal Revenue Service

32. _____ West again

33. First person singular or present indicative of be

35. *Physician's Desk Reference* (short name)

36. Also

41. One who inherits the estate of another

44. Abbreviation for Alzheimer's disease

47. Natural ability to know or perceive

48. Ralph Crandon's best pal, _____ Norton

49. Collection of Old Norse poems called the Elder or Poetic _____ , assembled in the early 13th century

52. Abbreviation for guided affective imagery

53. Money received for exchange of labor or goods during a specific time period

55. Prefix of: word indicating a disease that usually ends in death or either end of a transportation line

60. Vietnamese unit of weight

61. To form a mental image or picture of

At this point, you've read many pages and reviewed a lot of information on your memory. You've done a lot of work and have challenged many beliefs. But what should you do with all this work? Will it become an inseparable part of your life, or will it just collect dust in some dark corridor of your mental garage? Your continued effort will be necessary to make RARE–DREAM part of your daily life. Continue to use what you have learned to help you remember. Challenge yourself to learn new ways of remembering by trying new techniques based on premises within the book. Use this book as a springboard, a primer on how to be a master of your memory. Continue your spring cleaning and discard the junk that's cluttering your memory.

Edgar's Garage One Last Time

Edgar's garage was filled with junk during spring cleaning. We had you bend your memory around all his junk multiple times in this workbook. As they say, one man's junk is another man's treasure. We hope that Edgar's garage served as a barometer for the growth of your memory. Let's take one last visit to Edgar's garage in order to integrate all the principles of the RARE–DREAM memory design. One last time, relish the items in Edgar's garage and absorb the words "relax," "attend," "rehearse," "envision," and continue to "develop" "rational" and "emotionally" "adaptive" "mindsets."

After years of meandering and broken promises, the day came when Edgar finally decided to clean out his garage. It had not been exhaustively cleaned for over twenty years. It was filled with toys, tools, and just plain junk. Even a couple of old garbage bags didn't make it out to the curb one Tuesday night long ago. As he weeded through the piles of memories, the first thing he decided to throw out was a box of old broken watches that had been collecting dust for years. After that he threw out some old lamps that were the cornerstone of his first apartment. He found an old radio that he decided to throw out, along with a stack of newspapers that had accumulated over the years. He then found a pile of books. One of the books was *Moby-Dick*, the first book he had ever fallen in love with. As a boy he fantasized about battling the huge white whale. Edgar believed that in some way his love for *Moby-Dick* had a large impact on his decision to join the Navy.

He then found some old hubcaps and gently placed them in the garbage pile. He found an old pile of records, including an old Bing Crosby record so warped that it looked like a miniature mountain range. Poor Bing, all warped and scratched, he thought to himself. He then threw out a small and unusable barbecue grill that had deteriorated over the years. Some old phone books saved for no apparent reason, directly into the trash. His eyes lit up when he uncovered an old glass bottle he had found on the beach years ago. He picked up the bottle, and running his hand across it, he noted the cold feel of the glass on his skin. He enjoyed the smoothness of the feel. He felt that he could still smell a hint of saltwater and the coarse feel of sand on the bottle. He decided to keep this bottle. He found the power drill he thought he had lost years ago underneath a dusty table.

He found an old unopened can of Spam luncheon meat that had somehow found its way into the garage. He thought to himself that this would go well with a couple of fried eggs and buttered toast.

He found an old hammer that he put into his toolbox. He then came across a model of Apollo 13 that he had given to his son on the hot summer in 1969 that Neil Armstrong had spoke those famous words, "One small step for man, one giant leap for mankind." He also found a wooden baseball bat that felt heavy in his hands. He swung the bat into his left hand and felt the sharp sting of the heavy, smooth, and refined wood in his hand. He could still hear the crack of this bat, harkening back to his son's Little League days. He then turned to the first dress that he ever wore. It was a beautiful pink silk dress that fit him perfectly. It was backless and it really turned heads when he would go shopping in it. He smiled as he gently placed it in the garbage bag. He threw away an old television set that he never got around to fixing. He decided to keep an old checkers game with all the pieces still intact. He decided to quit for the day and engage his wife in a sporting game of checkers.

✐ ✗ Exercise: What Kind of Treasures Do You Remember?

Every piece of Edgar's junk that you remember becomes a treasure. Give it your best shot.

1. _____
2. _____
3. _____
4. _____
5. _____
6. _____
7. _____
8. _____
9. _____
10. _____
11. _____
12. _____
13. _____
14. _____
15. _____
16. _____
17. _____
18. _____
19. _____
20. _____

Congratulations to those of you who got them all correct. Bigger congratulations to those of you who didn't get them all correct yet maintained a positive mindset.

We hope that you've found this book both helpful and enjoyable. Remember what Mrs. Franklin said in the beginning of the book. Take the time to enjoy the small things. Remember, "Each of us is put here on earth to learn, share, love, appreciate, and give of ourselves. None of us knows when this fantastic experience will end. It can be taken away at any moment. Perhaps this is God's way of telling us that we must make the most out of every single day. So we would like you all to make us a promise. From now on . . . find something beautiful to notice."

One last note; we need to change a word in our acronym. The "D" for "develop" no longer applies. You have already developed a rational and emotionally adaptive mindset. Now you can change your D into "durable" and continue to maintain a durable, rational, emotionally adaptive mindset!

Appendix A

Glossary of Terms Related to Memory and Health Care

Abstraction: Considered higher-order functioning. Ability to draw parallels of an unrelated concept to a specific situation or idea.

Acalculia: Disturbance in the ability to perform simple or complex arithmetic problems.

ACE Inhibitor: Angitensin Converting Enzyme Inhibitor. Drugs used mainly for the treatment of heart disease and high blood pressure.

Acetylcholine: Neurotransmitter within the body believed to be involved in memory functioning.

Acquisition: The process by which the brain develops a code after exposure to information to be remembered. This becomes a record of the experience.

Acuity: Sharpness of a stimulus.

Acute: The sudden onset of a crucial disease process.

Adiadokokinesia: Inability to stop a motor movement and initiate a movement in the opposite direction.

Affect: The observable mood or emotional state of an individual.

Ageism: Term used to describe the overt and covert discrimination of the elderly.

Agnosia: Inability to recognize various objects by perception of the senses.

Agrammatism: Inability to arrange words in grammatical sequence or to form an intelligible sentence.

Agraphia/Dysgraphia: Disturbance in writing intelligible words.

Ahylognosia: The inability to differentiate qualities of materials such as weight or texture.

Akathisia: Restless leg syndrome.

Akinesia: Partial loss or reduction of voluntary movement.

Alexia/Dyslexia: Reading impairment.

Alexithymia: Inability to identify or describe feelings.

Alternating attention (Attention switching): The ability to switch from one stimulus to another.

Ambivalence: Refers to the coexistence of polarized or opposite feelings toward a situation or object. Involves the use of the unconscious to hold the conflicting emotion temporarily at bay. Dynamic psychotherapeutic models view this as a potential cause of anxiety and internal conflict.

Amnesia: Loss of memory about the events within a distinct period of time.

Amusia: Defect in the perception of music.

Analgesic: Pain medication.

Anemia: Condition caused by decreased red blood cell count.

Aneurysm: A deformity in the wall of an artery that can result in a hemorrhage.

Anomia: Difficulty in finding the correct word for a person, place, or thing.

Anosmia: Loss of the ability to smell.

Anosodiaphoria: An unconcern for one's paralysis.

Anosognosia: A severe neglect in which the person fails to recognize his deficit.

Anoxia: Lack of oxygen to the brain resulting in cell damage.

Anterograde amnesia: Difficulty in learning new information and in consolidating information about continuing events.

Anticholinergic: Medications used to block the activity of acetylcholine. Acetylcholine is responsible for many activities within the nervous system and is one of the key neurotransmitters involved in memory. Side effects of anticholinergics often involve short-term memory deficits and confusion.

Anticoagulation: Thinning of the blood. Preventing blood clots from forming by slowing down the clotting process. Coumadin and heparin are two common drugs used as blood thinners.

Anticonvulsant: Medication used to reduce the possibility of a seizure. Common anticonvulsants include: Tegretol, Dilantin, Mysoline, and phenobarbital.

Antidepressant (Thymoleptic): Medications used to treat the symptoms of depression. Three major classifications include:

1. *Tricyclics (TCA):* including (a) tertiary amines: amitriptyline, doxepin, imipramine, (b) secondary amines: nortriptyline, protriptyline, desipramine.

2. *Monoamine Oxidase Inhibitors (MAO's):* including isocarboxazid, phenelzine, tranylcypromine.

3. *Selective Serotonin Reuptake Inhibitors (SSRI's):* including Prozac, Zoloft, Paxil.

There is also another classification of antidepressants that fall into the broad heading of atypical.

Antiparkinson drugs: Drug used to treat the symptoms of Parkinson's disease.

Apallic Syndrome: Disease process marked by diffuse bilateral degeneration of the cerebral cortex with spared subcortical function.

Apathy: Disinterested and unconcerned attitude often seen in dementia and depression.

Aphasia/Dysphasia: Inability to use language to communicate and/or comprehend due to brain cell damage. Impairment in speech. Dysphasia is a milder form of aphasia. Receptive aphasia is impairment in the comprehension of speech. Expressive aphasia is difficulty in verbally expressing oneself.

Aphasia: expressive: Inability to express oneself verbally, while knowing what one wants to communicate.

Aphasia: fluent: Use of language at a normal rate of speed that has limited meaning.

Aphasia: global: Limited or no ability to comprehend or produce communication.

Aphasia: nonfluent: Mostly intact comprehension marked by poor expressive ability. Usually characterized by broken speech and impoverished articulation.

Aphasia: receptive: Difficulty grasping what others express.

Aphemia: Solitary loss of articulation or ability to express oneself in speech while maintaining ability to write or understand spoken language (expressive aphasia).

Apractognosia: Disorder that consists of several apraxic and agnostic syndromes stemming from an impairment of spatial perception.

Apraxia: Inability to perform single intentional motor movements that is not due to the loss of co-ordination, motor control, or sensation. Dyspraxia refers to limited ability to carry out movement.

Apraxia: constructional: Inability to reproduce geometrical shapes or assemble simple puzzles.

Apraxia: ideomotor: Inability to perform intentional motor movement due to a breakdown in the ability to coordinate instructions from previous movements.

Arousal: State of alertness governed by the reticular activating system. The reticular activating system is located in the brain stem and extends from the medulla to the thalamus.

Art therapy: Development of motors skills, creativity, perceptual abilities, and self-esteem through artwork.

Articulation: Use of the lips, tongue, teeth, and palate to form words.

Aspiration: Food or fluid in the lungs.

Associated reaction: The secondary unintentional movement that follows another intentional movement.

Association: Your mind stores memory in a series of associations that are tied together in a logical manner. Association serves as a trigger that stimulates the retrieval of the specific memory needed. Association can be used as a tool in both recall and encoding.

Astereognosia (Tactile Agnosia): Inability to recognize objects through the sense of touch.

Asymbolia: Inability to use or comprehend words, gestures and/or other types of symbols.

Ataxia: Uncoordinated voluntary muscle movements due to damage within the cerebellum or basal ganglia. Other movement disorders are usually ruled out before this diagnosis is given.

Atrophy: A wasting away of a portion of the body (for instance, muscles, organs) due to inactivity, lack of nutrition, or nerve damage.

Attention: Purposeful focus of sensory system(s) toward a stimulus.

Attention: alternating: Purposeful focus of attention from one stimulus to another.

Attention span: The amount of time one is able to focus attention.

Attention-sustained: Continual focus of attention on one stimulus; concentration.

Attentional capacity: The ability to focus and control attention.

Auditory agnosia: Inability to recognize differences in sound that is not due to a hearing impairment.

Autotopagnosia: Impairment in the recognition of body parts. A defect in the comprehension of body scheme.

Awareness: Ability to perceive internal and external stimuli.

Balance: Ability to maintain upright position through continual adjustment of movement and equilibrium signals.

Barbiturate: A medication that causes a hypnotic state or state of drowsiness. Can have effects on memory functioning.

Belief system: Internalized views of self, others, and the environment. Consists of feelings, thoughts, and behaviors.

Benzodiazepines: Class of medications used for the treatment of seizures and anxiety. Side effects include depression, confusion, memory deficits, and impaired coordination.

Beta-amyloid: Toxic substance found in brain plaques. Usually associated with Alzheimer's disease. It is believed that a defect in the regulating action of some enzymes (lysosomal proteases) may be responsible for the release of beta-amyloid.

Beta-blocker: Heart medication mainly used for the treatment of high blood pressure. The mechanism of action results in dilated blood vessels and slowed heart rate.

Bilateral: Occurring on both sides of the body.

Body image: Internal representation of one's body that focuses more on one's feelings and thoughts of one's body rather than the actual structure.

Body scheme: A postural model of one's body. Believed to be the basis of motor functions as it relates to how one perceives the position of the body and the relationship of body parts.

Bradykinesia: Slowing in the execution of motor movements.

Brain dead: Permanent loss of all levels of brain functioning.

Brain injury: Damage to the brain that results in loss of one or more functions. Classified as mild, moderate, and severe.

Brain injury: acquired: Impairment in cognitive functioning due to the sustainment of head injury.

Brain injury: closed: Tissue damage within the brain resulting from the collision of the head with another object.

Brain injury: penetrating: Impairment in brain functioning due to direct damage of brain tissue from an object.

Brain injury: traumatic: Damage to brain tissue due to an incident of injury.

Brain plasticity: The ability of the undamaged portion of the brain to assume functions of the damaged portion.

Brain scan: Imaging of the brain after injection of a radioactive dye.

Bronchodilator: Medication that opens the bronchial tubes of the lungs.

Calcium channel blocker: Medication used in the treatment of high blood pressure.

Cerebral angiography: Medical procedure where dye is injected into an artery so that the vascular system can be examined through X-ray.

Cerebral compression: The compression of brain tissue due to swelling, hematoma, tumor, or aneurysm.

Cerebral hemorrhage: Massive bleeding into the brain.

Cerebral infarct: Death of a region of the brain due to significantly diminished blood supply.

Cerebral spinal fluid: Fluid within the CNS.

Cerebral vascular accident (CVA): Commonly referred to as stroke. Destruction of brain tissue due to a lack of blood flow due to bleeding or blockage.

Cholesterol: Fatty substance found throughout the body. Sustained high levels result in hardening of the arteries and other cardiovascular diseases and subsequent memory deficits.

Chorea (Choreiform movements): Asynchronous, irregular movements that appear to proceed semipurposively from one part of the body to another.

Chronic: Disease process of long duration.

Chunking: A mnemonic technique where several pieces of related information are placed in a central concept for ease in remembering.

Cognitive flexibility: The ability to see things from different perspectives and to remain flexible in thinking.

Cognitive theory of memory: Surmises memory functioning to be like a computer. The mind accepts input through perception, stores it in memory, processes it through thought, and acts on it in reaching decisions.

Cogwheel rigidity: Continual rhythmical interruption of passive movement, slight catch with each movement.

Color agnosia: Inability to recognize differences in color.

Competence: mental: Refers to an individual's ability to handle personal affairs. Having adequate mental abilities for daily functioning.

Congestive heart failure: Inadequate pumping of the heart resulting in fluid accumulation in body tissues.

Copy theory: One of the oldest known theories pertaining to memory which dates back to ancient Greek philosophers. We perceive an object, which creates a mental copy in our minds.

Connectionism: Belief that theories of the mind and memory should be based on the study of the brain's actual functioning.

Constructional apraxia: Inability to copy designs in two or three dimensions.

Cortex: Outer layer of the brain. Alzheimer's disease usually affects the cortex.

Corticosteroids: Medications used for their anti-inflammatory property.

Circumlocution: Use of another word or phrase in place of a word that cannot be remembered.

Clonus: Series of rhythmic jerks following the stretching of a muscle.

Declarative memory: Portion of long-term memory that stores factual information.

Delayed recall: The ability to remember information after a sustained period of time.

Delirium: Sudden onset of symptoms that include confusion, fluctuating levels of consciousness, and disorientation. Delirium is often reversible.

Delusions: Firmly held false beliefs despite evidence to the contrary.

Dementia: A cognitive impairment or loss of mental ability, particularly related to deficits in memory. Also includes impairment in speech, judgment, thought, and personality changes. A classification for as many as sixty etiologies.

Demyelination: The loss of the protective coating (myelin) on nerve fibers that act to speed up nerve impulses.

Depth of processing model of memory: Concept supported by Craik and Lockhart (1972). This concept purports that effective memory is contingent upon the kinds of operations carried out while encoding information, and that retention is determined by the characteristics that are emphasized during the initial encoding process. According to this model, information that is encoded in a more personally meaningful way is more likely to be recalled.

Diabetes mellitus: Disease in which the pancreas is unable to produce insulin resulting in the improper processing of sugar. Can lead to memory deficits among other medical complications.

Distractibility: Difficulty in sustaining attention due to the interference of another stimulus.

Diuretic: Commonly referred to as a water pill. Medication that assists the kidneys in ridding the body of salt and water.

Divided attention: The ability to perform or attend to two different tasks simultaneously.

DREAM: Developing **R**ational and **E**motional **A**daptive **M**indsets.

Dressing Apraxia: Inability to dress oneself due to a disorder in body scheme or motor planning.

Dysarthria: Impairment in speech marked by weakness or slowness of speech musculature.

Dysdiadochokinesia: Impairment of simple alternating movements such as touching fingers and thumb sequentially. Results from damage to the cerebellum.

Dysgraphia: Impaired ability to write. Agraphia is the inability to write.

Edema: Accumulation of fluid in the body that results in swelling.

Elaboration: The level of processing involved with learning information.

Electroencephalography (EEG): Measure of electrical activity of the brain taken from surface electrodes on the scalp.

Embolism: A clot or other obstruction that is carried from a larger vessel into a smaller one. It obstructs the circulation of blood and results in damaged brain tissue. A thrombosis is a formed clot that remains at the point at which it formed.

Emphysema: Swelling of the alveoli in the lungs resulting in difficulty in breathing.

Encoding: Process of learning.

Envision: Principle that guides the teaching of visual imagery. Relates to the process of elaboration during encoding. It incorporates all of the senses, not just vision.

Enzyme: Chemical within the body that acts to speed up other chemical reactions.

Episodic memory: Information about particular memories associated with the time and place that you learned the information. Traumatic memories are stored in this form.

Essential tremor: Tremor that is inherited and usually postural in nature.

Etiology: Cause of a disease or condition.

Explicit memory: Conscious retrieval of memory resulting in recollection of data from the past.

Figure ground: Refers to the foreground and the background. Impairment entails the inability to distinguish the two.

Finger agnosia: One's inability to distinguish one's own fingers.

Form constancy: Ability to attend to subtle variations in form.

Generalization: The ability to transfer knowledge learned in one context to other contexts.

Gerstmann syndrome: Syndrome derived from a lesion in the dominant hemisphere that includes dysgraphia, finger agnosia, right/left discrimination, and dyscalculia.

Glaucoma: Visual degenerative disease whereby abnormally high pressure builds up inside the eyes. Results in permanent impairment if not treated.

Guided affective imagery: A waking dream technique in psychotherapy, used in brief therapy and group therapy.

Heart block: Disease where the heart's electrical conduction system becomes disrupted resulting in abnormal heartbeat.

Hemianopsia: Visual field deficits that involve blindness in one half of the visual field.

Hemiparesis (Hemiplegia): Paralysis of one side of the body.

Histamine: Chemical within the body associated with allergic reactions. Produces many changes within the body including: decreased blood pressure, increased secretions from salivary glands and stomach, dilation of small blood vessels, swelling, and itching. Histamine blockers are a group of medications used primarily to treat allergic reactions. They have also been studied for the treatment of Alzheimer's disease.

Homonymous hemianopsia: Blindness in right or left visual field in both eyes.

Hormone: Chemical produced within a gland that travels within the bloodstream to affect another part of the body.

Hygiene: The science, conditions, and practices that serve to promote or preserve health.

Hypertension: High blood pressure.

Hypokinesia: Slowing in the initiation of movements.

Hypothermia: A condition that results from overexposure to cold temperatures that can result in memory deterioration.

Ideational apraxia: Inability to carry out automatic activities even when the concept of the task is understood.

Ideomotor apraxia: Inability to initiate gestures or perform purposeful motor tasks even though the task is understood.

Implicit memory: Memory that comes to mind or influences one's behavior even though there is no conscious recollection.

Infection: Disease that is the result of a microorganism within the body. Bacterial infections are often treated with antibiotics. Viral infections are not as treatable by medications. Viral infections include: a cold, flu, AIDS.

Insight: Person's awareness of his or her problem.

Interactive imagery: Consists of a mental picture that is vivid and distinctive with at least two objects interconnected in some way.

Lateral: Occurring on one side of the body.

Learning: The ability to change behavior to adapt to the environment. Change in an individual's perceptions due to experience. Closely linked to memory.

Long-term memory: What most people call memory. It is the stored, permanent information that we have committed to memory to be retrieved and used later.

Long-term register: Equivalent to long-term memory. Where information is stored then retrieved, updated, and restored as necessary.

Macrosomatognosia: Perception of one's body as very large due to a disorder in the body scheme.

Metamorphopsia: Visual distortion of objects even though objects are accurately recognized. Often associated with a lesion in the parietal lobe.

Microsomatognosia: Perception of one's body as very small due to a disorder in the body scheme.

Memory: The process of taking information from one's environment through the senses and organizing and storing this information in the form of representations. Also the ability to recall these representations at a later time.

Memory: auditory: The ability to recall a series of number, names, words, etc., presented orally. An individual with an auditory memory impairment may need constant reminders of instructions presented orally.

Memory: delayed: Recall of information after a set delay of time, typically ten minutes or more. Typically tested with an interference presented during the waiting period to prevent rehearsal.

Memory: episodic: Memory of events in a person's life. Typically stored and recalled according to time. Usually more vulnerable to injury than semantic memory probably due to minimal opportunities for rehearsal.

Memory: fund of information: An estimation of the amount of information that an individual retains about their past.

Memory: immediate: The ability to recall information immediately after presentation. Tied directly to attention.

Memory: long-term: Refers to the ability to recall information thirty minutes or more after presentation. Requires storage and retrieval of information.

Memory: remote: Information that a person is able to recall about the past. When referring to injury, it usually refers to information that the individual can recall prior to injury. Information from delayed memory becomes remote memory after several months.

Memory: semantic: Learned factual information usually encoded through repetition.

Memory: short-term: Also referred to as working memory. Amount of limited information that an individual can hold in conscious awareness. Usually limited to several minutes and seven to nine bits of information.

Memory spot: Central location to place daily used items such as keys, wallet, etc.

Memory: visual: The ability to store and recall pictures, figures, and text via the input of information through visuo-perceptual channels. Information may be encoded using auditory or visual representations independent of the mode of presentation.

Mental capacity: Amount of information that an individual can process in a given period of time.

Mental disability: A general concept referring to a disabling mental condition due to injury, illness, severe emotional disorder, or mental retardation.

Metamemory: Pertains to self-knowledge and self-perceptions about memory.

Method of loci technique: Consists of remembering things by visually placing what you want to remember in set places that are familiar to you.

Mnemonic: Specific techniques and tips used to improve memory functioning.

Motor apraxia: Loss of motor memory patterns resulting in loss of purposeful movement.

Movement tremor: Tremor that occurs during purposeful movement. If it occurs during the initiation of movement it is referred to as an *initial tremor*. If the tremor occurs during the movement it is referred to as a *transitional tremor*. If the tremor occurs during the end of a movement it is referred to as *terminal tremor*.

Multi-infarct dementia: Dementia caused by a series of strokes.

Myasthenia gravis: Chronic condition that often ends in general weakness and paralysis.

Myoclonus: Brief repetitive muscle contractions stemming from the CNS.

Narcotic: Addictive medication used for the treatment of pain. Side effects include cognitive slowing and memory impairment.

Nativism: Originated with Plato. Belief that knowledge is innate and present at birth. Opposite of the tabula rasa belief that we are born as "blank slates" and knowledge is accumulated throughout our life span.

Nervous system: Includes the brain, spinal cord, and nerves in the body.

Neurological imaging: Techniques used to obtain images of the brain and spinal cord. Two most common procedures are computed tomography (CT) and magnetic resonance imaging (MRI). Others include: single photon emission computed tomography (SPECT) and positron emission tomography (PET).

Neurotransmitters: Chemical substances in the brain that conduct electrical impulses from one cell to another.

New Agers: Term given to older adults who are currently defining new roles for the aged.

Nonsteroidal anti-inflammatory drugs (NSAID): Class of medications that include aspirin and ibuprofen used to treat pain and swelling. Currently being studied for the treatment and management of progressive dementias such as Alzheimer's disease.

Oculomotor deficits: Defect in the voluntary movement of the eyes or in the ability to gaze from side to side or upward and downward.

Paralalia: A speech deficit. Usually involves the production of a sound different than the one desired.

Paraphasia: Replacement of one word for another because the desired word cannot be remembered.

Parkinson's disease: Progressive nervous system disorder that results in uncoordinated motor movements, tremors, lack of facial expression, rigidity of muscles, and difficulty walking. Parkinson's disease is different from parkinsonism, which results in only a portion of the above symptoms and is often caused by the side effects of medications or drugs.

Perception: Ability to accurately interpret internal and external sensory information.

Pica: Eating nonfood substances. Often seen in later stages of dementia.

Planotopokinesia: Disorganization of discriminative spatial judgment.

Prosopagnosia: Inability to recognize faces and distinguish differences in faces.

Postural abnormalities: Stooped posture, stiffness.

PQRST: Stands for "preview," "question," "read," "summarize," and "test." Used as a way to rehearse and organize information and enhance attention skills (Sandman 1993).

Preparatory set: A mental warm-up, preparing yourself and your mind for the specific abilities needed in an upcoming situation. Mentally rehearsing in your head all the activities, demands, and potential difficulties that may occur in an impending situation.

Preparatory review: The act of taking a step back from a demanding task in order to review and adjust your performance. It's much the same as a preparatory set, except you're taking the time to do it after you've already started a task. It's a mental pit stop. It helps prevent confusion and frustration.

Procedural memory: Portion of long-term memory that stores information on how to do something.

Pseudo dementia: Dementia symptoms that are caused by the onset of depression and which are almost always reversible.

Psychosis: Mental illness in which the person suffers from disordered thinking, bizarre behavior, hallucinations, illusions, and/or delusions.

RARE: **R**elaxation, **A**ttention, **R**ehearsal, and visual imagery (**E**nvision).

Recall: Ability to retrieve information previously stored in memory.

Recognition: Ability to retrieve information previously stored in memory with the aid of a reminder.

Rehearsal: Viewed as a method to sustain information in the working memory long enough for the information to be encoded. Process of repeating information to be remembered.

Resting tremor: Tremor involving several muscle groups that is apparent during rest but tends to disappear during purposeful movement.

Retention: The capacity to remember. Rehearsal is one of the most important factors involved in retaining the information that we have been exposed to.

Retrieval: Obtaining information that has been stored in long-term memory. Once the information is successfully stored, it must be retrievable in order to be useful. For information to be retrieved it first must be stored effectively. Retrieval cues and reminders can help in this process.

Retropulsion: Tendency to fall backwards when walking.

Search: The ability to find a particular stimulus within the context of similar stimuli.

Secondary memory: Memory that was recently converted to long-term memory.

Selective attention: The ability to attend to one stimulus while blocking out another.

Semantic memory: All the general information that we have accumulated in our long-term memories. Semantic memory can be further broken down into declarative memory and procedural memory. Declarative memory stores information about facts (like who, what, when, where). Procedural memory stores information on how to do something (e.g., how to change the spark plugs in your car).

Sensory filters: Interface between senses and memory. Point at which information is taken from the environment through sight, smell, taste, touch, or sound.

Serotonin: Neurotransmitter in the body and the brain that is believed to be partially responsible for the regulation of mood.

Schizophrenia: Mental disorder that results in psychosis, delusions, hallucinations, and a general breakdown in reality perception.

Short-term memory store: Interface between sensory filters and long-term memory. Enables one to encode the information whereupon it is stored in the long-term register.

Somatic complaints: Physical symptoms such as headache, gastrointestinal discomfort, pains, and dizziness that may be attributable to emotional discomfort.

Somatotopagnosia: Unawareness of body structure and failure to recognize parts of the body and their relationship to each other.

Statins: Class of medications used to treat high cholesterol. These include: Mevacor, Lescol, and Zocor. These medications have been identified as possibly causing memory impairment.

Subcortical dementia: Dementia that is caused by abnormalities in the brain below the cortex. Alzheimer's disease is usually associated with the cortex. Parkinson's disease is usually subcortical. Symptoms included in subcortical dementias are: movement disorders, cognitive slowing, executive dysfunction, memory impairment, mood and personality changes.

Sun downing: Increased agitation and disruptive behaviors in dementia patients during the evening and early night.

Sustained attention (concentration): The application of mental effort in a purposeful, sustained manner.

Syncope: Fainting spells usually caused by transient cerebral ischemia due to circulatory insufficiency to the brain.

Systemic lupus erythematosus (SLE): Commonly referred to as lupus. Chronic, progressive disease marked by disruptions to multiple organs and blood vessels, skin irritation, and arthritis. Often results in intermittent impaired cognitive functioning.

Tactile agnosia: Inability to recognize objects by touch even though peripheral sensory nerves remain intact.

Tardive dyskinesia: Condition usually caused by the long-term side effects of antipsychotic medications that results in continued involuntary movements of the mouth, tongue, and other muscle groups within the body.

Tertiary memory: Long-term memory of the distant past. This memory is the last to be affected by Alzheimer's disease and is rarely affected by depression.

Thyroid: Large gland in the neck that serves to regulate body growth through secretion of thyroxine. Thyroid disorders can result in hyperthyroidism or hypothyroidism and can result in disturbances in mood and memory, among other disorders.

Tic: Repetitive, sudden, transient, and stereotyped movements with a limited distribution. Prolonged tics are referred to as "dystonic."

Transient ischemic attacks: Often referred to as "mini-strokes." Usually of rapid onset and brief duration. Due to temporary insufficient blood supply to the brain.

Tremor: Rhythmic and repetitive movements of a body part. Resting tremor is one occurring at rest; action (kinetic or intention) tremor occurs during movement; postural tremor is observed when the affected body part is voluntarily held against gravity.

Unilateral body agnosia: Neglect of the left side of the body.

Unilateral neglect: Inability to integrate or use sensory information from the left side of the body.

Unilateral spatial agnosia: Neglect of the left side of visual space.

Verbal apraxia: Difficulty in forming and organizing intelligible words although the musculature structure within the face and head remains intact.

Vigilance: The ability to detect rarely occurring signals over a prolonged period of time.

Visual objective agnosia: Inability to recognize objects.

Visual spatial agnosia: Deficit in perceiving spatial relations between objects or in relation to self.

Working memory: Contains all that we are conscious of and working on right now. Other terms associated with working memory include: immediate, active, or primary memory.

$\mathbf{A}_{\textbf{ppendix}}$ B

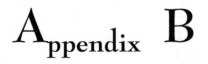

Memory Journal

Name _____ Date _____

Memory Event _____

_____

_____

Self-Talk (Thoughts) _____

_____

_____

_____

Feelings _____

_____

_____

_____

Additional Notes: _____

_____

_____

_____

Memory Journal

Name _____ Date _____

Memory Event _____

_____

_____

Self-Talk (Thoughts) _____

_____

_____

_____

Feelings _____

_____

_____

_____

Additional Notes: _____

_____

_____

_____

Memory Journal

Name _____ Date _____

Memory Event _____

_____

_____

Self-Talk (Thoughts) _____

_____

_____

_____

Feelings _____

_____

_____

_____

Additional Notes: _____

_____

_____

_____

Memory Journal

Name _____ Date _____

Memory Event _____

_____

_____

Self-Talk (Thoughts) _____

_____

_____

_____

Feelings _____

_____

_____

_____

Additional Notes: _____

_____

_____

_____

Memory Journal

Name _____ Date _____

Memory Event _____

_____

_____

Self-Talk (Thoughts) _____

_____

_____

_____

Feelings _____

_____

_____

_____

Additional Notes: _____

_____

_____

_____

Memory Journal

Name _____ Date _____

Memory Event _____

_____

_____

Self-Talk (Thoughts) _____

_____

_____

_____

Feelings _____

_____

_____

_____

Additional Notes: _____

_____

_____

_____

Memory Journal

Name _____ Date _____

Memory Event _____

_____

_____

Self-Talk (Thoughts) _____

_____

_____

_____

Feelings _____

_____

_____

_____

Additional Notes: _____

_____

_____

_____

Appendix C

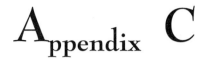

Resources for New Agers

For many of the resources listed it may be necessary to consult your phone directory for the office nearest you.

AAN Education and Research Foundation—(800) 879-1960, www.aan.com

Agency for Healthcare Administration—(800) 342-0828. Publishes information on nursing homes.

AGS Foundation for Health and Aging—(212) 755-6810, www.healthinaging.org

Alzheimer's Association, Inc.—National and local chapters. National number is (800) 272-3900, www.alz.org

Alzheimer's Disease Education and Referral Center (ADEAR)—(800) 438-4380. Contains a database available to the public on the latest advances in medications in treating the disease: www.alzheimers.org.

Alzheimer's Foundation—(918) 481-6031

Alzheimer Resource Centers—Consult your local phone directory.

American Academy of Neurology—(612) 695-2791, (800) 879-1960, www.aan.com

American Academy of Physical Medicine & Rehabilitation—(800) 825-6582, www.aapmr.org

American Association of Electrodiagnostic Medicine—(507) 288-0100, www.aaem.net

American Association of Neuroscience Nurses—(888) 557-2266, www.aann.org

American Association of Retired Persons (AARP)—Consult your local phone directory. Provides a wide range of services including legal and financial advisement.

American Association of Retired Persons (AARP) Andrus Foundation—(800) 775-6776, www.andrus.org

American College of Emergency Physicians—(800) 798-1822, www.acep.org

American Council for Headache Education—(800) 255-ACHE, www.achenet.org

American Epilepsy Society—(860) 586-7505, www.aesnet.org

American Headache Society—(856) 423-0043, www.ahsnet.org

American Heart Association—(800) 242-8721

American Neurological Association—(612) 545-6284, www.aneuroa.org

American Occupational Therapy Association—(301) 652-2682

American Osteopathic Association—(800) 621-1773, www.aoa-net.org

American Parkinson Disease Association, Inc.—(800) 223-2732, (718) 981-8001, www.apdaparkinson.com

American Red Cross—Consult your local phone directory for local office.

American Society of Neuroimaging—(612) 545-6291, www.asnweb.org

American Society of Neurorehabilitation—(612) 545-6324, www.asnr.com

American Stroke Association (Division of the American Heart Association)—(888) 478-7653, www.StrokeAssociation.org

The Amyotrophic Lateral Sclerosis Association (ALS)—(800) 782-4747

Area Agency on Aging—Consult your local phone directory.

Association of University Professors of Neurology—(612) 545-6724, www.aupn.org

Brain Injury Association—(800) 444-6443, www.biausa.org

Child Neurology Society—(651) 486-9447, www.umn.edu

Citizens United for Research in Epilepsy (CURE)—(630) 734-9957, www.cureepilepsy.org

Consortium of Multiple Sclerosis Centers—(877) 700-CMSC, www.mscare.org

Department of Elder Affairs—Check your local phone directory under State Agencies.

Depression Awareness, Recognition, and Treatment—(800) 421-4211

Dystonia Medical Research Foundation—(800) 377-3978, www.dystonia-foundation.org

Easter Seal Society—Consult your local phone directory for local office.

Elder Services Division—City and county-based services for seniors.

Eldercare—Consult directory for location. Eldercare Locator (800) 677-1116.

Epilepsy Foundation of America—(800) EFA-1000, www.EpilepsyFoundation.org.

Hospice—Consult directory for local office. National Hospice (800) 658-8898.

Michael J. Fox Foundation for Parkinson's Research—(800) 780-7644, www.MichaelJFox.org

Movement Disorder Society—(414) 276-2145, www.movementdisorders.org

Multiple Sclerosis Association of America—(800) 833-4MSA, (800) 532-7667, www.msaa.com

Muscular Dystrophy Association—(602) 529-2000, (800) 572-1717, www.mdausa.org

National Brain Tumor Foundation—(800) 934-CURE, www.braintumor.org

National Chronic Care Consortium—(952) 814-2652, www.nccconline.org

National Council on Aging—(800) 424-9046

National Family Caregivers Association—(800) 896-3650, www.nfcacares.org

National Headache Foundation—(888) 643-5552, www.headaches.org

National Institute on Aging—(800) 222-2225, (301) 496-1752

National Institute on Health—(301) 496-4000

National Institute of Neurological Disorders and Stroke—(800) 352-9424, www.ninds.nih.gov

National Multiple Sclerosis Society—(800) FIGHT-MS, www.nmss.org

National Organization for Rare Disorders (NORD)—(800) 999-6673, www.rarediseases.org

National Parkinson Foundation, Inc.—(800) 327-4545, www.parkinson.org

National Stroke Association—(800) STROKES (787-6537), www.stroke.org

Paralyzed Veterans of America—(800) 424-8200, www.pva.org

Parkinson's Action Network—(800) 850-4726

Parkinson's Disease Foundation—(212) 923-4700, (800) 457-6676, www.pdf.org

The Parkinson's Institute—(800) 786-2978

Respite Care—Consult your local phone directory. Provides assistance with health care.

Senior Centers—Consult your local phone directory.

Social Security Administration—Medicare and Medicaid. (800) 772-1213.

Society for Neuroscience—(202) 462-6688, www.sfn.org

United Parkinson Foundation—(312) 733-1893

United Way—Consult your local phone directory.

U.S. Department of Health and Human Services—(800) 358-9295

Veteran's Administrations—Provides a wide variety of assistance to veterans and their families. Consult your local phone directory.

Visiting Nurse Association—Provides medical assistance. Consult your local phone directory.

WE MOVE (Worldwide Education and Awareness for Movement Disorders—(800) 437-6682, www.wemove.org

Widowed Persons Service—(800) 424-3410

Appendix D

Review of Major Structures of the Brain and Their Functions

This portion of the book is not necessary to read as part of the formal memory-enhancement program presented in this workbook. It is technical in nature and is intended for those more interested in the structures of the brain. It is also intended as a future reference if you find that you need to look up specific information on areas of the brain and how they relate to memory.

Amygdala: Responsible for emotional integration of sensory input and memories.

Basal ganglia: Located deep in the hemispheres. The basal ganglia are made up of the globus pallidus, caudate nucleus, and the amygdala. Forms circuit with the cortex. Important in the regulation of movement and in habit learning. Works closely with frontal lobes.

Brain stem: Connection from spinal cord to lower areas of the brain. Responsible for autonomic functions such as heart rate, blood pressure, etc. Motor and sensory neurons pass through the brain stem.

Broca's area: Located in the left frontal lobe. Involved in the production of fluent speech.

Caudate nucleus: Part of the neostriatum, which is part of basal ganglia. Receives projections from the neocortex and connects through the putamen and globus pallidus to the thalamus and finally to the motor area of the cortex.

Cerebellum: The back portion of the brain that assists in coordinating movement. Damage often results in ataxia.

Cerebrum: Largest part of the brain. Upper portions of the brain believed to be predominately responsible for higher-order functions. Divided into the left and right cerebral hemisphere.

> **Left cerebral hemisphere:** In most people the left cerebral hemisphere is responsible for speech, math, reading, and writing. Damage to the left hemisphere often results in problems with verbal communication and problems with movement on the right side of the body.

> **Right cerebral hemisphere:** In most people the right cerebral hemisphere is responsible for visuospatial skills, direction, attention, and the regulation of emotions. Damage to this area will affect left-sided body movements and visuospatial abilities.

Corpus callosum: Connects the two hemispheres of the brain. Allows for communication between the two hemispheres.

Frontal lobes: Responsible for higher-order functioning (judgment, abstraction, and motivation), production of speech, and has influence on personality. Damage results in difficulty with verbal expression, difficulty concentrating, and lack of emotional control. In the back of the frontal lobes are the motor areas that control voluntary movements. Damage results in contralateral paralysis or paralysis on the opposite side of the body.

Hippocampus: Structure in the brain believed to be responsible for the processing and coordination of memory functioning. It is the end point of the cortex and the ultimate destination of multiple cortical and subcortical processes.

Neurons: Cells in the brain that store and process information.

Neurotransmitters: Chemicals produced by the neurons that carry information from neuron to neuron. Specific neurotransmitters are responsible for specific tasks (for instance, dopamine is responsible for movement).

Occipital lobes: Located in the back of the brain. Responsible for regulation of sight.

Parietal lobes: The front parts (anterior) of the parietal lobes are responsible for tactile discrimination and recognition. The back part (posterior) of the parietal lobe is responsible for attention. The left parietal lobe is responsible for reading, writing, arithmetic, and performance of learned information. Its other function is speech. The right parietal lobe is responsible for the comprehension of visuospatial relationships and understanding facial expressions and tones in speech.

Substantia nigra: Connects basal ganglia to the midbrain. Provides dopamine to the basal ganglia.

Temporal lobes: Important for memory. When information enters the sensory registers it is briefly stored here and then sent to long-term memory or lost. The bottom section (ventral portion) of the temporal lobes regulates the recognition of faces and objects (note that this is a different function than recognizing facial expressions). The left portion of the temporal lobe (lateral) is important for processing auditory information.

Thalamus: Responsible for the relay of sensory information. Coordinates information with the temporal lobes and serves a primary function in memory.

Wernicke's area: Located in the rear of the superior temporal gyrus. Believed to be involved in the comprehension of speech.

Appendix E

Answers to Exercises and Puzzles

Answers are presented in chronological order of appearance in book.

Answers to Edgar and His Garage Quest

1. box of old broken watches
2. old lamps
3. old radio
4. a stack of newspapers
5. a pile of books
6. some old hubcaps
7. an old pile of records
8. a small and unusable barbecue grill
9. some old phone books
10. an old glass bottle
11. power drill
12. an old can of Spam
13. an old hammer
14. an old model of the Apollo 13
15. a wooden baseball bat that felt heavy in his hand
16. an old television set
17. a beautiful pink silk dress
18. an old checkers game

Answer to S Paragraph

Number of S's in paragraph = 28

Answers to Method of Numerical Association

The items were: hangers, computer disks, pencils, starch, magazine, staples, and a new iron.

Answers to Semantic and Episodic Memory Exercise

1. Semantic
2. Episodic
3. Episodic

4. Semantic
5. Semantic
6. Semantic

Answers to Systems of Memory

The five systems of memory are:

1. Working memory
2. Episodic memory
3. Perceptual memory
4. Procedural memory
5. Semantic memory

*Episodic and semantic memory together make up long-term memory

Answer to Verbal Translation of Visual Information

Draw a square. In the upper right corner of the square, draw a circle slightly smaller than the square lying on top of the square. Draw a line that bisects the upper right corner of the square and ends in the center of the circle. The line has an arrow on it at the point that it ends in the circle. Finally draw a small circle inside the square in the lower left corner of the square. Blacken this small circle.

Answer to Visual Translation of Verbal Information

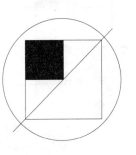

Answers to Recognition of Edgar's Garage Items

1. Yes; 2. No; 3. Yes; 4. No; 5. Yes; 6. No; 7. Yes; 8. Yes; 9. No; 10. No;
11. Yes; 12. No; 13. Yes; 14. No; 15. No; 16. No; 17. Yes; 18. No; 19. Yes; 20. Yes

Answers to Categories of Potentially Reversible Dementia

D rugs and Alcohol toxicity
E ar and eye problems
M etabolic and endocrine abnormalities
E motional Problems
N utritional deficiencies
T raumas or tumors
I nfection processes
A therosclerotic complications

Answers to Reading Comprehension Quiz

1. False; 2. True; 3. True; 4. True; 5. True; 6. False; 7. False; 8. False; 9. False; 10. False; 11. False; 12. True; 13. True; 14. True; 15. True; 16. False; 17. False; 18. True; 19. True; 20. True.

Answers to Crossword Puzzle

References

American Medical Association (AMA) Department of Drugs. *AMA Drug Evaluations Annual.* 1992. Chicago: American Medical Association.

American Psychiatric Association. 1994. *Quick Reference to the Diagnostic Criteria from the Diagnostic and Statistical Manual of Mental Disorders.* 4th ed. Washington DC: American Psychiatric Association.

Andrews, R. 1993. *Columbia Dictionary of Quotations.* New York: Columbia University Press.

Anschutz, L., C. J. Camp, R. P. Markley, and J. J. Kramer. 1987. Remembering mnemonics: A three-year follow-up on the effects of mnemonics training in elderly adults. *Experimental Aging Research* 13:141-143.

Atkinson, R. C., and R. M. Shiffrin. 1968. Human memory: A proposed system and its control processes. In *The Psychology of Learning and Motivation,* vol. 2, edited by K. W. Spence and J. T. Spence. Orlando, FL: Academic Press.

Ayd, F. J. 1995. *Lexicon of Psychiatry, Neurology, and the Neurosciences.* Baltimore: Williams and Wilkins.

Backman, L., and L. G. Nilsson. 1985. Prerequisites for lack of age differences in memory performance. *Experimental Aging Research* 11(2):67-73.

Baddeley, A. D., B. A. Wilson, and F. Watts, eds. 1998. *Handbook of Memory Disorders.* New York: John Wiley and Sons.

Bandura, A. 1989. Regulation of cognitive processes through perceived self-efficacy. *Developmental Psychology* 25:729-735.

Bandura, A. 1986. *Social Foundations of Thought and Action: A Social Cognitive Theory.* Englewood Cliffs, NJ: Prentice Hall.

Bandura, A. 1982. Self-efficacy mechanism in human agency. *American Psychologist* 37:122-147.

Bandura, A. 1977. Self-efficacy: Toward a unifying theory of behavioral change. *Psychological Review* 84:191-215.

Barr, A., R. Benedict, L. Tune, and J. Brandt. 1992. Neuropsychological differentiation of Alzheimer's disease from vascular dementia. *International Journal of Geriatric Neuropsychology* 7:621-627.

Barrett-Connor, E., and D. Kritz-Silverstein. 1993. Estrogen replacement therapy and cognitive function in older women. *JAMA* 269:2637-2641.

Beck, A. T., A. J. Rush, B. F. Shaw, and B. Emery. 1979. *Cognitive Therapy of Depression.* New York: Guilford Press.

Beck, A. T. 1967. *Depression: Clinical, Experimental, and Theoretical Aspects.* New York: Hoeber.

Berkow, R., and A. J. Fletcher, eds. 1992. *The Merck Manual* 16th ed. Rahway, NJ: Merck Research Laboratories.

Best, D. L., K. W. Hamlett, and S. W. Davis. 1992. Memory complaint and memory performance in the elderly: The effects of memory-skills training and expectancy change. *Applied Cognitive Psychology* 6(5):405-416.

Birge, S. J., and K. F. Mortel. 1997. Estrogen and the treatment of Alzheimer's disease. *American Journal of Medicine* 103(3A):36S-45S.

Birge, S. J. 1996. is there a role for estrogen replacement therapy in the prevention and treatment of dementia? *The Journal of American Geriatrics Society* 44(7):865–870.

Breitner, J. C. S., and K. A. Welsh. 1995. An approach to diagnosis and management of memory loss and other cognitive syndromes of aging. *Psychiatric Services: Journal of the American Psychiatric Association* 46:29-35.

Brink, T. L., J. A. Yesavage, O. Lum, P. Heersema, M. B. Adey, and T. L. Rose. 1982. Screening tests for geriatric depression. *Clinical Gerontologist* 1:37-44.

Brookmeyer, R., S. Gray, and C. Kawas. 1998. Projections of Alzheimer's disease in the United States and the public health impact of delaying disease onset. *American Journal of Public Health* 88(9):1337-1342.

Burkhardt, C. R, C. M. Filley, B. K. Kleinschmidt-DeMasters, S. de la Monte, M. D. Norenberg, and S. A. Schneck. 1988. Diffuse lewy body disease and progressive dementia. *Neurology* 38:1520-1528.

Buttini, M., M. Orth, S. Bellosta, H. Akeefe, R. E. Pitas, T. Wyss-Coray, L. Mucke, and R. W. Mahley. 1999. Expression of human apolipoprotein E3 or E4 in the brains of ApoE -/- Mice: Isoform-specific effects on neurodegeneration. *Journal of Neuroscience* 19:4867-4880.

Camp, C. J., J. W. Foss, A. B. Stevens, C. C. Reichard, L.A. McKitrick, and A. M. Hanlon. 1993. Memory training in normal and demented elderly populations: The E-I-E-I-O Model. *Experimental Aging Research* 19:277-290.

Campbell, R. J. 1989. *Psychiatric Dictionary*. New York: Oxford University Press.

Carlson, N. 1994. *Physiology of Behavior*. Needham Heights, MA: Allyn & Bacon.

Carroll, Lewis. 1872. *The Columbia Dictionary of Quotations*. New York: Columbia University Press, 1993.

Cherrier, M., S. Craft, S., Plymate, et al. 1998. Effects of testosterone on cognition in healthy older men. *Endocrinology Abstracts* 98:643.

Cicerone, K. P., and D. E. Tupper. 1990. Neuropsychological rehabilitation: Treatment of errors in everyday functioning. In press. To appear in *Neuropsychology of Everyday Life: Issues in Development and Rehabilitation,* edited by D. E. Tupper and K. P. Cicerone. Boston: Klumer Academic Publishing.

Cooper, J. A., H. J. Sagar, N. Jordan, N. S. Harvey, and E. V. Sullivan. 1991. Cognitive impairment in early untreated Parkinson's disease and its relationship to motor disability. *Brain* 114:2095-2122.

Craik, F. I. M., and J. M. McDowd. 1987. Age differences in recall and recognition. *Journal of Experimental Psychology: Learning, Memory, and Cognition* 13:474-479.

Craik, F. I. M., and R. S. Lockhart. 1972. Levels of processing: A framework for memory research. *Journal of Verbal Learning and Verbal Behavior* 11:671-684.

Crook, T., R. T. Bartus, S. H. Ferris, P. Whitehouse, G. D. Cohen, and S. Gershon. 1986. Age-associated memory impairment: Proposed diagnosis criteria and measures of clinical change. Report of a National Institute of Mental Health work group. *Developmental Neuropsychology* 2:261-276.

Cummings, J. L., H. V. Vinters, G. M. Cole, and Z. S. Khachaturian. 1998. Alzheimer's disease: Etiology, pathophysiology, cognitive reserve, and treatment opportunities. *Neurology: Current Perspectives in Alzheimer's Disease* 51(1):S2-S14.

Dellefield, K. S., and G. J. McDougall. 1996. Increasing metamemory in older adults. *Nursing Research* 45(5):284-290.

Economics and Statistics Administration, U.S. Department of Commerce, U.S. Census Bureau, Population Division. 1995. *Statistical Brief—Sixty-five Plus in the United States.* May.

Ellis, A., and R. Grieger eds. 1977. *Handbook of Rational-Emotive Therapy,* vol. 1. New York: Springer.

Ellis, A. 1970. *The Essence of Rational Psychotherapy: A Comprehensive Approach to Treatment.* New York: Institute for Rational Living.

————. 1962. *Reason and Emotion in Psychotherapy.* New York: Lyle Stuart.

Eslinger, P. J., A. R. Damasio, A. L. Benton, and M. VanAllen. 1985. Neuropsychological detection of abnormal mental decline in older persons. *Journal of the American Medical Association* 253:670-674.

Farlow, M. R., and R. M. Evans. 1998. Pharmacological treatment of cognition in Alzheimer's dementia. *Neurology* 51(1):536-544.

Fischer, E., and J. T. Noland. 1991. *What's So Funny About Getting Old?* Minneapolis: Compcare Publishers.

Folstein, M. F., S. E. Folstein, and P. H. McHugh. 1979. Psychiatric syndromes in Huntington's disease. *Advances in Neurology* 23:281-289.

Folstein, M. F., S. E. Folstein, and P.H. McHugh. 1975. Mini-mental state: A practical method for grading the cognitive state of patients for the clinician. *Journal of Psychiatric Research* 12:189-198.

Frank, J. D. 1985. Therapeutic components shared by all psychotherapies. In *Cognition and Psychotherapy,* edited by M. J. Malony and A. Freeman. New York: Plenum.

Freter, S., H. Bergman, S. Gold, H. Chertkow, and A. M. Clarfield. 1998. Prevalence of potentially reversible dementias and actual reversibility in a memory clinic cohort. *CMAJ* 159(6):657-662.

Gathercole, S. E., and A. D. Baddeley. 1993. *Working Memory and Language.* Hove, England: Erlbaum.

Gearing, M., S. S. Mirra, J. C. Hedreen, S. M. Sumi, L. A. Hansen, and A. Heyman. 1995. Consortium to establish a registry for Alzheimer's disease (CERAD). Part X. Neuropathology confirmation of the clinical diagnosis of Alzheimer's disease. *Neurology* 45:461-466.

Glasgow, R. E., R. A. Zeiss, M. Barrera, and P. M. Lewinsohn. 1977. Case studies on remediating memory deficits in brain damaged individuals. *Journal of Clinical Psychology* 33:1049-1054.

Goodwin, D. W., B. Powell, D. Bremer, H. Hoine, and J. Stern. 1969. Alcohol and recall: State dependent effects in man. *Science* 163:1358.

Haase, G. R. 1977. Disease presenting as dementia. In *Dementia,* 2d ed., edited by C. E. Wells. Philadelphia: F.A. Davis.

Hachinski, V. C., P. Potter, and H. Merskey. 1987. Leuko-araiosis. *Archives of Neurology* 44:21-23.

Hamilton, M. 1960. A rating scale for depression. *Journal of Neurology, Neurosurgery, and Psychiatry* 23:56.

Hanninen, T., M. Hallikainen, K. Koivisto, et al. 1995. A follow-up study of age-associated memory impairment: Neuropsychological predictors of dementia. *Journal of the American Geriatrics Society* 43:1007-1015.

Harper, P. S. 1992. The epidemiology of Huntington's disease. *Human Genetics* 89(4):365-76.

Hebert, L. E., P. A. Scherr, L. A. Beckett, et al. 1995. Age-specific incidence of Alzheimer's disease in a community population. *JAMA* 273:1354-1359,

Heilman, K. M., L. Doty, J. T. Stewart, D. Bowers, and L. Gonzalez-Rothi. 1995. *Helping People with Progressive Memory Disorder*. Gainesville, FL: University of Florida Health Science Center.

Heilman, K. M., and E. Valenstein, eds. 1985. *Clinical Neuropsychology*, 2d ed. New York: Oxford University Press.

Henderson, V. W. 1997. Estrogen, cognition, and a woman's risk of Alzheimer's disease. *American Journal of Medicine* 103:11-18.

Hermann, D. J. 1987. Task appropriateness of mnemonic techniques. *Perceptual and Motor Skills* 64:171-178.

Hertzog, C. D., F. Hultsch, and R. A. Dixon. 1989. Evidence for the convergent validity of two self-report metamemory questionnaires. *Developmental Psychology* 25:687-700.

Heyman, A., G. G. Fillenbaum, K. A. Welsh-Bohmer, M. Gearing, S. S. Mirra, R. C. Mohs, B. L. Peterson, and C. F. Pieper. 1998. Cerebral infarcts in patients with autopsy-proven Alzheimer's disease: CERAD, Part XVIII. Consortium to Establish a Registry for Alzheimer's Disease. *Neurology* 51(1):159-162.

Hier, D. B., K. Hagenlocker, and A.G. Shindler. 1985. Language disintegration in dementia: Effects of etiology and severity. *Brain Language* 25:117-133.

Hill, R. D., C. Allen, and P. McWhorter. 1991. Stories as a mnemonic aid for older learners. *Psychology and Aging* 6(3):484-486.

Hill, R. D., C. Allen, and K. Gregory. 1990. Self-generated mnemonics for enhancing free recall performance in older learners. *Experimental Aging Research* 16(3):141-145.

Hill, R. D., C. Simeone, and M. Storandt. 1990. The effects of memory skills training and incentives on free recall in older learners. *Journal of Gerontology* 15:227-232.

Holtzman, D. M., K. R. Bales, S. Wu, P. Bhat, M. Parsadanian, A. M. Fagan, L. K. Chang, Y. Sun, and S. M. Paul. 1999. Expression of human apolipoprotein E reduces amyloid-beta deposition in a mouse model of Alzheimer's disease. *Journal of Clinical Investigation* 103(6):R15-R21.

Holmes, Sir Oliver Wendell. 1889. Letter, 27 May 1889, to poet and reformer Julia Ward Howe on her seventieth birthday. *The Columbia Dictionary of Quotations*, Columbia University Press, 1993. Caedmon recordings reproduced by arrangement with HarperCollins Publishers.

Hsia, A. Y., E. Masliah, L. McConlogue, Y. Gui-Qui, G. Tatsuno, K. Hu, D. Kholodenko, R. C. Malenka, R. A. Nicoll, and L. Mucke. 1999. Plaque-independent disruption of neuronal circuits in Alzheimer's disease mouse models. *Proceedings of the National Academy of Sciences, USA* 96:3228-3233.

Huntington's Disease Collaborative Research Group. 1993. A novel gene containing a trinucleotide repeat that is expanded and unstable on Huntington's disease chromosomes. *Cell* 72:971-983.

Hyman, B. T., T. Gomez-Isla, M. Briggs, H. Chung, S. Nichols, F. Kohout, and R. Wallace. 1996. Apolipoprotein E and cognitive change in an elderly population. *Annals of Neurology* 40:55-66.

Johnson, K. A., R. A. Sperling, B. L. Holman, J. S. Nagel, and J. H. Growdon. 1992. Cerebral perfusion in progressive supranuclear palsy. *Journal of Nuclear Medicine* 3:704-709.

Johnson, Samuel. 1759. *The Columbia Dictionary of Quotations*. New York: Columbia University Press, 1993.

Kaiser, F. E. 1999. Erectile dysfunction in the aging man. *Medical Clinics of North America* 63: 1267-1278.

Kaye, J. A. 1998. Diagnostic challenges in dementia. *Neurology: Current Perspectives in Alzheimer's Disease* 51(1).

Katzman, R., D. Galasko, T. Saitoh, L. J. Thal, and L. Hansen. 1995. Genetic evidence that the lewy body variant is indeed a phenotypic variant of Alzheimer's disease. *Brain and Cognition* 28:259-265.

Khachaturian, A. S. 1994. Scientific opportunities for developing treatments for Alzheimer's disease: Proceedings of research planning workshop 1. *Neurobiology of Aging* 15:S-11-S-15.

Kliegl, R., J. Smith, and P. B. Baltes. 1990. On the locus and process of magnification of age differences during mnemonic training. *Developmental Psychology* 6:894-904

Kolb, B., and I. Q. Whishaw. 1995. *Fundamentals of Human Neuropsychology,* 4th ed. New York: W.H. Freeman and Company.

Koltai, D. C., and K. A. Welsh-Bohmer. 2000. Geriatric neuropsychological assessment. In *Clinician's Guide to Neuropsychological Assessment* 2nd ed., edited by R. D. Vanderploeg. Mahwah, NJ: Lawrence Erlbaum Associates.

Laaksonen, R. 1994. Cognitive training methods in rehabilitation of memory. In *Brain Injury and Neuropsychological Rehabilitation,* edited by A. Christensen and B. P. Uzzell. New Jersey: Lawrence Erlbaum Associates.

Lachman, M. E., S. L. Weaver, M. Bandura, E. Elliot, and C. J. Lewkowicz. 1992. Improving memory and control beliefs through cognitive restructuring and self-generated strategies. *Journal of Gerontology* 47(5):293-299.

Lachman, M. E., M. Bandura, S. L. Weaver, and E. Elliot. 1995. Assessing memory control beliefs: The memory controllability inventory. *Aging and Cognition* 2(1):67-84.

Lam, R. E., M. C. Tierney, and E. Boyle. 1998. Does depression in memory-impaired elders predict Alzheimer's Disease? *Journal of the American Geriatrics Society* 46(9):S34.

Landauer, T. K, and R. A. Bjork. 1978. Optimal rehearsal patterns and name learning. In *Practical Aspects of Memory,* edited by M. M. Gruneberg, P. Morris, and R. Sykes. London: Academic Press.

Lapp, D. 1984. Commitment: Essential ingredient in memory training. *Clinical Gerontologist* 2(1):58-60.

Larson, E. B. 1991 Geriatric medicine. *Journal of the American Medical Association* 265:1325-1326.

Lawton, M. P, P. A. Parmelee, I. R. Katz, and J. Nesselroade. 1996. Affective states in normal and depressed older people. *Journal of Gerontology* 51:P309-P316.

LeDoux, J. E. 1994. Emotion, memory and the brain. *Scientific American* 270(6):50–57.

Leirer, V. O., D. G. Morrow, J. I. Sheikh, and G. M. Pariante. 1990. Memory skills elders want to improve. *Experimental Aging Research* 16(3):155-158.

Lezak, M. D. 1995. *Neuropsychological Assessment.* 3d ed. New York: Oxford University Press.

Lichtenberg, G. C. 1993. *The Columbia Dictionary of Quotations.* New York: Columbia University Press.

Loewen, E. R., R. J. Shaw, and F. I. M. Craik. 1990. Age differences in components of metamemory. *Experimental Aging Research* 16(1):43-48.

Losonczy, K., T. B. Harris, and R. J. Havlik. 1996. Vitamin E and vitamin C supplement use and risk of all-cause and coronary heart disease in older persons: The established populations for epidemiologic studies of the elderly. *American Journal of Clinical Nutrition* 64:190-196.

Luh, C. W. 1922. The conditions of retention. *Psychological Monographs* 31(3).

Maltby, N., G. A. Broe, H. Creasey, A. F. Jorm, H. Christensen, and W. S. Brooks. 1994. Efficacy of Tacrine and lecithin in mild to moderate Alzheimer's disease: Double blind trial. *The British Medical Journal* 308:879-883.

The Medical Letter, Inc. 1997. *The Medical Letter on Drugs and Therapeutics.* New York: The Medical Letter, Inc. 39:53-54

McCrae, R. R, D. Arenberg, and P. T. Costa. 1987. Declines in divergent thinking with age: Cross-sectional, longitudinal and cross sequential analyses. *Psychology and Aging* 2:130-137.

McGlone, J., S. Gupta, D. Humphrey, S. Oppenheimer, T. Mirsen, and D. R. Evans. 1990. Screening for early dementia using memory complaints from patients and relatives. *Archives of Neurology* 47:1189-1193.

Morley, J. E., and H. M. Perry. 1999. Androgen deficiency in aging men. *Medical Clinics of North America* 83:1279-1289.

Morley, J. E. 1993. Management of impotence: Diagnostic considerations and therapeutic options. *Postgraduate Medicine* 93(3):65-72.

Morris, J. C., A. Heyman, R. C. Mohs, J. P. Hughes, G. Van Belle, G. Fillenbaum, E. D. Mellits, C. Clark, and the CERAD investigators. 1989. The Consortium to Establish a Registry for Alzheimer's Disease (CERAD). Part 1. Clinical and neuropsychological assessment of Alzheimer's disease. *Neurology* 39:1159-1165.

Morris, J. C., R. C. Mohs, H. Rogers, G. Fillenbaum, and A. Heyman. 1988. CERAD clinical and neuropsychological assessment of Alzheimer's disease. *Psychopharmacology Bulletin* 24:641-651.

Moss, M. B., M. S. Albert, and T. L. Kempner. 1992. Neuropsychology of frontal lobe dementia. In *Clinical Syndromes in Adult Neuropsychology: The Practitioner's Handbook*, edited by R. F. White. New York: Elsevier.

Mulnard, A., C. W. Cotman, C. Kawas, et al. 2000. Estrogen replacement therapy for treatment of mild to moderate Alzheimer's disease. *JAMA* 283:1007-1015.

Murdoch, B. E., H. J. Chenery, V. Wilks, and R. S. Boyle. 1987. Language disorders in dementia of the Alzheimer's type. *Brain Language* 31:122-137.

National Academy of Sciences. 1989. *Recommended Daily Allowances.* 10th ed. Washington D.C.: National Academy Press.

National Institute of Aging, National Institutes of Health. 1999. *Progress Report of Alzheimer's Disease.* NIH Publication No. 99-4664. Washington, DC: Department of Health and Human Services.

National Institute of Mental Health. 1995. *Basic Behavioral Science Research for Mental Health. Rockville, MD: National Institute of Mental Health.*

Neely, A. S., and L. Baeckman. 1993. Long-term maintenance of gains from memory training in older adults: Two 3½ year follow-up studies. *Journal of Gerontology* 48(5):233-237.

Nicklaus, Jack. 1993. *The Columbia Dictionary of Quotations.* New York: Columbia University Press.

Ogrocki, P. K., and K. A. Welsh-Bohmer. 2000. Assessment of cognitive and functional impairment in the elderly. In *Neurodegenerative Dementias: Clinical Features and Pathological Mechanisms*, edited by C. M. Clark and J. Q. Trojanowski. New York: McGraw-Hill.

Oken, B. S., D. M. Storzbach, and J. A. Kaye. 1998. The efficacy of ginkgo biloba on cognitive function in Alzheimer's disease. *Archives of Neurology* 55(11):1409-1415.

Parente, R., and M. Stapleton. 1993. An empowerment model of memory training. *Applied Cognitive Psychology* 7:585-602.

Perry, R., I. McKeith, and E. Perry, eds. 1996. *Dementia with Lewy Bodies: Clinical, Pathological and Treatment Issues.* Cambridge: Cambridge University Press.

Perlmutter, M. 1978. What is memory aging the aging of? *Developmental Psychology* 14:330-345.

Petersen, R. E., G. E. Smith, S. C. Waring, R. J. Ivnik, E. G. Tangalos, and E. Kokmen. 1999. Mild cognitive impairment—Clinical characterization and outcome. *Archives of Neurology* 56: 303-308.

Physicians' Desk Reference. 2001. Montvale, NJ: Medical economics company, inc.

Plassman, B. L., and J. C. S. Breitner. 1996. Recent advances in the genetics of Alzheimer's disease and vascular dementia with an emphasis on gene-environment interactions. *JAGS* 44:1242-1250.

Poon, L. W. 1985. Difference in human memory with aging: Nature, causes, and clinical implications. In *Handbook of the Psychology of Aging*, 2d ed., edited by J. Birren and K. Schaie. New York: Van Nostrandt Reinhold.

Poon, L. W., L. Walsh-Sweeney, and J. L. Fozard. 1980. Memory skill training for the elderly: Salient issues on the use of imagery mnemonics. In *New Directions in Memory and Aging: Proceedings of the George A. Talland Memorial Conference*, edited by L. W. Poon, J. L. Fozard, L. S. Cermak, D. Arenberg, and L. W. Thompson. Hillsdale, NJ: Erlbaum.

Poorkaj, P., T. D. Bird, E. Wijsman, E. Nemens, R. M. Garruto, L. Anderson, A. Andreadis, W. C. Wiederhold, M. Raskind, and G. D. Schellenberg. 1998. Tau is a candidate gene for chromosome 17 frontotemporal dementia. *Annals of Neurology* 43:815-825.

Postman, L., and L. Rau. 1957. Retention as a function of the method of measurement. *University of California Publications in Psychology* 8:217-270.

Preston, J. D., J. H. O'Neil, and M. E. Talaga. 1999. *Handbook of Clinical Psychopharmocology for Therapists*, 2d ed. Oakland, CA.: New Harbinger Publications.

Quayhagen, M. P., M. Quayhagen, R. R. Corbeil, P. A. Roth, and J. A. Rodgers. 1995. A dialectic remediation program for care recipients with dementia. *Nursing Research* 44(3):153-159.

Rebok, G. W., and L. J. Balcerak. 1989. Memory self-efficacy and performance differences in young and old adults: The effect of mnemonic training. *Developmental Psychology* 25(5):714-721.

Reed, S. K. 1992. *Cognition*. Pacific Grove, CA: Brooks/Cole Publishing Company.

Roberts, H. 1981. Perspective on vitamin E as therapy. *Journal of the American Medical Association* 246:129-130.

Robertson-Tchabo, E.A. 1980. Cognitive-skill training for the elderly: Why should "old dogs" acquire new tricks? In *New Directions in Memory and Aging: Proceedings of the George A. Talland Memorial Conference*, edited by L. W. Poon, J. L. Fozard, L. S. Cermak, D. Arenberg, and L. W. Thompson. Hillsdale, NJ: Erlbaum.

Robertson-Tchabo, E. A., C. P. Hausman, and D. Arenberg. 1976. A classical mnemonic for older learners: A trip that works! *Educational Gerontology* 1:215-226.

Roses, A. D. 1995. Apolipoprotein E genotyping in the differential diagnosis, not prediction, of Alzheimer's disease. *Annals of Neurology* 38:6-14.

Russell, R. M. 1997. New views on RDAs for older adults. *Journal of the American Dietary Association*. 97:515–518.

Sabiston, D. S., ed. 1997. Alzheimer's Disease. *Duke Medical Update* 4(1).

Sandman, C. A. 1993. Memory rehabilitation in Alzheimer's disease: Preliminary findings. *Clinical Gerontologist* 13(4):19-33.

Sano, M., C. Ernesto, R. G. Thomas, M. R. Klauber, K. Schafer, M. Grundman, P. Woodbury, J. Growdon, C. W. Cotman, E. Pheiffer, L. S. Schneider, and L. J. Thal. 1997. A controlled trial of selegline, alpha-tocopherol, or both as treatment for Alzheimer's disease. The Alzheimer's disease cooperative study. *New England Journal of Medicine* 336(17):1216-1222.

Saunders, A. M., K. Schmader, J. C. Breitner, M. D. Benson, W. T. Brown, L. Goldfarb, D. Goldgaber, M. G. Manwaring, M. H. Szymanski, N. McCown, K. C. Dole, D. E. Schmechel, W. J. Strittmatter, M. A. Pericak-Vance, and A. D. Roses. 1993. Apolipoptotein E-E4 allele distributions in late onset Alzheimer's disease and in other amyloid forming diseases. *Lancet* 342:710-711.

Schenk, D., R. Barbour, W. Dunn, G. Gordon, H. Grajeda, T. Guido, K. Hu, J. Huang, K. Johnson-Wood, K. Khan, D. Kholodenko, M. Lee, Z. Liao, I. Lieberburg, R. Motter, L. Mutter, F. Soriano, G. Shopp, N. Vasquex, C. Vandevert, S. Walker, M. Wogulis, T. Yednock, D. Games, and P. Seubert. 1999. Immunization with A-Beta attenuates Alzheimer's disease-like pathology in the PDAPP mouse. *Nature* 400(6740):173-177.

Scogin, F., and M. Prohaska. 1993. *Aiding Older Adults with Memory Complaints*. Sarasota, FL: Professional Resource Press.

Scogin, F., M. Storandt, and L. Lott. 1985. Memory-skills training, memory complaints, and depression in older adults. *Journal of Gerontology* 40(5):562-568.

Selye, Hans. 1976. *Stress in Health and Disease*. Woburn, MA: Butterworth.

Sheikh, J. I., J. A. Yesavage, J. O. Brooks, L. F. Friedman, P. Gratzinger, R. D. Hill, A. Zadeik, and T. Crook. 1991. Proposed factor structure of the geriatric depression scale. *International Psychogeriatrics* 3:23-28.

Sheikh, J. I., R. D. Hill, and J. A. Yesavage. 1986. Geriatric depression scale (GDS): Recent evidence and development of a shorter version. *Clinical Gerontology: A Guide to Assessment and Intervention*. New York: The Haworth Press.

———. 1986. Long-term efficacy of cognitive training for age-associated memory impairment: A six-month follow-up study. *Developmental Neuropsychology* 2(4):413-421.

Sherrington, R., E. I. Rogaev, Y. Liang, E. A. Rogaeva, G. Levesque, M. Ikeda, H. Chi, C. Lin, G. Li, and K. Holman. 1995. Cloning of a gene bearing mis-sense mutations in early onset Alzheimer's disease. *Nature* 375:754-760.

Siegler, I. C, L. W. Poon, D. J. Madden, and K. A. Welsh. 1995. Psychological aspects of normal aging. In *Textbook of Geriatric Psychiatry*, 2d ed., 105-127. edited by E. W. Busse and D. G. Blazer. Washington DC: American Psychiatric Press.

Smith, J. S., and L. F. Kiloh. 1981. The investigation of dementia: Results in 200 consecutive admissions. *Lancet* 1:824-827.

Smith, A. D. 1980. Age differences in encoding, storage, and retrieval. In *New Directions in Memory and Aging: Proceedings of the George A. Talland Memorial Conference*, edited by L. W. Poon, J. L. Fozard, L. S. Cermak, D. Arenberg, and L. W. Thompson. Hillsdale, NJ: Erlbaum.

Snowdon, D. A., L. H. Greiner, J. A. Mortimer, K. P. Riley, P. A. Greiner, and W. R. Markesbery. 1997. Brain infarction and the clinical expression of Alzheimer's disease: The nun study. *Journal of the American Medical Association* 277(10):813-817.

Snowdon, D. A., S. J. Kemper, J. A. Mortimer, P. A. Greiner, D.R. Wekstein, and W. R. Markesbery. 1996. Linguistic ability in early life and cognitive function and Alzheimer's disease in late life: Findings from the nun study. *Journal of the American Medical Association* 275:528-532.

Snyder, P. J., and P. D. Nussbaum. 1998. *Clinical Neuropsychology: A Pocket Handbook for Assessment*. Washington DC: American Psychological Association.

Sohlberg, M. M., and C. A. Mateer. 1987. Effectiveness of an attention training program. *Journal of Clinical and Experimental Neuropsychology* 9(2):117-130.

Soto, C., E. M. Sigurdsson, L. Morelli, R. A. Kumar, E. M. Castano, and B. Frangione. 1998. Beta-sheet breaker peptides inhibit fibrillogenesis in a rat brain model of amyloidosis: Implications for Alzheimer's therapy. *Nature Medicine* 4:822-826.

Stankov, L. 1988. Aging, intelligence and attention. *Psychology and Aging* 3(2):59-74.

Stewart, W. F., C. Kawas, M. Corrada, and E. J. Metter. 1997. Risk of Alzheimer's disease and duration of NSAID use. *Neurology* 48:626-632.

Stigsdotter, A., and L. Backman. 1989. Multifactorial memory training with older adults: How to foster maintenance of improved performance. *Gerontology* 35:260-267.

Stigsdotter-Neely, A. S., and L. Backman. 1993. Long-term maintenance of gains from memory training in older adults: Two 3½-year follow-up studies. *Journal of Gerontology* 48(5):233-237.

———. 1995. Effects of multifactorial memory training in old age: Generalizability across tasks and individuals. *Journal of Gerontology* 50B(3):134-140.

Strittmatter, W. J., A. M. Saunders, D. Schmechel, M. Pericak-Vance, J. England, G. S. Salvesen, and A. D. Roses. 1993. Apolipoprotein E: High-avidity binding to beta-amyloid and increased frequency of type 4 allele in late-onset familial Alzheimer's disease. *Proceedings of the National Academy of Sciences USA* 90:1977-1981.

Tabrizi, S. J., R. S. Howard, J. Collinge, M. N. Rossor, and F. Scaravilli. 1996. Creutzfeldt-Jakob disease in a young woman. *Lancet* 347:945-948.

Thompson, T. L., C. R. Filley, W. D. Mitchell, K. M. Culig, M. LoVerde, and R. L. Byyny. 1990. Lack of efficacy of hydergine in patients with Alzheimer's disease. *New England Journal of Medicine* 323:445-448.

Tomlinson, B. E., G. Blessed, and M. Roth. 1970. Observations of the brains of demented old people. *Journal of Neurological Science* 11:205-242.

Treat, N. J., L. W. Poon, J. L. Fozard, and S. J. Popkin. 1978. Toward applying cognitive skill training to memory problems. *Experimental Aging Research* 4(4):305-319.

Tuling, E. 1972. Episodic and semantic memory. In *Organization and Memory*. New York: Academic Press.

Verghese, J., G. Kuslansky, M. J. Katz, M. Sliwinski, H. A. Crystal, H. Buschke, and R. B. Lipton. 2000. Cognitive performance in surgically menopausal women on estrogen. *Neurology* 55(6):872-874.

Verhaeghen, P., A. Marcoen, and L. Goossens. 1992. Improving memory performance in the aged through mnemonic training: A meta-analytic study. *Psychology and Aging* 7(2):242-251.

Verhaeghen, P., N. V. Ranst, and A. Marcoen. 1933. Memory training in the community: Evaluations by participants and effects on metamemory. *Educational Gerontology* 19:525-534.

Villardita, C. 1993. Alzheimer's disease compared with cerebrovascular dementia: Neuropsychological similarities and differences. *Acta Neurologica Scandinavica* 87:299-308.

Wagner, M. T., and D. L. Bachman. 1996. Neuropsychological features of diffuse lewy body disease. *Archives of Clinical Neuropsychology* 11:175-184.

Walsh, P. C. 1995. *The Prostate: A Guide for Men and the Women Who Love Them*. Baltimore: The Johns Hopkins University Press.

Weatherall, D. J., J. G. Ledingham, and D. A. Warrel, eds. 1983. *Oxford Textbook of Medicine*. New York: Oxford University Press. 24:14.

Wechsler, D. 1987. *Wechsler Memory Scales-Revised (WMS-R)*. San Antonio, TX: Psychological Corp.

Welsh, K. A., S. Mirra, G. Fillenbaum, M. Gearing, D. Beekly, and S. Edland. 1996. Neuropsychological and neuropathological differentiation of Alzheimer's disease from other dementias: The CERAD experience. *Journal of the International Neuropsychological Society* 2:12.

Welsh, K. A., N. Butters, R. C. Mohs, D. Beekly, S. Edland, G. Fillenbaum, and A. Heyman. 1994. The Consortium to Establish a Registry of Alzheimer's Disease (CERAD) Part V: A normative study of the neuropsychological battery. *Neurology* 44:609-614.

Welsh, K. A., N. Butters, J. Hughes, R. C. Mohs, and A. Heyman. 1992. Detection and staging of dementia in Alzheimer's disease: Use of the neuropsychological measures developed for CERAD. *Archives of Neurology* 49:448-452.

———. 1991. Detection of abnormal memory in mild cases of Alzheimer's disease using CERAD neuropsychological measures. *Archives of Neurology* 48:278-281.

Welsh-Bohmer, K. A., and P. D. Ogrocki. 1998. Clinical differentiation of memory disorders in neurodegenerative disease. In *Memory in Neurodegenerative Disease*, edited by A. I. Troster. New York: Cambridge University Press.

Welsh-Bohmer, K. A., M. Gearing, A. M. Saunders, A. D. Roses, and S. M. Mirra. 1997. Apolipoprotein E genotypes in a neuropathological series from the Consortium to Establish a Registry for Alzheimer's Disease (CERAD). *Annals of Neurology* 42:319-325.

Welsh-Bohmer, K. A., and J. M. Hoffman. 1996. Positron emission tomography neuroimaging in dementia. In *Neuroimaging II: Clinical Applications*, edited by E. Bigler. New York: Plenum Press.

West, R. L. 1995. Compensatory strategies for age-associated memory impairment. In *Handbook of Memory Disorders*, edited by B. A. Wilson and F. N. Watts. New York: John Wiley & Sons Ltd.

West, R. L., and T. H. Crook. 1992. Video training of imagery for mature adults. *Applied Cognitive Psychology* 6:307-320.

Wheeler, M. A. 2000. A comparison of forgetting rates in older and younger adults. *Aging, Neuropsychology and Cognition* 7(3):179-193.

Woolf, Virginia. 1993. *The Columbia Dictionary of Quotations*. New York: Columbia University Press.

Xu, X., D. Yang, T. Wyss-Coray, J. Yan, L. Gan, Y. Sun, and L. Mucke. 1999. Wild-type but not Alzeheimer-mutant amyloid precursor protein confers resistance against p53-medicated apoptosis. Proceedigns of the National Academy of Sciences, USA, 96:7547–7552.

Yaffe, K., T. Blackwell, R. Gore, L. Sands, V. Reus, and W. S. Browner. 1999. Depressive symptoms and cognitive decline in nondemented elderly women: A prospective study. *Archives of General Psychiatry* 56(5):425-430.

Yaffe, K., G. Sawaya, I. Lieberburg, and D. Grady. 1998. Estrogen therapy in postmenopausal women: Effects on cognitive function and dementia. *JAMA* 279:688-695.

Yesavage, J. A. 1989. Techniques for cognitive training of memory in age-associated memory impairment. *Archives of Gerontology Geriatrics* 1:185-190.

Yesavage, J. A., J. Sheikh, E. Decker-Tanke, and R. Hill. 1988. Response to memory training and individual differences in verbal intelligence and state anxiety. *American Journal of Psychiatry* 145(5):636-639.

Yesavage, J. A. 1984. Relaxation and memory training in 39 elderly patients. *American Journal of Psychiatry* 141(6):778-781.

Yesavage, J. A., and R. Jacob. 1984. Effects of relaxation and mnemonics on memory, attention and anxiety in the elderly. *Experimental Aging Research* 10(4):211-214.

Yesavage, J. A. 1983. Imagery pretraining and memory training in the elderly. *Gerontology* 29:271-274.

Yesavage, J. A., T. L. Brink, T. L. Rose, O. Lum, V. Huang, M. B. Adey, and V. O. Leirer. 1983. Development and validation of a geriatric depression screening scale: A preliminary report. *Journal of Psychiatric Research* 17:37-49.

Yesavage, J. A., and T. L. Rose. 1983. Concentration and mnemonic training in the elderly with memory complaints: A study of combined therapy and order effects. *Psychiatry Research* 9:157-167.

Yesavage, J. A., T. L. Rose, and G. H. Bower. 1983. Interactive imagery and affective judgements improve face-name learning in elderly. *Journal of Gerontology* 38(2):197-203.

Zarit, S. H., K. D. Cole, and R. L. Guider. 1981. Memory training strategies and subjective complaints of memory in the aged. *Gerontologist* 21(2):158-164.

Zarit, S. H., D. Gallagher, and Kramer. 1981. Memory training in the community aged: Effects on depression, memory complaint, and memory performance. *Educational Gerontology* (6):11-17.

Zarit, S. H. 1980. *Aging and Mental Disorders: Psychological Approaches to Assessment and Treatment*. New York: Free Press.

About the Authors

Douglas J. Mason, LCSW, Psy.D. and Michael Lee Kohn, Psy.D. are very connected with the community that this book will serve. The book grew out of award-winning treatment strategies they developed to treat this population.

Douglas Mason is a Neuropsychology Fellow and Clinical Associate at the Duke University Medical Center and the Bryan Alzheimer's Disease Research Center.

Michael Kohn is a forensic psychologist at Eastern State Hospital in Williamsburg, Virginia.

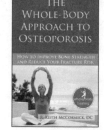